AND HOW SHALL YOU KNOW ALL PARABLES?

A Thematic Framework for Understanding
The Gospels Based on the Parable of the Sower
(A Discipling Tool)

JOHN WEDLOCK

To Vance, a compatriot in
many ways – teaching the Word of God,
serving in the U.S. Navy, and teaching
young people. May God richly bless
you and your dear family.

John Wedlock

ISBN 978-1-64028-686-3 (Paperback)
ISBN 978-1-64028-687-0 (Digital)

Christian Faith Publishing, Inc.
296 Chestnut Street
Meadville, PA 16335
www.christianfaithpublishing.com

Printed in the United States of America

ACKNOWLEDGEMENTS

Grateful thanks to:

God, my Father, for all His provisions in my life and in the writing of this book. "Every good thing given is from above, coming down from the Father of lights."

Jesus Christ, my redeemer and king, for my salvation and His Word upon which this book is based.

The Holy Spirit, my guide and teacher, for His power to persevere and not get weary during the 45 years of the development and writing of this book.

My parents who taught me the ways of the Christian ethic.

Mr. Frank Braxton who not only knew about Jesus but who had a personal relationship with Jesus and explained that to me when I was a new believer.

Bob Muhlig who took me to a Navigators' Bible study when I was a new believer.

Authors whose writing stimulated my thinking over the years – Larry Crabb, John Fischer, Gordon MacDonald, M. Blaine Smith, and Dallas Willard.

Gene Pickett who has been a good friend and my "Barnabas".

All of the brothers and sisters in the various Sunday school and ABF classes in which I taught the Gospels for their questions of clarification.

All of the men to whom I taught (one on one) over the years for the encouragement of seeing their walk with the Lord.

All the great English teachers at Lockwood Jr.-Sr. High School and my mother (an English teacher) for teaching me how to write.

Bob and Betty Morgan for providing a lap-top computer on which I composed the book.

Cherie Collins and my daughter, Amy, for technical support with the computer!

Pastor John Goasdone who labored *many* hour doing the initial edit.

Gina Burkett and John Howat for doing the computer graphics for the diagrams.

Jeff and Diane Fineran, Bruce and Marjorie Wedlock, Bernie and Gale Norman, Todd Nichols, John and Maria Alfred, Brian and Lorna Caulfield, Gene and Sis Pickett, Rob and Cathy Hsu, Bob and Betty Morgan, and Dave Ferrara for the financial support needed to publish the book.

My wife of 56 years, Louise, who was a ready sounding board, an essential encourager, and a wonderful helpmate in so many ways.

CONTENTS

DIAGRAMS

APPENDICES

INTRODUCTION
Come and See...Jesus

One day, when I was reading in the Gospel of Mark, I came upon a verse in chapter four that really caught my attention:

> And He (Jesus) said to them (the disciples), "Do you not understand this parable? **And how will you understand all parables?**" (Mark 4:13)

The parable about which Jesus is speaking is the "Parable of the Sower," and this verse really peaked my interest. It seems that Jesus is suggesting that this is *the* basic parable that needs to be understood; or, perhaps, the understanding of other parables depends on an understanding of the "Parable of the Sower." Whatever the case, I was convinced that the understanding of *this* parable was pivotal to my understanding of scripture, and subsequently, to my spiritual growth.

I began my study by reading the parable in each of the Gospels in which it appears: Matthew 13:3–8, 18–23; Mark 4:3–20; and Luke 8:4–15. I read these passages over and over. As I did, I began to realize that the different types of soils that Jesus is describing represent the different types of people that are in the world, the response of these different types of people to hearing the Word of God, and the result of their response. (see Appendix I)

The first type of soil that Jesus describes is the **"wayside."** The wayside is where people walked; and, as a result, the soil is packed down and hard. Consequently, the seed falling on this ground is not able to penetrate the hard surface. The birds, which easily can see the seed lying in the open, come and devour it. Jesus says that the response of the "wayside," or hard-soil people, is that they hear the Word of God, but do not understand it. The result of this response is that Satan takes the Word of God out of their heart so that they will not believe and be saved. I see these people as the **hard** people.

The second type of soil that Jesus describes is the "**rocky soil.**" This rocky soil represents an area of ground with a small amount of soil on top and solid ledge beneath. When the seed falls on this soil, it is able to penetrate the surface, germinate, and grow up quickly into a healthy young plant. However, the ledge prevents the plant from extending its roots deeply into the soil. When the sun becomes very hot, the plant wilts because its roots are not deep enough to obtain the water it needs in order to be sustained. Jesus says that the response of the rocky-soil people to the Word of God is that they hear it and receive it with joy. The result of this response to the Word of God is that these people stumble or "fall away" when troubles or persecutions arise because of the Word. I see these people as the **shallow** people.

The third type of soil that Jesus describes is the "**thorny soil.**" This area of ground abounds with thorny weeds. When the seed falls on this soil; it is able to penetrate the surface, germinate, and grow into a healthy plant. However, the thorny weeds grow up, choke the plant by denying it nutrition and light, and prevent the plant from being able to bear fruit. Jesus says that the response of the thorny-soil people to the Word of God is that they hear the Word, and without reflection, "go on their way." The result is that these people allow the cares and worries of the world and the deceitfulness of riches to strangle their lives to the point where they are unproductive for God. I see these people as the **spiritually unproductive** people.

The fourth type of soil that Jesus describes is the **"good soil."** When the seed falls on the good soil, it penetrates the surface, germinates, grows into a healthy plant, and bears much fruit. Jesus says that the response of the good soil people to the Word of God is that they hear it, receive, understand it, and keep it. The result is that these people are productive for God. I see these people as the **spiritually productive** people.

I had gained some understanding about the soils in the "Parable of the Sower," but I wanted to know more. When I accepted Jesus as my personal Savior and Lord, I felt compelled to know Him—to have the "mind of Christ" (1 Cor. 2:16). In order to get to know Him, I began to study each of the Gospel books—Matthew, Mark, Luke, John, and Acts (I consider Acts part of the "good news"). As I studied, I began to perceive a major theme in each of these books. I also began to realize that there is a relationship between each of the soils in the "Parable of the Sower" and each of the themes of the Gospel books, with the exception of the Gospel of John. (see Appendix II)

First, I noticed that the Gospel of Mark is emphasizing the problem of man's pride and the hardness that it causes in the heart of man. Is Mark talking about the wayside-soil people? The Gospel of Luke seems to be emphasizing man's lack of steadfast faith and the shallowness it causes in man's heart. Is Luke talking about the rocky-soil people? The Gospel of Matthew is pointing out man's disobedience and the distraction that leads man's heart away to a spiritually unproductive life. Is Matthew talking about the thorny-soil people? The Book of Acts describes the apostles' ministry and their witness of Jesus, both accomplished through the power of the Holy Spirit. Acts also describes the spiritually productive blessings and conversions that this ministry and witness brought to the hearts of many people. Is Luke talking about the good-soil people?

You can imagine the excitement I felt as I began to see God's order in all of this. However, there was one remaining book to connect—the Gospel of John. There are four soils depicted in the "Parable of the Sower," and there are five books. God is too orderly, and the Gospel of John is too important for there not to be a connection. The Gospel of John talks about repenting from sin and being "born again." This is personally realized by believing that Jesus took the punishment for our sin upon His body, and provided forgiveness for that sin by the shedding of His blood. John is describing spiritual regeneration, and spiritual regeneration is how people cross over from being the not-so-good soil (hard, rocky, thorny, or any combination thereof) to being good soil. This is how the Gospel of John fits into the "Parable of the Sower."

Next, I noticed that, perhaps, there was a progressive relationship among soils in the Parable of the Sower and the related themes of the Gospels and Acts. This progressive relationship, I began to see, is related to and provides a framework for our spiritual growth and maturity (see Appendix III). I saw that we need to have servant-like humility (opposite to the "wayside soil") in order to "see and believe in" Jesus, and to be able to receive a Jesus-focused spirituality. If we have Jesus-focused spirituality (transformation from natural focus to supernatural focus), we will be focused on Jesus, and as a result, will love Him more. If we love Jesus, the more we will trust Him and develop a steadfast faith (opposite to the "rocky soil") in Him. If we have a steadfast faith in Jesus, the more we will develop a devoted obedience (opposite to the "thorny soil") to Him. If we have a devoted obedience to Jesus, the more we will follow the leading of the Holy Spirit. The more we follow the leading of the Holy Spirit, the more we will be spiritually productive (the same as the "good soil"). If we are spiritually productive through the power of the Holy Spirit, we will be amazed at the mighty works of God done through us to others. When we see the mighty works of God done through us, we will be humbled before God. When we are humbled before God, we will see Jesus more clearly; and the cycle will begin again and continue. If we are following this pattern, we will be growing in our spiritual maturity and will be following the two commandments of Jesus, love God and love your neighbor.

At the same time as all of this was happening, I was studying motivational theory in my work as an educator. I discovered that man is ultimately not motivated to action by *external* stimuli, but by an attempt to satisfy his *intrinsic* needs (see Appendix IV). I began to see a connection between each of man's intrinsic needs and each of the paired themes of the "Parable of the Sower" and the Gospel books (see Appendix V). One of the intrinsic needs is a sense of worth. Is man attempting to meet this need through pride rather than humility (wayside soil/hard people/Mark)? Another need is freedom. Is man attempting to meet this need by considering choices in the natural realm only rather than including consideration of choices in the spiritual realm as well (transformation/saved people/John)? Another need is power. Is man attempting to meet this need solely through reliance on his own reason rather than a steadfast faith in God (rocky soil/shallow people/Luke)? Another need is security. Is man attempting to meet this need by attempting to provide for himself in his own power rather than allowing God to provide for him (thorny soil/spiritually unproductive people/Matthew)? Another need is meaning. Is man attempting to find meaning in the church and through the power of the Holy Spirit (good soil, spiritually productive people/Acts)? Another need is joy. Is man going to find joy independent of the satisfaction of all his other needs or is he going to find joy in the *satisfaction of all of his needs in God?* The connection of the intrinsic needs to the paired themes of the "Parable of the Sower" and the Gospel books was striking. Had God created man with all of these intrinsic needs that **only *He* could satisfy?**

I began to see that the intrinsic needs are also progressively related and that the nature of the progression is based on the type of relationship in which we find ourselves. (see Appendix VI). The most basic need is the *personal* need of *security*, which is satisfied by physiological provision. The next level of need is the *interpersonal need* of *worth*, which is satisfied by love and acceptance. The next level of need is the *managerial* needs of *freedom*, satisfied by choice, and *power*, satisfied by trust. The next level is the *organizational* need of *meaning*, which is satisfied by purpose within something larger than ourselves. Another need is *joy*, which is satisfied by the meeting of all of the above needs and fun.

Realizing the specific connections among the themes of each of the soils in the "Parable of the Sower," the themes of the Gospel books and Acts, and man's intrinsic needs was a gift from God and was quite exhilarating (see Appendix VII). What has followed is years of study, application, reflection, and teaching based on this framework. So I invite you, in the name of Jesus and the power of the Holy Spirit, to "come and see Jesus" based on this framework provided by Him, to be challenged to respond to what you see, and to grow in your spiritual maturity!

FRAMEWORK FOR SPIRITUAL MATURITY

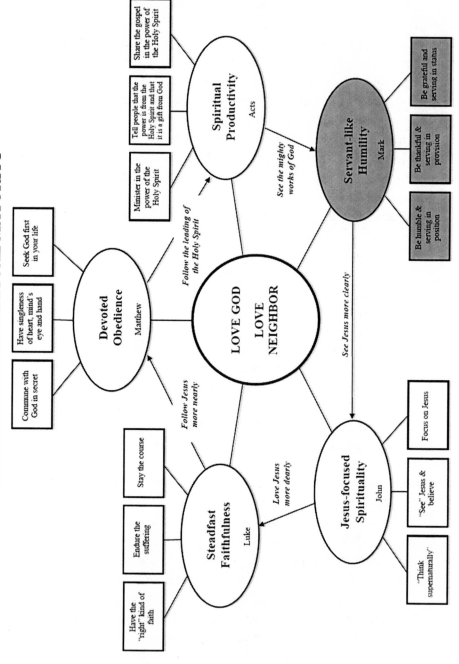

SECTION I

Servant-Like Humility

Listen to this! Behold, the sower went out to sow; as he was sowing, some seed fell beside the road, and the birds came and ate it up...These are the ones who are beside the road where the word is sown; and when they hear, immediately Satan comes and takes away the word which has been sown in them. (Mark 4:3, 4, 15)

I began my quest for the "mind of Christ" with a fresh study of the Gospel books, and I started with the book of Mark. It was the shortest of all of the Gospel books and seemed to be the easiest to understand. Also, in my previous readings in Mark, I had noticed the frequent use of the words, "hard" and "hardness" in Jesus' description of the state of people's hearts. This caused me to reflect back on the "Parable of the Sower." The **"wayside soil,"** I remembered, was where the people walked, and it was packed down and hard. I made the connection at this point that the theme of the Gospel of Mark might be concerned with hardness. I read and meditated on the Book of Mark with the concept of hardness of the heart in mind. What began to emerge was the theme that **selfish pride** was the cause of the **hardness**.

Reflecting on my understanding of human intrinsic needs, it occurred to me that the need related to pride was that of personal worth. We all want to have a sense of worth, and most of the time, our sense of worth is determined by the amount of love and acceptance we feel from those around us. In our early life, it is the love and acceptance we feel from our parents and family that gives us a sense of worth. Later in life, it is the love and acceptance we feel from our teachers, our coaches, our spouses, our bosses, our peers, etc., that also gives us a sense of worth. However, what if for some reason we do not feel love and acceptance from those around us? What if we feel "walked on" like the "wayside soil?" Some of us will choose to remain in the suffering of our sense of worthlessness. Others will try to take control of gaining their sense of worth by themselves without the unsolicited love and acceptance of others. Both choices are not good and represent the **"wayside soil."** If we choose to remain in our suffering, we will withdraw, become suspicious of all attempts by others to love and accept us, and harden ourselves to all those attempts. If we choose to try to take control of gaining our sense of worth, we will try (in our "Adam" nature) to raise ourselves up in our own eyes and in the eyes of others. If we do so, we become prideful and hard. The choice we really need to make is to humble ourselves and allow ourselves to sense the love and acceptance of Jesus, a love-and-acceptance that is absolute and unchanging. A sense of Jesus' **love and acceptance** will give us a **true** sense of **worth**.

Something else confirmed all of this. I read the section on the Gospel of Mark in *The New Bible Commentary, Revised*, which said that, "The Gospel was probably written for Gentile readers in general, but particularly for Romans" (p. 851). What was the prominent characteristic of the ancient Romans? I believe that it was their pride; and perhaps, the theme of this particular gospel was to directly address that issue.

Reading in chapter ten of the Gospel of Mark, I found a concise presentation concerning man's problem with selfish pride which also reveals the "mind of Christ" concerning pride and humility. In the next three chapters, we will examine the three types of pride that causes hardness in man's heart and the contrasting humility that is the remedy to man's prideful hardness.

FRAMEWORK FOR SPIRITUAL MATURITY

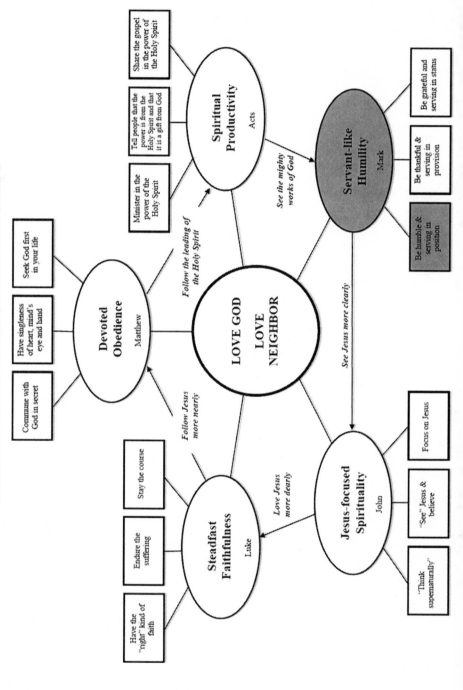

CHAPTER 1

Take a Knee:
Be Humble in Position

Pride of position.

"Pride of position" is one form of pride that is presented in Mark, chapter ten, verses 1–13. A husband in the Hebrew culture of the time was the absolute ruler of his household. His **position** was above that of his wife just because he was the husband. Husbands, as described in verses 1–12, were considering their position in relation to their wives only, and not also in their relationship to God. They had lost sight of God, in His position over them, and what God would think concerning their actions. As a result, they became prideful and began to use their position over their wives to raise themselves up. They were divorcing their wives because of "some uncleanness" (Deut. 24:1–4), which was extended by some to mean "anything not pleasing to the husband." Perhaps, the wife could not provide a son and heir for him. Perhaps, the wife had become unhealthy, old, or unattractive. Whatever the case, these husbands were divorcing their wives not for just cause but, rather, for the cause of their own pride (vv. 2–9). They would divorce their wives in order to raise themselves up in their own eyes and the eyes of other men. They felt that by doing this, they would gain a sense of worth. When questioned further about this issue by His disciples, Jesus emphasizes the importance of the marriage commitment by connecting remarriage after divorce to adultery (vv. 10–12). The Hebrew men, even the Pharisees themselves, were blinded and hardened by their pride, had become inconsiderate of their wives, and would not let the Word of God penetrate their hearts. Jesus tells them that this is all due to the **hardness** of their hearts (Mark 10:5).

Now the men of today, as the Hebrew men of old, also have position in society. They can be husbands, fathers, elder brothers, office managers, company bosses, teachers, civic leaders, deacons, elders, etc. The women of today also have position in society. They can be mothers, elder sisters, office managers, company bosses, civic leaders, deaconess, etc. In addition, men or women can have position because of their physical size, intellectual ability, athletic ability, physical beauty, wittiness, agility, physical strength, etc. There is nothing wrong with having position over others. Problems develop, however, when we lose sight of our position in relationship to God and begin to use our position to raise ourselves up. We forget that God is in position *above* us and forget what *He* thinks is right. We begin to think only about our relationship with those *beneath* us in position and what is right in *our own* eyes. We use, and abuse, others to raise ourselves up in an attempt to give ourselves a sense of worth. It is like the parable of the "wicked servant" (Matt. 18:23–35). In this parable, a servant is forgiven his debt by the king, turns around and has a fellow servant imprisoned for being indebted to him, and is found out and punished for his actions by the king. The servant has lost sight of his relationship to the king who is above him in position and is thinking only about his relationship with his fellow servant who owes him money. When we lose sight of our relationship with God, we become selfish, inconsiderate of others, hard, and prideful. We push others down and use them to raise ourselves up. What happens as a result is hurtful and destructive to others and us.

Experiencing pride of position.

Before my conversion, I held many different positions. I was a Yale graduate, a husband, a father, an officer in the United States Navy, a high-school teacher, a high-school basketball coach, etc. I was very proud of who I was in all of my positions. However, I selfishly abused the power of my positions to the detriment of those around me—my wife, my children, the enlisted men under my command, my students, the basketball players on my team, etc. I realized (at times) that my actions were inappropriate, and I was concerned about that. However, my "pride of position" would never allow me to publicly acknowledge it. If I did, I feared that it would affect my sense of worth and cause others around me to esteem me less. This would have had an adverse effect on my sense of worth, and that was unacceptable to me at that time. I was a **hard** person!

I remember an incident in which I demonstrated the prideful hardness of heart in my position as a husband. I was driving to the store with my wife, Louise. I came to an intersection and did not stop. Louise informed me that I had run a stop sign. I was sure that I had not and told her in no uncertain terms that I had not. On the return trip from the store, Louise pointed out the stop sign located at the intersection. Without hesitation, I told her that someone must have come in the intervening time and installed it. I was the husband; that was that, and no discussions, please! I was in the position of husband. If I for a moment thought that I had done something wrong, it would affect my sense of worth. This might cause others to esteem me less and not accept me. Therefore, I absolutely denied that I was wrong, was inconsiderate of my wife, and went on. This is an example of the selfish "pride-of-position" that blinds men and women and hardens their hearts so that the Word of God cannot penetrate.

Humility in position.

The opposite of selfish "pride-of-position" is servant-like "humility-in-position" and is presented in verses 13–16 of Mark, chapter ten.

A rabbi in Jewish culture held a very high position in that culture. His time was considered very valuable and should have been given to studying and teaching the Word of God. Usually, only the rabbi's disciples were permitted access to him.

In contrast, children in the Hebrew culture were of very low position. Certainly, it would have been considered beneath the position of a rabbi to spend his valuable time with children. Yet Jesus, a rabbi, humbles himself in his position and permits children to come to him (v. 14). Jesus is serving the children in that He is giving recognition to them. We know how children feel important when adults or famous people give them recognition. This is in sharp contrast to the Hebrew men who in a prideful manner are abusing their position as husbands by divorcing their wives for no just cause. Are these men serving their wives? Even Jesus' disciples rebuke those who had brought the children to Him (v. 13). Where are the hearts of the disciples? Jesus indicates that *all* people, even those in great positions, must humble themselves as children before God if they expect to enter God's kingdom (v. 15). They will need to leave the issue of their worth in God's hands.

Experiencing humility in position.

At one point in my life as a believer, I served in the position of Social Studies Chairman in a public school. The school superintendent and the school principal of this school seemed to be having problems with some of the teachers in the Social Studies Department. I was appointed to the position of chairman of the department in spite of a very qualified internal candidate. The principal pretty much told the teachers in the department that I was coming there to "straighten them out." You can imagine the attitude of the teachers toward me when I arrived at the school. I had to try to find a way to show the teachers that I was in the position to serve them and not to lord it over them. I learned that there was a process by which the teachers received their weekly teaching supplies. Part of that process was that the supplies would be delivered by a student. I decided, instead, to deliver the supplies myself. I felt that this might provide a picture of my desire to serve them and an opportunity to ask them if there was any other way that I might serve them. Slowly, they began to see that my desire in my position was to serve them.

Contrasting scriptural examples of how to use "position."

I found that Mark, chapter fourteen, provided a good view of the application of the concept of selfish "pride-of-position" contrasted against the concept of servant-like "humility-in-position." I examined each of the people described in this chapter and attempted to determine who was being selfishly prideful in their position and who was exhibiting servant-like humility in their position.

Those, I found, who were being selfishly prideful in their position were numerous. The chief priests, scribes, and the council all have position in Hebrew society in that they are the religious leaders. Yet, they selfishly use the power of their position in order to plot the death of Jesus (v. 12). It appears that Jesus has become a threat to their position, and they want to rid themselves of Him. The manner in which they carry out the plot is extremely deceitful. They consort together in a deceitful way in order that the Hebrew people will not blame them for Jesus' death (vv. 1–2). They also consort deceitfully with Judas in order to capture Jesus (vv. 10–11). They bring forward false witnesses against Jesus (vv. 56–58). They do not participate personally in the capture of Jesus, but deceitfully send an armed crowd (vv. 43). It appears that these religious leaders are exhibiting selfish pride in order to protect their positions. They are taking the issue of their worth into their own hands and using dishonesty and deceit to accomplish their ends.

The disciples are selfishly prideful in their position as both disciples and men in the Hebrew culture. They are indignant about the woman who humbly and sacrificially pours her costly perfume upon Jesus (vv. 3–4). They feel, perhaps, that she should have given the perfume to them. Then, they would decide whether or not to anoint Jesus or to sell the perfume and give it to the poor. They scold her (vv. 5). This woman threatens their position as disciples and men, and they feel that they need to take the issue of their worth into their own hands (vv. 5).

Judas has position as a disciple of Jesus. He selfishly uses his position to betray Jesus in order to obtain money (vv. 10). This is in sharp contrast to the woman of no position who sacrificially pours out her costly perfume on Jesus. He deceitfully consorts with the chief priests about how he can betray Jesus; and, in return, the chief priests promise to pay him for his betrayal (vv. 11). Judas betrays Jesus with a deceitful kiss (vv. 44–45). Judas certainly takes the issue of self worth into his own hands.

Peter also has position as a disciple of Jesus, and in addition, he is considered the leader among all of the disciples. He in a prideful way indicates that even though all will fall away, he will not (vv. 29). When Jesus disagrees, Peter vehemently states that even if he faces death, he will not deny Jesus (vv. 31). His position as the leading disciple is being threatened. Peter, however, lies and denies his relationship with Jesus three times in order to save his life (vv. 66–72). Peter cannot go "all the way" as a servant and shows his nature to be that of an incomplete servant. Here, Peter's "position" as a "person who is alive" becomes more important to him than being a disciple of Jesus—as is the case with all the disciples in their flight (vv. 50–52). Peter's position of life versus possible death causes him to take his sense of worth into his own hands.

The only person in this chapter who is exhibiting servant-like humility in position is Jesus. Certainly, the leper and the woman with the perfume are exhibiting humility, but neither has any position. Jesus *has* position. He is the great Second Person of the Trinity, the Son of God, the Christ, the Messiah, etc. Jesus humbles himself in His position to eat at the home of a leper (vv. 3)! In the Hebrew culture of that time, lepers are considered the unclean of the unclean and the lowest of the low. For Jesus, a rabbi, to enter the house of a leper and eat there is considered far beneath His position. In addition, He accepts the anointing of his body by a woman (v. 3), another person of low position in society. He humbles himself in His position to do so. Obviously, He does not sense that this is a threat to His position or that this will affect His sense of worth. He probably knows what kind of effect His humble actions will have on the sense of worth of the leper and the woman. His actions of love and acceptance raise *their* sense of worth. This is similar to what He does by receiving the children. He *raises* their sense of worth. That's what Jesus is all about; **He raises people up!**

In preparing for the Passover, Jesus does not expect, in a prideful manner, his disciples to do all of the preparation for Him because of His position. He humbly provides a room, furnished and ready, for them to celebrate the Passover (vv. 13–15). He shares the bread and the cup of the Passover with His disciples and indicates that the bread and the cup represent the sacrificial death that he will experience in order to *serve* them and others by providing for their salvation (vv. 22–24). Here, the Master is humbly *serving* His people. Certainly, this was a revolutionary concept for those days, and how it must have raised the disciples' sense of worth. Jesus, however, does not seem to think that these actions will affect His sense of worth.

Jesus exhibits humility in position as he prays to the Father in the Garden of Gethsemane. Jesus falls to the ground in prayer to ask the Father if He has to allow Himself to be crucified (vv. 35–36a, 39). However, Jesus acknowledges that He is there to serve, and He submits to the Father's will (v. 36b). Here, Jesus puts his sense of worth, even His life, totally in the Father's hands. He goes "all the way," and His nature is that of a complete servant. He is confident that His Father will raise Him up.

Summary.

There are several gems of wisdom that we can glean from studying these portions of the Gospel of Mark. People who become prideful in their positions are extremely *self-serving* and often abuse the power of their position. They are almost obsessively preoccupied with raising themselves up in their own eyes and the eyes of others. They go to extremes of deceit, dishonesty, and even murder to preserve their position, especially when their position is threatened. Often, they push others down in order to raise themselves up. Sacrifice, in order to serve God or others, is not a thought that enters their minds. Their hearts become hard to the Word of God. It becomes increasingly difficult for them to humble themselves and to place their lives in God's hands. They become more and more set in this pattern of behavior to achieve a sense of worth. Ironically, this pattern of behavior never leads to the satisfaction of that need. Look where the young man's sense of worth is as he escapes naked (v. 51). Look where Peter's sense of worth is after he protects his own life by denying Jesus for the third time (v. 72). I call this type of "**wayside soil**" people the "**HARD PEOPLE.**"

On the other hand, people who are humble do not abuse the power of their position. They, instead, use it to serve God and others. Jesus is humble in His position as the great, righteous, Second Person of the Trinity. In all humility, He loves the lowly and unclean. He is not threatened, nor feels it below His position to do so. He touches them, and His recognition of them raises *them* up and gives *them* a sense of worth. Serving another person communicates a care and love for them, and a bonding between the two develops. God the Father's relationship with Jesus is like that. It is honest and open. Jesus is in prayer with His Father and is submissive to the Father's will. Jesus is not considering the eyes of others, but only His Father's eyes. Jesus humbly is willing to give His life at the Father's direction. This results in the *salvation* of many people in that some will be raised up, spiritually, at their death, and bodily, at the resurrection of the dead. In addition, humbly serving God usually results in benefits to others. **The glorification of God and the satisfaction of our need for a sense of worth comes when we humble ourselves, experience love and acceptance from God, and use any position that we are granted by God to serve others. *God* will raise us up and give us a sense of worth. We, then, will not be the "wayside soil." We are loving God and loving our neighbor. Servant-like humility, in the form of humbleness, is the "mind of Christ" concerning how we should behave in any "position" in which we find ourselves.**

> **People were bringing little children to Jesus to have him touch them, but the disciples rebuked them. When Jesus saw this, he was indignant. He said to them, 'Let the little children come to me, and do not hinder them, for the kingdom of God belongs to such as these. I tell you the truth, anyone who will not receive the kingdom of God like a child will**

**never enter it.' And he took the children in his
arms, put his hands on them and blessed them.
(Mark 10:13–16)**

Do we see Jesus a little more clearly?
Are we, in our various positions, humble and serving others?
Let' go on!

FRAMEWORK FOR SPIRITUAL MATURITY

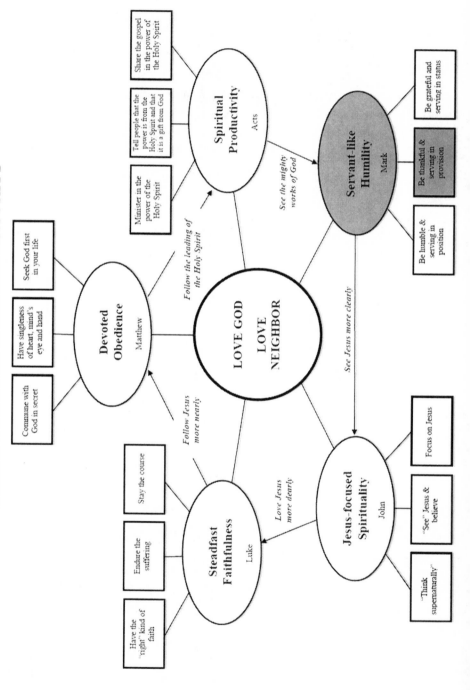

LOVE GOD LOVE NEIGHBOR

Devoted Obedience — Matthew
- Commune with God in secret
- Have singleness of heart, mind's eye and hand
- Seek God first in your life

Spiritual Productivity — Acts
- Minister in the power of the Holy Spirit
- Tell people that the power is from the Holy Spirit and that it is a gift from God
- Share the gospel in the power of the Holy Spirit

Servant-like Humility — Mark
- Be humble & serving in position
- Be thankful & serving in provision
- Be grateful and serving in status

Jesus-focused Spirituality — John
- "Think supernaturally"
- "See" Jesus & believe
- Focus on Jesus

Steadfast Faithfulness — Luke
- Have the "right" kind of faith
- Endure the suffering
- Stay the course

Follow the leading of the Holy Spirit

See the mighty works of God

See Jesus more clearly

Follow Jesus more nearly

Love Jesus more dearly

CHAPTER 2

From Whom All Blessings Flow: Be Thankful In Provision

Pride of provision.

A second form of pride presented in chapter 10 of the Gospel of Mark (vv. 17–22) is **"pride of provision."** A man in the Hebrew culture of that time was expected to be righteous, and that his prosperity would be interpreted as a reward from God for his righteousness. This, in turn, would give a man a great sense of worth. The man, described in verse 17, believes that *he* has been providing for *his own* righteousness, and the resulting rewards, by observing all of the "commandments" from his youth (v. 20). He feels great pride and a sense of worth in such provision for himself. This is really an illusion. What he does not understand is that both the provision of righteousness and its rewards are really the work of God. However, he has discovered one thing that he feels that he cannot provide for himself—eternal life. He asks Jesus what he needs to do to inherit eternal life (v. 17). Jesus responds by telling him to sell all that he possesses and to give the money to the poor (v. 21). Jesus tells him that if he does this, he will have treasure in heaven (v. 21). Jesus also instructs him to follow Him (v. 21). Jesus is really telling him to acknowledge and rely totally on the true provider of all things—God. The man is sad because the pride he has in providing for himself and his sense of worth connected to that pride, are threatened (v. 22). He is not truly thankful for all that God has provided for him. His pride has blinded him, and it seems that he will not let the Word of God, Jesus, penetrate his hard heart. The man goes away saddened and grieving because of the **hardness** of his heart.

Jesus expands on the problem of pride of provision with his disciples. He tells them that it will be hard for those who are wealthy to enter the kingdom of God (vv. 23–25). Because the Jews had always believed that their prosperity was a sign that God was pleased with them, the disciples are amazed and even astonished at His words (vv. 24, 26). Jesus goes on to tell His disciples that trusting in their own provision will not result in their entering the kingdom of God (v. 25). Jesus says that if anyone is willing to give up striving to provide for themselves, *God* will provide for them abundantly (vv. 27–30). Furthermore, Jesus indicates that those who seem to be providing "successfully" for themselves will be "last" in His eyes, and those who seek God's provision will be "first" (v. 31). Those who rely thankfully on God's provision will be raised up and will receive a great sense of worth through this manifestation of God's love and acceptance.

In today's society, some men and women also are working toward "righteousness and its reward." There is nothing wrong with that unless we forget our relationship to God and begin to believe that we are providing these things ourselves. If we believe that we are providing for ourselves, we will begin to develop a pride of provision and will use that pride in an attempt to give ourselves a sense of worth.

Experiencing pride of provision.

The "pride-of-provision" issue that plagued me for years was that of owning a house and yard. I would find myself working to the extreme in order to maintain and improve both my house and my yard. One day, I was raking leaves in my front yard and thinking to myself, "What a beautiful yard God has provided for me. Thank, you, Lord!" In the middle of my thankful praise to the Lord, I heard a voice behind me. One of my friends that lived up the street was on a walk and was passing by my house. My friend said to me, "John, your yard always look so good; *you* do such a good job." What a temptation to cross the line and feel that I had provided for myself! Was I working so hard to be a thankful good steward of the things that the Lord had provided for me; or was *I* working so hard to show everyone around me how well I had provided for myself and my family, thereby enhancing my sense of worth? The answer depended on where my heart was on any given day. On the days that the answer to the latter question was "yes," I was exhibiting "pride of provision" and was not being thankful to God. The "pride of provision" blinds men and women and hardens their hearts so that the Word of God, Jesus, cannot penetrate.

Thankfulness in provision.

The opposite to "pride of provision" is "thankfulness in provision" and is presented in verses 32–34. Jesus and His disciples are on the road to Jerusalem, and they were all aware of what was going to happen there (v. 32). No matter, Jesus is out in front (v. 32). He has the "point." His disciples are amazed at Jesus, and all that followed Him were fearful (v. 32). Jesus then describes to His disciples how He will be scourged and killed when He gets to Jerusalem (vv. 33–34). However, Jesus is persevering because He knows that God the Father will provide for him in that "Three days later He will rise again" (v. 34). Jesus is thankful and relying on the *Father's* provision to raise Him up.

Experiencing thankfulness in provision.

Shortly after my conversion, needy young people were placed in my path. My wife, Louise, and I were living in a three-bedroom apartment with our three young children at the time. On one Christmas Eve, an eighteen-year-old boy knocked on our door needing a place to stay. We took him in. Shortly thereafter, a seven-year-old boy, whose family was breaking down, came to live with us. Then, a fifteen-year-old girl, who had been hospitalized with hepatitis contracted through drug use, came to stay. Louise and I felt that the Lord wanted us to take care of these children. However, our apartment was too small to house everyone. We began looking for a house to rent and found a perfect place. The only problem was that the owner wanted a full year's rent in advance. We did not have the resources in and of ourselves to raise that kind of money, but the Lord did. We prayed; and in the three weeks that followed, God provided the full year's rent. Wow, did God provide, raise us up, and give us a sense of worth? Thank you, Lord!

After we moved into the house, Louise and I took in more young people who were having problems. In the "giving up everything department," all of our personal possessions were either destroyed or stolen—literally the clothes off of our backs and the shoes off of our feet. In addition, we needed $1500 per month more than my income in order to provide for the young people. I recall the day in our second year of ministry when both the rent and the electric bill were overdue. Payment had to be made by the next day or the ministry would come to an end. We prayed. That night, Louise and I were scheduled to speak at the local Lions Club. We did so, not mentioning to anyone the specifics of our current need. After we finished speaking, donations unexpectedly came forward from the members. Don't you know that the donations totaled, to the penny, the amount that we needed to pay the rent and electric bill! Wow, again! Thank you, Lord! We need to seek God's provision in our lives and not try to do it all on our own.

Contrasting scriptural examples of perception of and action concerning provision.

Chapter 15 of the Gospel of Mark provides a good example of the application of the concept of perception and action concerning provision. I looked at the characters in this chapter and tried to figure out who was focused on pridefully providing for themselves, and who was thankfully waiting on God's provision.

In verses 1–29, the concept that emerges is one of people using (and abusing) others in order to provide gain for themselves and raise themselves up. Because of envy, the chief priests, elders, scribes and the whole council bring Jesus before Pilate and *accuse* Him of many things (vv. 1, 3, 10). Jesus is beginning to overshadow these religious leaders. Taking their provision into their own hands, they *accuse* Him before Pilate and stir up the crowd to release Barabbas instead of Jesus (v. 11). The crowd is *using* Jesus as they seek to please their religious leaders (vv. 13, 15). Pilate does what is politically expedient for himself by *delivering* Jesus to the crowd (vv. 6–9, 15). The soldiers are *using* Jesus in order to provide entertainment for themselves (vv. 16–20). All of the above characters are not thankfully seeking God's provision in their lives, but are using another (specifically Jesus) in order to provide for themselves. Jesus, on the other hand, is silent before His accusers (v. 4). He is not using and abusing others in order to provide for himself. Those in the crowd feel that their sense of worth can be maintained if everyone else is doing the same thing. Often, people go along with the crowd in order to gain a sense of justification for their own behavior. Obviously, these people are not thankfully waiting on the provision of God. Conversely, Jesus does not provide for himself, but awaits the provision of God, the Father (vv. 34–36, Ps. 22). The provision of the Father is that the veil of the temple is torn in two symbolizing that, through the sacrifice of Jesus on the cross, everyone (not only the high priest) now can have access to God. When we thankfully wait on God's provision for us, it always ends up benefiting others and increases our sense of worth.

Having faith and confidence in God's provision is the theme of verses 39–47. The "women" are still following Jesus and risking their own lives by doing so (vv. 40–41, 47). They have faith and confidence that God will provide for them. Joseph of Arimathea, who is a rich and respected leader, risks everything he has by claiming the body of Jesus (vv. 42–46). Joseph is trusting in God to provide for him. We need to step out in faith as we serve Jesus, thankfully trusting in God's provision as we go.

Summary.

There are several things we can learn from these parts of the Gospel of Mark. As a result of perceived self-provision, some people become prideful, and use and abuse others in order to provide for themselves. Then, in order to justify their actions, they draw others into a similar behavior. They do not thankfully exhibit faith and confidence in God's provision, but only have faith and confidence in their own provision. I call these types of **"wayside soil"** people the **"HARD PEOPLE."**

On the contrary, people who thankfully have faith and confidence in God's provision do not use or abuse other people or need to justify their behavior. The women and Joseph of Arimathea exhibit humble faith and confidence in God's provision as they cared for the body of Jesus. Jesus, himself, has humble faith in the Father's provision for Him, and we see how Jesus' faith is justified by the tearing of the temple veil. Thankfully, having faith in God's provision usually results in benefits to others. **The glorification of God and the satisfaction of our need for a sense of worth come when we receive and acknowledge thankfully God's provision for us, experience the love and acceptance from God in His provision for us, and use that provision to serve others. God will raise us up and give us a sense of worth. We, then, will not be the "wayside soil." We are loving God and loving our neighbor. Servant-like humility in the form of thankfulness is the "mind of Christ" concerning our provision.**

> **"Jesus looked at him and loved him. 'One thing you lack,' he said. 'Go, sell everything you have and give to the poor, and you will have treasure in heaven. Then come, follow me.'" (Mark 10:21)**

Do we see Jesus a little more clearly?
Are we thankful and using God's provision to serve others?
Let's go on!

FRAMEWORK FOR SPIRITUAL MATURITY

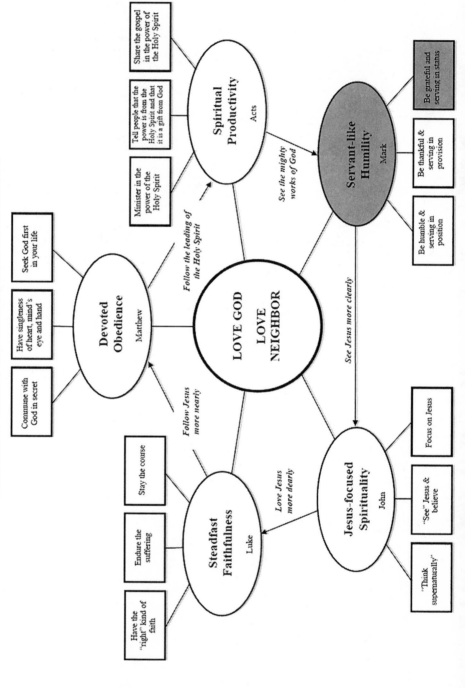

CHAPTER 3

Last But Not Least:
Be Grateful in Status

Pride of presumption.

A third form of pride presented in chapter ten (vv. 35–41) is the **"pride of presumption"** that others should serve us. James and John look upon Jesus as their teacher (v. 35). They ask Jesus to let them sit next to Jesus in His glory in heaven (vv. 35–37). They are pride fully caught up in their relationship with Jesus that they presume and expect that Jesus will automatically serve them in any way that they want. They are ungrateful (differs from thankful in that, after receiving, more is expected) and not satisfied with their status. In their prideful presumption, they are blind to the service that will be required of them in order to gain proximity to Jesus in heaven (vv. 38–40). The pride of presumption that Jesus should serve them clouds their sight and will not allow the Word of God, Jesus, to penetrate their hearts. James and John make an ungrateful request of Jesus because of the **hardness** of their hearts.

Experiencing pride of presumption.

I remember that early in my marriage to Louise, I presumed that, as my wife, she should serve me. I was a high school teacher and basketball coach at the time, and my arrival at the end of the workday was very unpredictable. However, I expected my dinner to be hot and on the table when I walked through the door. Somehow, Louise managed to do it even with our three very small children underfoot. I had no thought of serving her, but pridefully presumed that she should serve me in the manner that I demanded. Obviously, I was ungrateful in presuming that Louise should serve me in this way. This kind of ungrateful pride hardens our hearts so that the Word of God, Jesus, cannot penetrate.

Gratefulness in status.

The opposite to "pride of presumption" that others should serve us is "gratefulness in status" in relationship to God and others. This is found in verses 42–45 of chapter 10. Jesus tells his disciples that they are on the wrong track if they are seeking high position so that they can cause others to serve them (vv. 42–43). He tells them that those that would be great and chief among them shall be a servant and slave to the others (vv. 43–44). He says that He came not to be served, but to serve others (v. 45). His service to others is truly in the extreme in that He gives his life for them! God does not want us sitting around presuming about our place in heaven or our high place anywhere else and waiting for others to serve us. He wants us gratefully serving Him and others.

Experiencing gratefulness in status.

After my conversion, I can remember struggling with the concept of serving God, my wife, my children, my students, the players on the basketball team that I was coaching, my boss, my fellow teachers, my brothers and sisters in Christ, others in need, etc. The spirit was willing, but the flesh was most certainly weak. I was grateful for Louise and wanted to serve her by helping her so that she could become all that God wanted her to be. However, sometimes, that meant taking care of the children, doing the laundry, cooking, housecleaning, etc. I can recall vividly the ambiguous feelings of desire-to-support and resentment. It was only through the reading of God's Word and constant prayer on my part, the patience of Job on Louise's part, and the power of the Holy Spirit on God's part that I was able to begin to break through this particular barrier of pride.

One time, my grandson (age 17 at the time) and two of his friends came to visit us in Florida. We took them to Orlando and rented a hotel room for a few days. The morning after the first night's stay, we were all getting ready to go to the theme parks. I wandered out into the hall and overheard one of the housemaids saying to another that she had thirty-six rooms to clean that day. I came back into the room and told the boys that they needed to organize their belongings in such a way to make it easier for the housemaid to clean. One of the boys responded, "That's what she gets paid for." What an ungrateful response! We sat right down on the floor and did a Bible study on Mark 10:35–45. Later, we went to an all-you-can-eat pizza place, and the boys really went to town. As a result, the plates began to pile up on the table. I saw my grandson whisper something to the other boys, and they began to clean and stack the empty plates on the table. This made things much easier for the busboy.

One good way to avoid the temptation of presuming that others should serve us is to, in turn, serve them. In this way, we can show our gratefulness. My wife, Louise, is amazing at this. Those people who serve her quickly find themselves being served *by her*. We can go to a restaurant, and in five minutes, the waitress will be sharing her problems with Louise. If we go to someone's house for dinner, she is in the kitchen helping. If we are staying somewhere away from home, she will be ministering to the housemaids, the desk clerks, the maintenance people, the dining room staff, etc. She is the personification of gratefulness in status.

Contrasting scriptural examples of gratefulness in status.

Chapter 16 of the Gospel of Mark provided me a good view of the application of the concept of "pride of presumption" contrasted against the concept of "gratefulness in status." I examined each of the characters in this chapter and attempted to determine who was ungratefully presuming others should serve them and who was being grateful in status.

Mary Magdalene; Mary, the Mother of James; and Salome start out well, but fear gets in the way. They all bring sweet spices that they might anoint the body of Jesus (v. 1). They come to his sepulcher as soon as they can, not knowing how they will roll away the large stone from the entrance (v. 2). These women are not presumptuously waiting for someone to serve them. They are grateful for all that Jesus had done for them, and they are seeking to serve Him. However, after their encounter with the angel, they do not follow through in their serving. They are told to go and tell the disciples what they have seen; but due to *fear*, they do not tell the disciples (vv. 5–8). My sense is that their fear stemmed from not feeling "worthy" to tell the men.

Mary Magdalene responds to seeing Jesus in a grateful and serving way. She goes and tells the disciples what she has seen (vv. 9–10). The "two walking" also respond in grateful service to Jesus by going and telling the disciples that they have seen Him (v. 12).

The disciples, however, do not listen to Mary Magdalene (v. 11) or the "two walking" (v. 13). The eleven disciples, I am sure, feel that Jesus was closest to them; and, therefore, would appear to *them* first, not to a woman or to two "lesser" disciples. The eleven disciples, I believe, have a bad case of ungrateful "pride of presumption."

Finally, Jesus appears to all of the disciples at once and reproaches them for their unbelief and the **hardness** of their hearts (v. 14). Then, he exhorts them to a life of grateful service—"Go into all the world and preach the gospel to all creation" (v. 15). The disciples respond by doing as he commanded—"And they went out and preached everywhere, while the Lord worked with them, and confirmed the word by signs that followed." (v. 20).

Summary.

There is something we can learn from these portions of the gospel of Mark. People, whose pride is as a result of being presumptuous about their relationship to God and others, are not grateful, but *expect* God and others to serve *them*. I call these people the **HARD PEOPLE**.

On the other hand, Jesus expects His followers to be grateful for their status and to serve Him by going into the world and preaching the gospel. In verse 20, we see that His disciples do just that. The response of love and acceptance by Jesus in giving them such a great responsibility must have given the disciples a great sense of worth. **The glorification of God and the satisfaction of our need for a sense of worth come when we are grateful to God and are not expecting more than He has already provided, experience love and acceptance from God in the responsibilities that He gives to us, and serve Him and others unreservedly. God will raise us up and give us a sense of worth. We, then, are not the "wayside soil." We are loving God and loving our neighbor. Servant-like humility in the form of gratefulness is the "mind of Christ" concerning our status.**

> **You know that those who are regarded as rulers of the Gentiles lord it over them, and their high officials exercise authority over them. Not so with you. Instead, whoever wants to become great among you must be your servant, and whoever wants to be first must be slave of all. For even the Son of Man did not come to be served, but to give his life as a ransom for many. (Mark 10:42b-45)**

Do we see Jesus a little more clearly?
Are we grateful for our status and serving others?
Let's go on!

Summary
Section I

All the concepts concerning pride that we have seen in chapter ten are exhibited in the story of blind Bartimaeus. There is Bartimaeus begging by the side of the road (v. 46). Does he have any pride of position? He is a blind beggar, a man of no position. Does he have any pride of provision? He is a blind beggar, a man who relies totally on the provision of others. Does he have any pride of presumption that others will serve him? He is a blind beggar, a man who can neither presume nor expect that anyone will serve him. He is totally humbled by his circumstances and his status.

Bartemaius may be physically blind, but he perceives who Jesus is and cries out, "Jesus, thou Son of David, have mercy on me!" (vv. 47–48). The words, "Son of David," in these times had the same meaning as "Messiah" to the people. What Bartimaeus is really is saying is "Jesus, Messiah." He also perceives Jesus as holy and great and himself as sinful and small. He cries out, "have mercy on me" (vv. 47–48). Jesus, the rabbi of great position, calls Bartimaeus, the blind beggar of low position (v. 49), just as he did with the children. Bartimaeus casts away his garment (v.50), which is probably his only possession; and by doing so humbles himself and implies that his provision is totally in Jesus' hands. Because of his faith in Jesus, Bartimaeus is healed (v. 52). What a provision from Jesus! However, Bartimaeus is not ungrateful about his healing but gratefully serves Jesus by "following him in the road" (v. 52).

The Pharisees, the "rich" man, and James and John as depicted in chapter 10 are spiritually blind, "wayside soil," and "hard" people; and the Word of God cannot penetrate their hearts. None of these have the "mind of Christ." Bartimaeus is not the "wayside soil," and the Word of God, Jesus, penetrates his heart. Bartimaeus has spiritual sight; he sees who Jesus is! Bartimaeus humbles himself before Jesus, has faith on Jesus' provision, and Jesus heals him and raises him up. Bartimaeus is not presumptuous about being served but gratefully serves Jesus. Bartimaeus seems to have the "mind of Christ" concerning humility.

God is trying to touch the "hard ("wayside soil") people" through His Word. If they allow His Word to penetrate their hearts, they can experience His love and acceptance, give the glory to God, and be raised up to have a *true* sense of worth in Him. Where are we in all of this? Are we like the Pharisees, the rich man, and James and John; or are we like Bartimaeus? Are we spiritually blind, or do we have spiritual sight? Do we try to raise ourselves up in our own eyes and the eyes of others, or are we seeking, sensing and experiencing *God's* love and acceptance? Are we selfishly proud, or are we humble servants? Are we the "wayside soil" or not the "wayside soil?" Do we have the "mind of Christ?"

The glorification of God and the satisfaction of our need for a sense of worth come when we experience love and acceptance from God and use humbly any position we may have been granted in order to serve others, be thankful for God's provision for us and use it to serve others, and be grateful for our status and serve Him and others unreservedly. If we do this, we will have servant-like humility and will not be the "wayside soil." We are loving God and loving our neighbor. This is the "mind of Christ" concerning servant-like humility.

> **The time has come," he said. "The kingdom of God is near. Repent and believe the good news! (Mark 1:15)**

> Do we see Jesus a little more clearly?
> Do we want to see Jesus clearly enough
> to increase our belief in Him?
> Let's go on!

Note: If you want to pursue the theme of "servant-like humility" further in the Gospel of Mark, turn to Appendix VIII-A for a study outline. The outline provides for a macro study (based on a micro study) of the scripture and is written in an application format.

FRAMEWORK FOR SPIRITUAL MATURITY

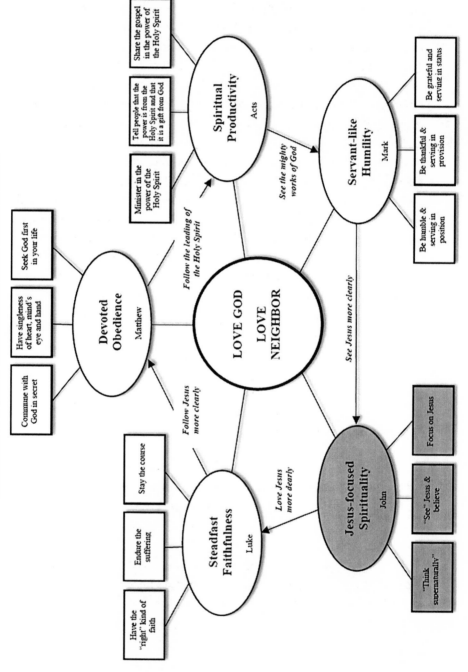

SECTION II

Jesus-Focused Spirituality

Symbolically, in the Bible, darkness represents everything that is not of God, including sin. As we are all born with the sin of Adam upon us; we, consequently, are all "in the dark." We cannot look past our sinful self, our sinful reason, and our sinful will. It all blinds us. We are the "wayside soil" in the Parable of the Sower which is unable to receive the seed, the Word of God, which falls upon it. While the seed lies upon the hard ground which is unable to receive it; the birds, Satan, come and snatch it away. There is no chance that the seed will penetrate the soil and come to life. Certainly, the theme of the Gospel of Mark helps us to understand that the sin of pride causes spiritual blindness that immobilizes us in the darkness of our sin.

Symbolically, in the Bible, light represents everything that is of God, including holiness. The light shines on all of us in the darkness of our sin; but because of our spiritual blindness, we cannot see it. We are the "wayside soil" in the Parable of the Sower, and our hardness needs to be broken up and softened. If that can happen, then the seed, the Word of God, can penetrate and germinate before the birds, Satan, snatch it away. Again, the Gospel of Mark helps us to understand that it is humility that helps in the lifting of our spiritual blindness. Humility breaks open the hardness of our pride. We begin to be able to look past our sinful self, our sinful reason, and our sinful will; and we begin to see spiritually. Remember that in Mark 14, we saw that the people who were able to "see" Jesus first were those who were the most humble. They were beginning to gain their spiritual sight. When we become humble and begin to gain our spiritual sight, we begin to see the Light, Jesus. We begin to see more clearly the holiness of the Light, Jesus, and realize the sinful darkness of ourselves. Jesus, the Word of God and the Light, begins to penetrate our sinful darkness.

In the beginning was the Word, and the Word was with God, and the Word was God. He was in the beginning with God. All things came into being through Him, and apart from Him nothing came into being that has come into being. In Him was life, and the life was the Light of men. The Light shines in the darkness, and darkness did not comprehend it. There came a man sent from God, whose name was John. He came as a witness, to testify about the Light, so that all might believe through him. He was not the Light, but he came to testify about the Light. There was the true Light which, coming into the world, enlightens every man. He was in the world, and the world was made through Him, and the world did not know Him. He came to His own, and those who were His own did not receive Him. But as many as received Him, to them He gave the right to become children of God, even to those who believe in His name, who were born, not of blood nor the will of the flesh nor of the will of man, but of God. And the Word became flesh, and dwelt among us, and we saw His glory as of the only begotten from the Father, full of grace and truth. (John 1:1–14)

In the above passage, the "Word" is Jesus and the "Light" is Jesus. When we are humble, we will begin to see the Light and the Word, Jesus. Jesus, the Light and the Word, will penetrate our sinful darkness and bring us to spiritual life. How this penetration and coming to spiritual life takes place is what the Gospel of John is all about. The Gospel of John does not present one of the themes in the Parable of the Sower, but rather, the manner in which the seed penetrates the hard soil and comes to life. It represents the way Jesus, the Light and the Word, penetrates our sinful darkness and brings us to spiritual life.

Reflecting on my understanding of human intrinsic needs, the need related to "coming to spiritual life" is that of freedom. In our "Adam" nature, we are bound in slavery to our sinful lives and ultimately to death, which is God's punishment for our sinful lives. We *have* no choice. We sin and wallow in the guilt of that sin. The oppression of our sin and the depression that accompanies our guilt plagues us daily. Jesus, the Light and the Word, is the only way through which we gain choice in our lives. Through the breaking of His body on the cross, Jesus took the punishment for our sin upon Himself and freed us from the oppression of a totally sinful life. Through the shedding of His blood on the cross, Jesus obtained forgiveness for our sin and freed us from eternal death and the depression of guilt related to our sin. If we believe this, Jesus will send the Holy Spirit to reside in us, and we will be spiritually transformed. Through the power of the Holy Spirit, whom Jesus sent to reside within us; we have the power to choose God, to resist the temptation of sin, and to choose righteousness. This new power to *choose* righteousness and life instead of sin and death provides us with the ultimate sense of *freedom*.

Chapter three of the Gospel of John provides a great description concerning the way in which we come to spiritual life and reveals the "mind of Christ" concerning spiritual transformation. This section outlines the three steps that enable us to be spiritually transformed. In the next three chapters we will focus on each of these three steps.

FRAMEWORK FOR SPIRITUAL MATURITY

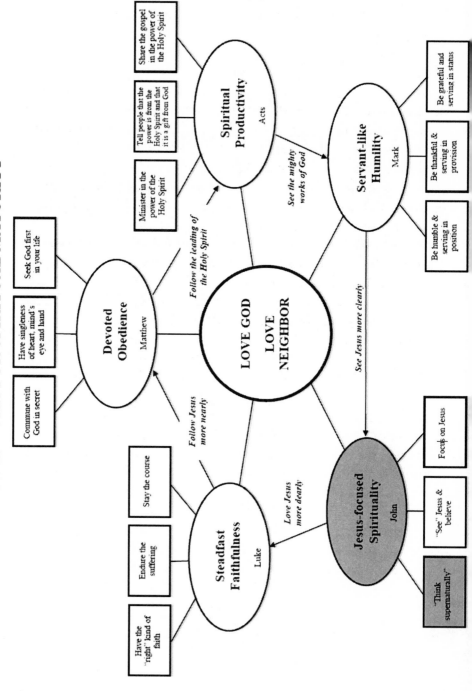

CHAPTER 4

Out of the Box:
Think Supernaturally

The first step to Jesus-focused spirituality has to do with the prerequisite for spiritual transformation and the manner in which we "come" to Jesus. "Coming" to someone means to enter his or her presence. We can enter another person's presence in a number of ways such as saying "hello," shaking hands, asking "What's Up?" or "How are you?," etc. The question is, however, how do we "come" to Jesus? How do we enter *His* presence?

Thinking past our self.

In chapter three of John's Gospel, Nicodemus "comes" to Jesus. Nicodemus is a Pharisee, a spiritual leader of the Jews, and a man of great position. However, this man of great position "comes" to Jesus at night (v. 2). Most probably, Nicodemus comes at night because he does not want to be seen with the controversial Jesus. Jesus had just created quite a disturbance in the temple (John 2:13–22). Nicodemus surely is concerned about losing his position as a spiritual leader if he is seen with such a controversial person as Jesus. Nicodemus "comes" to Jesus in a guarded way; he comes under the cover of darkness (3:1). The pride he has in his position causes him to "come" in secret. He cannot think past himself. He can only "think naturally" in that a public meeting with Jesus might affect his position with the other

Jewish leaders. He is not able to "think supernaturally" and trust God enough to come to Jesus openly.

Remember how Bartimaeus, the beggar, "comes" to Jesus? Unlike Nicodemus, Bartimaeus has no position about which to be concerned. He is able to think past himself, to think supernaturally, and to choose to trust Jesus. Bartimaeus throws off his cloak, probably his only possession, in front of the crowd and "comes" to Jesus *openly*!

Thinking past our reason.

Besides not "coming" to Jesus openly, Nicodemus comes to Jesus doubting His witness. At the Passover festival in Jerusalem many "believed in His name" because they saw the signs that He was doing (John 2:23). Although Nicodemus has witnessed the signs done by Jesus, he cannot think past his reason in the natural realm. The most he is willing to accept is that Jesus is a teacher who has come from God (v. 2). He can only accept that Jesus is a "teacher" from God and is bound in his thinking in the natural realm. He cannot think supernaturally, at this point, that Jesus is the Messiah.

Remember Bartimaeus, the beggar? He cries out to Jesus— "Jesus, Son of David." Saying "Son of David" is the same as saying "Messiah." Bartimaeus could not have seen, but only heard, of the signs that Jesus had done; yet he does not doubt Jesus' witness. He is able to think past his reason, to think supernaturally, and to choose to trust Jesus. To Bartimaeus, Jesus *is* the Messiah. There is *no doubt*!

Nicodemus comes to Jesus trying to rationally understand Jesus' teaching and direction. Jesus tells Nicodemus that he cannot see things supernaturally unless he is born again of the Holy Spirit (v. 4, 7). Nicodemus tries to reason with his mind and asks Jesus if he is required to enter his mother's womb a second time in order to be born again (v. 4). Nicodemus cannot think past his reason.

Remember Bartimaeus, the beggar? When Jesus asks what he wants, Bartimaeus asks Jesus to allow him to regain his sight. Bartimaeus understands that Jesus' signs were supernatural and that Jesus could, through supernatural means, heal his blindness. He is able to think past his reason, to think supernaturally, and choose to trust Jesus.

Thinking past our will.

Jesus explains that this rebirth cannot be understood in the natural realm (vv. 5–8). Nicodemus responds in amazement at the possibility of such things (v. 9). Jesus tells Nicodemus that, as a spiritual leader of the Jews, he should perceive things supernaturally (vv. 10–13). However, Nicodemus can only think naturally in that the signs can only be interpreted in the natural realm. He seems unwilling to accept the supernatural realm and the working of the Holy Spirit. His thinking is bound in the natural realm; and, for Nicodemus at this time, there is no choice.

Finally, there is nothing in scripture that indicates the immediate outcome of Nicodemus' encounter with Jesus. One is led to believe from what follows in John 3 that Nicodemus does not make an immediate change in his thinking. He certainly does not begin to follow Jesus publicly at that point in time. He cannot think past his will and continues to do what *he* thinks is appropriate. He is a slave to thinking in the natural realm and is unable to choose to do that which is God's will.

Remember Bartimaeous, the beggar? After Jesus heals his blindness, Bartimaeus immediately follows Jesus on the road. Bartimaeus begins to follow Jesus publicly. Bartimaeus no longer does what *he* wants to do. He now begins to do what *Jesus* wants him to do. He is able to think past his will, to think supernaturally, and to choose to follow Jesus.

The first step in coming to spiritual life has to do with the manner in which we "come" to Jesus. We must enter His presence openly, not doubting that He is the Messiah, and willing to accept the works of the Holy Spirit in the supernatural realm. We need to think supernaturally past our self, our reason, and our will!

Experiencing "thinking naturally."

Before my conversion, I was much like Nicodemus—thinking in the natural realm. In my youth, I had learned about Jesus, especially about the way in which he helped those in need. I interpreted these works and signs in the natural realm. Jesus, to me, was just a man who helped others, and that was a good thing to do. Both of my parents and my grandmother were teachers whose business was to help others. They reinforced the things that I had learned about Jesus. As a result, I embarked on a career in which my goal was to help people. I became a high-school teacher and an athletic coach doing works of help in the natural realm.

After a few years of teaching and coaching, I began to notice that my "helping of others" was not working very well. I was always quick to give *my* advice to others concerning how to solve their problems. However, most of the time, my advice turned out to be inappropriately timed and people often viewed my attitude as arrogant. I also found that I wanted other people to lean on me. I began to see that I was using the dependence of other people in order to satisfy my own need of worth. Many times, those whom I was "helping" fell flat on their faces when I was not around to serve as a crutch. I became jealous of others who were helping those whom *I* was helping. How would anyone know that a person had worked through a problem because of *my* help if others were helping as well? Certainly, my pride had become a big problem. Finally, I found real difficulty going past the point of my own pain (physically, emotionally, socially, financially, etc.) for others. I was able to give out of my abundance or spare time, but not out of that which I considered to be my own personal need or desires. My works to help other people were in the natural realm, and things were not going well. I saw no other alternatives from which to choose, and I felt trapped and helpless.

I was proud of my position as teacher and coach, and proud that I was able to provide for myself in those positions. I never opened myself to accept help from anywhere (having been raised in the Puritan ethic of New England probably did not help any). To do so, I felt, would indicate weakness on my part to those around me and would cause me to be diminished in their eyes. This certainly was a lonely type of existence. However, the problems related to seeking help beyond myself prevented me from reaching out. I began to study philosophy and psychology, but those studies did not help. I was thinking totally in the natural realm. Again, I saw no other choices with which I could resolve my problems.

I was not open to anyone else, including Jesus. My concept of Jesus at the time was that He was a good and wise teacher in the natural realm. I did not have a clue about Jesus as the Messiah in the supernatural realm. Hey, I did not even have a clear idea what a Messiah was! The working of the Holy Spirit in the supernatural realm never entered my mind, and I just continued to do things "my way." I could not see any other choices. Just as Nicodemus, I was unable to think past myself, my reason, and my will.

I remember one incident in my life at this time that showcased all of my difficulties of thinking in the natural realm. I was seated at a lunch table in the cafeteria of a high school with all of my fellow coaches. A boy, whom I had been helping in my social studies classroom, came up to me at the table and said, "Hello." The boy had long hair upon which the other coaches frowned (this was the mid-1960s). I could feel the glare of the coaches' eyes as they watched to see how I would interact with this boy. Would I be able to treat the boy with kindness and respect as Jesus would have? No, I would not. I operated in the natural realm and satisfied my own needs at the expense of another. I could not go past the point of my own pain for the boy and risk not being accepted by the coaches. I seemed to be totally predisposed to make choices in this way. I looked at myself afterward, and I did not like what I saw. I was saddened and depressed about my behavior. I was just like Nicodemus "coming" to Jesus; I was enslaved to thinking and operating in the natural realm and was not able to "see" Jesus.

Scriptural examples contrasting "thinking naturally" and "thinking supernaturally."

Chapter eighteen of the Gospel of John is a good place in which to examine the application of the concept of "thinking supernaturally."

Judas is definitely not thinking supernaturally. He is concerned only about himself. He "comes" to Jesus at night just as Nicodemus did (vv. 1–3). He does not "see" Jesus and comes to betray Him (v. 2). Judas does not come openly but secretly, accompanied by a detachment of soldiers (v. 3). Judas cannot think supernaturally past *himself* to "see" Jesus.

Peter is not thinking supernaturally, either, when he attempts to stop the capture of Jesus. He reasons that he will take matters into his own hands and protect Jesus (v. 10). Jesus remarks back to Peter that He is doing the will of His Father in the supernatural realm (v. 11). Jesus is thinking supernaturally; Peter is not. Peter cannot think supernaturally past his own *reason* in order to "see" Jesus.

Peter also is not thinking supernaturally when he denies Jesus (vv. 15–18). He cannot think past his own will and chooses to protect himself instead. It is the same with Annas, Caiaphas, and Pilate. (vv. 19–40). They all know that Jesus is not guilty, yet they proceed to convict him wrongly. They deal with Jesus in a politically expedient manner. All of those above cannot think supernaturally past their own *will* in order to "see" Jesus.

Jesus, on the other hand, is thinking supernaturally. He explains to Peter why He is *not* protecting Himself in the natural realm (v. 11). It is because Jesus *is* doing the will of His Father in the supernatural realm. Pilate asks Jesus if He is a king (v. 37). Jesus responds that he is not a king in the natural realm but a king in the supernatural realm (v. 37). He also says that those who are thinking supernaturally ("everyone who is of the truth") hear His voice (v. 37). Jesus is thinking and operating in the supernatural realm.

In John 18, everyone but Jesus is thinking in the natural realm. There is no choice for them because they cannot think past their self, their reason and/or their will. Jesus, however, is able to think in both the natural and supernatural realms. He has a choice; and He makes the choice in the supernatural realm, the will of His Father, "the cup which the Father has given Me, shall I not drink it?" (v. 11).

Summary.

Many things can be learned from the above portions of John's Gospel. True freedom can only come when we are able to think supernaturally past ourselves, our reason, and our will; all of which are the receptacles of our sin. Supernatural blindness precludes the possibility of making a supernatural choice. How can we make a supernatural choice if we cannot see it? We can only choose to think and operate in the natural realm; and, in a sense, we are bound there like slaves. We need to think past ourselves, our reason, and our will and consider the possibilities of the supernatural realm. **The glorification of God and the satisfaction of our need for a sense of freedom come when we have choice in the spiritual realm by "thinking supernaturally" past our self, our reason, and our will. God will reveal Himself to us. We are loving God and loving our neighbor. Jesus-focused spirituality, in the form of thinking supernaturally, is the "mind of Christ" concerning the perquisite first step in spiritual transformation.**

> **Nicodemus said to Him, "How can a man be born when he is old? He cannot enter a second time into his mother's womb and be born, can he? Jesus answered, 'Truly, truly, I say to you, unless one is born of water and the Spirit he cannot enter in the kingdom of God. That which is born of the flesh is flesh, and that which is born of the Spirit is spirit. Do not be amazed that I said to you, 'You must be born again.' The wind blow where it wishes and you hear the sound of it, but do not know where it comes from and where it is going; so is everyone who is born of the Spirit. (John 3:4–8)**

Are we thinking more supernaturally?
Do we see Jesus a little more clearly?
Let's go on!

FRAMEWORK FOR SPIRITUAL MATURITY

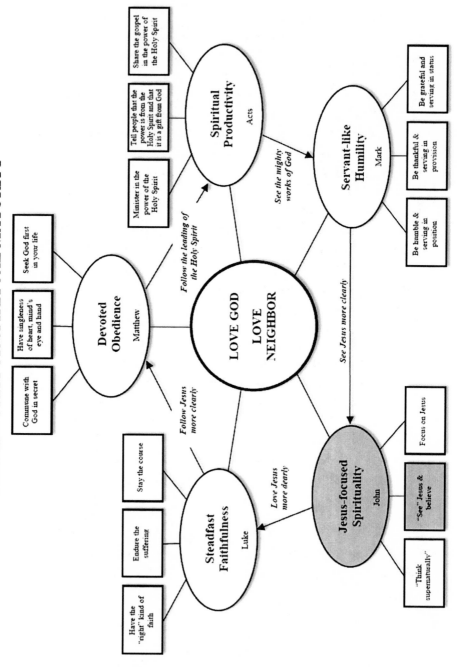

CHAPTER 5

Let There Be Light: "See" And Believe in Jesus

The second step to Jesus-focused spirituality is all about the transformation itself. This is a transformation that takes us from the natural realm to the supernatural realm. We all have experienced a natural birth into the natural realm, but we also must experience a spiritual birth into the supernatural realm. We must be "born again." The question is, then, what must happen for us to experience a spiritual birth?

Spiritual Birth.

After God had delivered the Israelites from slavery in Egypt, they had become discouraged on their journey. They spoke out against God and their leader, Moses. In doing this the Israelites sinned. God sent fiery serpents among the Israelites. These serpents bit the people and many of them died because of the venomous bite. The people came to Moses and asked him to intercede with God on their behalf. Moses prayed to God, and God responded. God told Moses to "Make a fiery serpent, and set it on a standard." It came to pass that if a serpent had bitten anyone, when he looked at the bronze *serpent*, he lived. (Num. 21: 4–9)

No one has ascended into heaven, but He who descended from heaven; the Son of Man. Just as Moses lifted up the serpent in the wilderness, even so must the Son of Man (Jesus) be lifted up; so that whoever believes in Him shall have eternal life. (John 3:13–15)

When we were born into the natural realm, we all inherited the sin of Adam. Adam, himself, was "bitten" by the serpent, Satan, in the Garden of Eden. Adam had sinned against God. His punishment for this included his eventual death (Gen. 3: 1–19) because the payment for sin is death (Rom. 6: 23). Adam's sin and the consequential punishment of death was passed on to all his descendants, which includes us (Rom. 5: 12). Adam was "bitten" by the serpent for his sin just as the Israelites were bitten by the serpents for their sin. Death was the subsequent consequence for both. It is because of the sin of Adam that we have inherited sin and that we, also, have been "bitten" by the serpent. At the very moment of our birth, we begin to die because of the venomous sin in ourselves.

What can be done in order to deliver us from the dilemma of sin and its consequences of eternal punishment and death? We need to look upon Jesus on the cross as the Israelites looked upon the bronze serpent on a standard in order not to die but to live (Rom. 5:14–21). What this means is that we need to understand and believe that even though we were sinners, Jesus Christ took the punishment and death of our sin upon Himself (Rom. 5: 8–11). We need to "see," or perceive, that Jesus is:

- *The Lord/Source of the Holy Spirit/Christ/Messiah/ Savior/Prophet/Healer* (John 4)—all in one
- *One Sent by God the Father* (John 5)—given all authority by the Father
- *The Bread of Life* (John 6). The person of substance who provides for our spiritual and eternal security.
- *The Source of the **Living Water*** (John 7). The person of life who enlivens and empowers us with the Holy Spirit.

- *The Light of the World* (John 8). The person of truth who *frees* us from all the lies about remaining in condemnation for our sin.
- *The Light of the World*—(John 9). The person of truth who *frees* us from all the lies about Him not being able to heal us (including from our sin).
- *The Door of the Sheep/The Great Shepherd* (John 10). The person of care who gives us a sense of *worth* through His love and acceptance.
- *The Resurrection and the Life* (John 11). The person of hope who gives us *joy* in that we will never die and will see the glory of God.
- *The King* (John 12). The spiritual King and Savior who gives us *meaning* by providing us the opportunity to serve in His kingdom and to glorify God.

(For a handout on the above, turn to Appendix IX)

If we repent of our sins and steadfastly believe these things; we will no longer be dying, nor shall we ever die, from the venomous bite of the serpent. We shall live forever!

Jesus goes on to state that "God so loved the world, that He gave His only begotten Son, that whoever believes in Him shall not perish, but have eternal life" (v. 16). Jesus goes on to state that He did not come into the world to judge it, but through Him it might be saved (v. 17). Jesus says that everyone that believes in Him is not judged, practices the truth, and comes to the Light so what they do can be seen as being done in God (vv. 18–20).

Experiencing spiritual birth.

On Easter Sunday morning in 1967, my wife, Louise, informed me that she was taking the children (John, age six; Mark, age five; and Amy, age two) to church. I had not attended church since my time in the Navy. Being a teacher, I was working another job in order to be able to support my family. This job involved my working thirty-two hours on the weekend and hindered me from attending church. However, I reached a point where I was not working that schedule any more, and Louise was inviting me to go to church with her. My first reaction was to tell her that only hypocrites go to church twice a year (Easter and Christmas). I told her that I would wait and go with her on the following Sunday. She indicated to me that, whatever the case, she was going on this Easter Sunday. I relinquished and told her that I would take the family. We went to a church that was located in the subdivision where we lived. As I walked up the steps of the church with my two boys in hand; my son, John, noticed a picture of the crucifixion in full color just inside the door. He asked me, "Dad, what do they do to you in here?" As we made our way inside, I began to tell him about Jesus and why He was on the cross. Once inside, we were given bulletins outlining the order of worship. On the cover was a drawing of two hands with holes in them. My son, Mark, asked me, "Dad, why do these hands have holes in them?" I told Mark that the holes in Jesus' hands came from the nails that were used to secure him to the cross. I told him how painful that must have been for Jesus; but that after Jesus died, he came back to life and did not have any more pain in his hands. We took our seats in the church, and the service began. As I continued explaining about Jesus to my young boys, all of a sudden, **I UNDERSTOOD IT FOR THE FIRST TIME!** I have very sensitive hands; and when I thought about Jesus choosing to allow the soldiers to nail his hands to the cross, I was overwhelmed by the power of that act. HE HAD GONE PAST THE POINT OF HIS OWN PAIN! Where did Jesus get that kind of power; it is not a natural kind of power. Where did Jesus get the kind of love that was behind His power to act; it was not a natural kind of love. In that instant I saw who Jesus is. Jesus is the "source of the living water," the "bread of life," the "great shepherd," and the "light of the world." At the same time, I saw who I was. Jesus was holy and great; I was sinful and small. I was humbled before him and began to cry. I realized, for the first, time that Jesus loved me enough to go past His own pain for my benefit, taking the punishment and death for my sin upon Himself. This was not a natural act; it was a supernatural act. Jesus is God, and He did this for me. I felt so special. I felt so loved. I sensed that God accepted me, and *His* acceptance was all that mattered to me. I no longer felt the need to seek the acceptance of other people. I felt as if someone had removed a huge load from my shoulders. I felt so free. It was for joy that I was crying. I cried until the end of the worship service. I cried as the congregation left the church. One older lady said to me, "You'll be all right, Sonny." She was right about that! I cried all the way home. I cried for three hours. Louise had to cancel a lunch date with another couple because I could not stop crying.

I identify so much with Isaiah in the temple, "Woe is me for I am ruined! Because I am a man of unclean lips, and I live among a people of unclean lips; and my eyes have seen the King, the Lord of hosts" (Isaiah 6:6); Job after listening to God speak out of a whirlwind, "I have heard of You by the hearing of the ear; but now my eye sees You. Therefore I retract, and I repent in dust and ashes" (Job 42:5–6); or Saul on the road to Damascus, "Who are you, Lord?" (Acts 9:5). *I had "seen" Jesus on the cross and believed in Him!*

Scriptural examples contrasting "no spiritual birth" and "spiritual birth."

Chapter 19 and 20 of the Gospel of John provides a good piece in which to examine the application of the concept of "seeing" and believing in Jesus. Chapter 19 deals with "seeing" Jesus and chapter 20 addresses believing in Him.

"Seeing" Jesus."

In verses 1–22 of chapter 19, an interesting irony emerges. It is Pilate, a gentile, who seems to "see" Jesus more clearly than the Jewish chief priests and officers. Pilate finds no guilt in Jesus (v. 6); seems to sense something different about Jesus (vv. 11–12); and writes a title, "JESUS THE NAZARENE, THE KING OF THE JEWS.," and puts it on the cross (v.19).

The Jewish chief priests and officers, on the other hand, do not "see" Jesus at all. They want Jesus to be crucified because they say that He made Himself out *to be* the Son of God (vv. 6–7), threaten Pilate with disloyalty to Caesar if he does not crucify Jesus (v.12), state that they have no other king, but Caesar (v.15), and protest about the title of "king" that Pilate puts on the cross (v. 21).

Certainly, Pilate does not "see" Jesus clear enough to believe in Him, but he certainly "sees" Jesus more clearly than the Jewish chief priests and officers. These Jews do not "see" Jesus at all and are trying to destroy Him.

In verses 22–25 and 29–37 of chapter 19, the Jews and the soldiers, neither of whom could "see" Jesus, unknowingly participate in the fulfillment of prophecy about the Messiah. In an attempt to stay within the law relating to the Sabbath day, the Jews ask Pilate to have the legs of those crucified broken in order to hasten death and have the bodies removed (v. 31). The soldiers break the legs of the two others crucified with Jesus; but when they come to Jesus, they notice that He is dead already and do not break His legs (vv. 32–33). This fulfilled the prophecy concerning the Messiah found in Exodus 12:46—"It (the Passover lamb) is to be eaten in a single house; you are not to bring forth any of the flesh outside the house, nor are you to break any of the bone of it." In order to make sure that Jesus was dead, the soldiers pierced his side with a spear and blood and water come out of the wound (v. 34). This fulfilled the prophecy concerning the Messiah found in Zechariah 12:10a—"I will pour out on the house of David and on the inhabitants of Jerusalem, the spirit of grace and supplication, so they will look on Me whom they have pierced." Here, we see another irony. The Jews and the soldiers do not "see" Jesus as He fulfills the prophecies that later will help others to "see" Jesus as the Messiah.

In verses 25–27 and 38–42 of chapter 19, we finally find some people who "see" Jesus. The disciple (probably John) standing nearby to the cross must "see" Jesus because he obeys Jesus and takes His mother into his own household (vv. 26–27). Joseph of Arimathea and Nicodemus must have "seen" Jesus because they risk everything to claim His body and bury it (vv. 38–42).

Believing in Jesus.

In chapter 20, we find different degrees of what it takes to believe in Jesus. John goes into the empty sepulcher, sees the grave clothes, and believes that Jesus has risen from the dead without actually seeing Him (vv. 5, 8). Mary sees Jesus, but does not believe He has risen until He speaks to her (vv. 14–16). The disciples believe that Jesus has risen when He appears in their midst (v, 19–22). Thomas does not believe that Jesus has risen because he was not present when Jesus appeared in the midst of the other disciples (vv. 24–25). However, Thomas is present the second time that Jesus appears in the midst of the disciples (v. 26). At this moment, Thomas sees Jesus and also believes that Jesus has risen (vv. 27–28). Jesus tells Thomas that he has *seen* and believed, but blessed are they that have *not seen* and yet believed (v. 29). John finishes chapter 20 with the following statement:

> **Therefore many other signs Jesus also performed in the presence of the disciples, which are not written in this book; but these have been written so that you may believe that Jesus is the Christ, the Son of God; and that believing you may have life in His name. (John 20:30–31)**

Summary.

Many things can be learned from the above portions of John's Gospel. True freedom can come only when we are transformed from the natural realm to the supernatural realm. This happens when we "see" and believe in Jesus. Once this happens, we experience spiritual birth. No longer are we bound in the natural realm to make natural choices and to die. We can operate in the supernatural realm, make supernatural choices through the power of the Holy Spirit, and live forever! **The glorification of God and the satisfaction of our need for a sense of freedom comes when we choose transformation from the natural realm to the supernatural realm through our "seeing" and believing in Jesus. God will transform us! We are loving God and loving our neighbor. Jesus-focused spirituality, in the form of "seeing" and believing, is the "mind of Christ" concerning the second step in spiritual transformation.**

For God so loved the world, that He gave His only begotten Son, that whoever believes in Him shall not perish, but have eternal life. (John 3:16)

Are we "seeing" and believing in Jesus more?
Do we love Jesus a little more dearly?
Let's go on!

FRAMEWORK FOR SPIRITUAL MATURITY

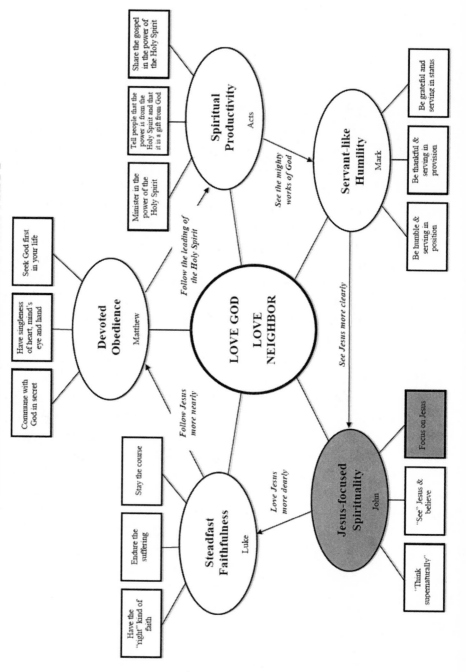

CHAPTER 6

Put on the Blinders:
Focus on Jesus

The third step in Jesus-focused spirituality is concerned with maintaining our focus on Jesus. Once we "see" and believe in Him, it is so important to keep our focus on Him. Focus means to center our attention on something with the purpose of seeing it more clearly. The something on which we need to focus is Jesus. When the pace and problems of every-day life press in on us, it is very easy for us to slip back into operating in the natural realm and to lose our focus. What can we do to ensure our focus stays on Jesus so that we can see Him more clearly?

Having a personal relationship with Jesus.

John the Baptist's disciples are focused on John the Baptist. They are a little concerned about the popularity of Jesus and query John about it (vv. 26–27). It is through John's response to his disciples that we see how to focus on Jesus.

John the Baptist "rejoices greatly" in being a friend of Jesus and in hearing His voice (v. 29). Having a relationship with Jesus and hearing His voice makes John's joy full.

We need to follow the example of John the Baptist and focus on our personal relationship with Jesus. We need to be satisfied completely with the Father's graciousness toward us through Jesus' work on the cross. It was through this act that the Father gave us eternal life and the opportunity to have such a close relationship with Jesus. What incredible gifts the Father has given to us (James 1:17). *Our joy, therefore, should be full.* However, we, as Christians, sometimes let the circumstances in our life begin to steal some of our joy. When we start to feel that we are losing some of our joy, we need to return to the foot of the cross and to our personal relationship with Jesus, especially through prayer and the reading of God's Word. A stronger sense of gratefulness to God will well up in our hearts, and the fullness of joy will be restored. We never know what the outcome of our circumstances will be; but we *do* know that as we go through them, our joy can remain full. People sometimes ask us if our cup of "this or that" is half empty or half full. When it comes to joy, our cup needs to be kept absolutely full. We do this by starting each day with our focus on Jesus and our personal relationship with Him. As a result, our "joy cup" will be full to the brim, and we will be prepared for any negative circumstances that confront us during the day.

Decreasing self; increasing Jesus.

Next, John the Baptist tells his disciples that he is no longer the focus. Jesus is now the focus, and John tells his disciples that he must decrease as the focus and Jesus must increase (v. 30). We need to focus less on ourselves, and more on Jesus. We must decrease as the focus in our daily lives, and Jesus must increase as the focus. We need to be thinking more and more about Jesus, and less and less about ourselves. This will flow from our personal relationship with him, which we will see more closely in Chapter 10.

Listening to Jesus, alone.

Finally, John the Baptist tells his disciples that they need to listen to Jesus alone because He was sent from heaven by God the Father (vv. 31–35). We need to pay very close attention to Jesus because He was sent by the Father. We need to study Jesus. What did He say? How did He say it? Why did He say it? What did He do? How did He do it? Why did He do it? Another important way to keep our focus on Jesus, therefore, is to read about Him in the Scriptures and keep our focus there.

Experiencing focusing on Jesus.

Shortly after I received Jesus, I was full of joy and was on fire to learn about Him. I poured through the Gospels in order to learn more about Him. One of my pastors jokingly called me the "red-letter" Christian (some Bibles have Jesus' words in red letters). I also found two men who "knew" Jesus (not just knew about Jesus), and I listened to them as they told me about Jesus and their relationship with Him. One was Bob Muhlig who took me to a Navigators' Bible study. The other was Mr. Frank Braxton, an eighty-year-old man from whom flowed a fountain of wisdom like a bubbling brook (Prov. 18:4).

My joy and my compulsion to learn about Jesus helped me to keep focused on Him in the days immediately after I received Him. However, I struggled with the piece about "focusing less on myself in my daily life and more on Jesus." The pace of my life at the time was busy. I was working, raising a family, studying for a graduate degree, etc., and I was having difficulty focusing on Jesus in my daily life. As a result, I came up with a plan. Every morning before I went to work I would put on a tie. When I would put on the tie in the morning, I would remember to place my focus on Jesus for the day. This worked well during the work-week. However, on Saturday, I would not put on a tie and would sometimes forget to place my focus on Jesus for the day. Just forgetting one day would sometimes lead to forgetting for a number of days even though I would put on a tie on those days. What I do today is to start the day in prayer and then continue in prayer throughout the day. This helps me to keep my focus on Jesus in my daily life. Also, I try to read scripture every day.

How else can we keep our focus on Jesus? Certainly, a focus upon Jesus on the cross and our personal relationship with Jesus are essential. In addition, I believe that chapters 13–17 of the Gospel of John provide further insight for us. We can focus on Jesus as the:

- *Humble Master washing His disciples' feet* (John 13) and responding by **humbly** washing each other's feet.
- *The Way, the Truth, the Life, and the only way to the Father* (John 14) and responding by being **focused on Jesus** and communing with the Father through the Holy Spirit.
- *True Vine in whom we, the branches, are to abide* (John 15) and responding by having **faith** in Jesus alone (not in ourselves nor any other person or thing.)
- *Sender of the Holy Spirit* (John 16) and responding by being **obedient** to the Word of God (Jesus) and the Holy Spirit.
- *Great unifier praying to the Father for unity* (John 17) and responding by allowing ourselves to be sanctified in truth and perfected in unity in that we may be spiritually productive (that the world may know that the Father sent Jesus and loves them).

(For a handout on this, turn to Appendix IX)

All of the above provides us with plenty of images on which to begin our focus on Jesus.

We need to be like John the Baptist. We should be full of joy in our relationship to Jesus, we should focus more on Him and less on ourselves, and we should learn about Him more and more because He speaks the words of God.

A scriptural example warning us about the problem of losing our focus.

There is an old saying about our bodies that states, "You are what you eat." I think that there should be another saying about our mind's eye that states, "You are what you focus on." On what have we been focused today or this past week? A possibility of our focus could be on ourselves and what we have been doing such as working at a job, taking care of our property, buying new clothes, eating, etc. Another possible focus could be our friends and family, people that are close to us. A third possible focus could be other people in the form of jealousy, coveting, etc. I believe that the apostle, John, is trying to warn us about the danger of these three types of focus in the 21st chapter of his Gospel.

Jesus has appeared to the disciples twice after his resurrection. However, the disciples are not constantly in His presence as before. It does not seem to have taken Peter very long to lose his focus on Jesus. He decides to go back fishing, and the disciples go with him (v. 3). They go back to their "old ways." The disciples go out in a boat to catch the fish, and Jesus appears to them on shore (v. 4). Jesus speaks to them, but they are so focused on their fishing that they do not recognize Him (v. 4). It is only when Jesus does a miracle (filling the net with fish) that John recognizes that the man on the shore is Jesus (vv. 6–7). Peter does not recognize Jesus until John tells him (v. 7). Jesus was not as visible to Peter as He had been before, and Peter had lost his focus on Jesus and gone back to his old ways. He could not see Jesus clearly because of his focus on himself and his "old ways."

Jesus asks Peter if he loves Him more than these (his friends). He not only asks Peter once; He asks him three times (vv. 15–17). Jesus knows that Peter may lose his focus on Jesus because of his friends, and will not do the work that Jesus has called him to do. It seems that Peter does not love Jesus dearly enough.

Finally, Jesus tells Peter about the death that Peter will experience as a result of following Jesus (vv. 18–19). Then Jesus says to Peter, "Follow me" (v. 19). Peter's response is to ask Jesus about what is going to happen to John. Here, Peter's focus leaves Jesus and comes to rest on John and John's future ministry (vv. 20–21). Jesus quickly corrects Peter by telling him that what happens to John is none of his business, and Jesus repeats his command to Peter, "You follow me" (v. 22). Jesus knows that Peter may compare his ministry with that of others and, as a result, lose his focus on Jesus. It seems that Peter is not willing to follow Jesus as nearly as he should have. (For a handout on the above, turn to Appendix X-B)

Hmm…this reminds me of a song, a song from *Godspell.*

Day by day,
Day by day,
Oh, dear Lord, three things I pray.
See Thee more **clearly,**
Love Thee more **dearly,**
Follow Thee more **nearly,**
Day by day.

One Sunday, I was asked to preach a sermon in a Native American church. I made an analogy between a Christian and a Native American warrior. Young Native American warriors probably had some fears about going into battle. They probably were afraid of knowing how to fight, afraid of dying, and afraid of being defeated. So what did they do? They did not focus on themselves, or their fear would have overtaken them. I understand that, instead, they focused on their war chief. He was the ultimate warrior. He knew how to fight. He knew how to stay alive. He knew how to win the battle. The young warriors would stay close to the war chief so that they could see him clearly and know how to fight in the battle. They would focus on him and do everything that he did. The young warriors would stay close to the war chief so that he would be close enough to help them if they were in trouble and would keep them alive. They knew that the war chief cared about them and would protect them. The young warriors stayed close to the war chief, followed him wherever he went during the battle, and would have a part in the winning of the battle. Whenever the war chief was killed in battle, the warriors would disengage the enemy and retreat. There was no one on whom to focus that could help them to know how to fight, stay alive, and win the battle. It was a bad omen.

Being a Christian warrior is much like being a Native American warrior. We are in a constant spiritual battle with the evil one and his followers. Our war chief in this battle is Jesus Christ. As warriors in battle, are we afraid of death? What do we do? Do we focus on ourselves and our wants and desires? No, because our fear in the end will overtake us. What we should do, then, is to focus on our war chief, Jesus Christ. He is the ultimate warrior. He knows how to fight the evil one. He knows how to stay alive eternally; He has conquered death and shown us through His resurrection. He has already won the victory all by Himself by taking the sin of the world, yours and mine, upon himself at the cross. The evil one is already defeated, and what is left is a mopping-up campaign. Is Jesus Christ the ultimate of ultimate war chiefs? Amen!

However, the battle continues today. What should we do today, and every day? Fight the battle without our war chief? This would not be too wise. We need to stay close to Jesus, our war chief, so that we can see Him clearly and know how to fight the battle. We need to focus on Him and do everything that He does. We need to stay close to Jesus so that if we get into trouble in the battle (even our own physical death) He will be close enough to help and keep us alive (eternally). We need to stay close to Jesus so that we can follow Him anywhere he goes during the battle (even places we would never dream of going) so that we can have a part in the winning of the battle.

So it is for a Christian warrior as it was for a Native American warrior except that our war chief, Jesus, will never be killed in the battle, we will never disengage the enemy, or retreat. There will always be our war chief, Jesus, on whom we can focus. He will help us to know how to fight, stay alive, and win the battle!

Experiencing keeping our focus on Jesus.

It is so important to have our focus on Jesus every moment of every day. One of my biggest battles came on December 2, 1987 when my son, age twenty-five, was killed in an automobile accident. If I had not started that day focused on Jesus, I do not know what would have been the result. However, because I was focused on Jesus that day, I was able to interpret supernaturally all that happened that day with His mind and to respond to everything with His heart. How sweet it is to have our focus on Jesus, the author and finisher of our faith.

73

"Turn your eyes upon Jesus.
Look full in His wonderful face,
And the things of earth will grow strangely dim
In the light of his glory and grace."

Scriptural examples about "keeping our focus on Jesus.

If for any reason we begin to lose focus on Jesus, Jesus will help us to restore our focus as He did with Peter in John 21. He will not deal with us harshly, but with gentleness. He will get our attention as He did with Peter and the fish (vv. 3–6). Then, He will invite us to eat with Him at a breakfast that He has already prepared (vv. 11–13). Next, He will ask us a tough question about how much we love Him (v. 15). If we can respond to this question by saying that we love Him more than anything, He will give us a command to feed and tend His lambs and sheep and to follow Him (vv. 15–19). If we question the destiny of other believers, He will tell us to mind our own business and to follow Him (vv. 20–23). If we can respond to Jesus' command, to follow, with a renewed sense of devotion, our focus will have been restored. Thank you, Jesus!

Summary.

Many things can be learned from the above portions of John's Gospel. True freedom can come only when we set and keep our focus on Jesus. Once this happens, we will not be distracted by the things of the natural realm and will be free to operate more consistently and victoriously in the supernatural realm. **The glorification of God and the satisfaction of our need for a sense of freedom come when we to choose to focus on Jesus. God will continue to transform us! We are loving God and loving our neighbor. Jesus-focused spirituality in the form of focusing on Jesus is the "mind of Christ" concerning the third step in spiritual transformation.**

> **He who comes from above is above all, he who is from the earth and speaks of the earth. He who comes from heaven is above all. What**

He has seen and heard, of that He testifies; and no one receives His testimony. He who has received His testimony has set his seal to this, that God is true. For He whom God has sent speaks the words of God; for He gives the Spirit without measure. The Father loves the Son and has given all things into His hand. He who believes in the Son has eternal life; but he who does not obey the Son will not see life, but the wrath of god abides on him (John 3:31–36)

Are we keeping our focus on Jesus a little more?
Do we love Jesus a little more dearly?
Let's go on!

Summary
Section II

All of the concepts concerning Jesus-focused spirituality can be seen in contrasting Nicodemus, Thomas, and Peter with Bartimaeus, the beggar. Initially, Nicodemus, Thomas, and Peter are not spiritually born. These men have different problems in the process. Nicodemus, at first, cannot "think supernaturally." Thomas, at first, cannot "see" and believe in Jesus. Peter, at first, cannot keep his focus on Jesus. Bartimaeus, on the other hand, **"thinks supernaturally"** (Bartimaeus thinks that Jesus has the supernatural power to heal). Bartimaeus **"sees" Jesus and believes** (Bartimaeus sees Jesus as the Messiah and believes in Him). Bartimaeus keeps his **focus on Jesus** (Bartimaeus follows Jesus on the road).

God is trying to regenerate people through His Word (the "seed") and His Holy Spirit. In this way, they will be able to choose the ultimate freedom of living in the supernatural realm. Where are we in all of this? Are we like Nicodemus, Thomas, and Peter; or are we like Bartimaeus? Have we taken advantage of the choice God has offered to us, or have we rejected that choice? Have we been born naturally only, or have we been born spiritually as well? Have we been transformed? Do we have the mind of Christ?

The glorification of God and the satisfaction of our need for a sense of freedom come when we experience the ultimate choice that God has provided for us to think supernaturally; to "see" Jesus and believe in Him; to focus on Jesus; and, as a result of all of this, to be spiritually transformed. We will be loving God and loving our neighbor. Jesus-focused spirituality in the form of thinking supernaturally, "seeing" and believing in Jesus, and focusing on Jesus is the "mind of Christ" concerning spiritual transformation.

> **To the Jews who had believed him, Jesus said, "If you hold to my teaching, you are really my disciples. Then you will know the truth, and the truth will set you free." (John 8:32–33)**

Do we love Jesus a little more dearly?
Do we love Him dearly enough to trust Him
more and to have more faith in Him?
Let's go on!

Note: If you want to pursue the theme of "Jesus-focused spirituality" further in the Gospel of John, turn to Appendix VIII-B for a study outline. The outline provides for a macro study (based on a micro study) of the scripture and is written in an application format.

FRAMEWORK FOR SPIRITUAL MATURITY

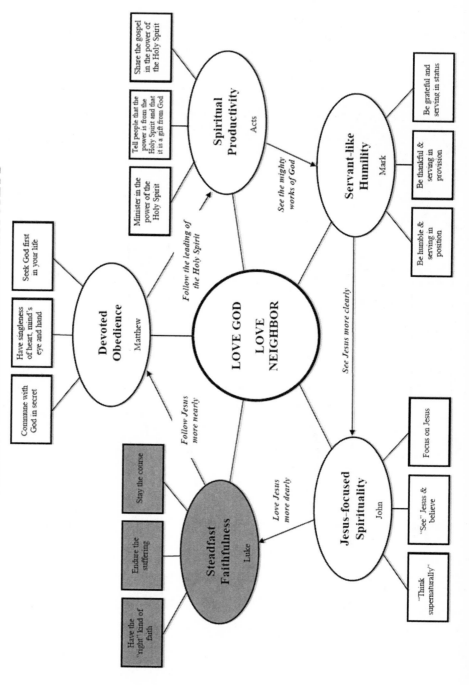

SECTION III

Steadfast Faithfulness

The sower went out to sow his seed; and as he sowed …seed fell on rocky soil, and as soon as it grew up, it withered away, because it had no moisture…Those on the rocky soil are those who when they hear, receive the word with joy; and these have no firm root; they believe for a while, and in time of temptation fall away. (Luke 8:5, 6, 13)

Now, if we are humble and find that our sense of worth comes from appropriating the love and acceptance of Jesus and if we have been spiritually transformed so that we possess the Holy Spirit and are truly free to choose to follow Jesus, then we are in the position to have faith in Jesus and fully submit and entrust ourselves to His power. However, the "Parable of the Sower" indicates that some who are in a position to have faith in Jesus do not fully submit and entrust themselves to His power, especially when they are tested. The "rocky soil" was a thin layer of soil that lay on top of a piece of solid ledge. The seed penetrated the soil, germinated, and sprang up. However, when the strong sunlight came upon the plant, it wilted. It wilted because its roots were unable to go deep because the rocky ledge stopped them. As a result, the plant wilted because it was not able to reach the water that was needed to sustain itself. In my reading in the Gospels, I had determined that the theme of the Gospel of Luke related to faithfulness and more specifically to a **faithfulness** that was **steadfast**.

Thinking back to my understanding of human intrinsic needs, the need related to **steadfast faithfulness** is **power**. In New Testament Greek the word, power, meant the "ability to do." We need to feel that we can **trust** in some source of **power** to accomplish the things we need to do. When we were young children, we trusted in the power of our parents to help us do things. Some of us, when we grew up, continued to trust in the power of our parents, other people, or things to help us accomplish what we needed to do. These remained in a dependent mode of behavior. Others, when we grew up, lost our trust in the power of our parents to help us do things and only trusted in our own internal power. These moved to an independent mode of behavior. Still others, operate somewhere in between these two modes of behavior. If we have come to spiritual life and are committed to following Jesus, we must give up our trust in the power of others, other things, and in our own power. We must trust in the power of Jesus, alone, and in the power of the Holy Spirit, which Jesus has provided for us. If we are like the "rocky soil," we will return to trusting in our own power and/or the power of others and other things when we encounter trouble and our faith in Jesus is tested (I call the "rocky soil" people the "shallow people"). Jesus says that these will "fall away" from following Him. We need to understand that following Jesus will require sacrifice on our part and that the sacrifice may result in suffering. However, if we are following Jesus and serving Him and others; we must **trust** that Jesus will provide the **power** of the Holy Spirit for us to be able to persevere to do whatever needs to be done, even when we encounter trouble and suffering. If we fully **trust** in Jesus, we will experience a great sense of **power** in the presence of the Holy Spirit in our lives, and we will be **steadfast** in our **faithfulness** to Jesus.

Chapter nine of the Gospel of Luke provides a concise presentation concerning man's problem with a lack of steadfast faithfulness, and reveals the "mind of Christ" concerning steadfast faithfulness itself. In Section III of this book, the three issues that cause a lack of steadfast faithfulness on the part of man will be explored. In the next three chapters, we will examine each of these three issues that contribute to a lack of steadfast faith in Jesus and how we can deal with them.

FRAMEWORK FOR SPIRITUAL MATURITY

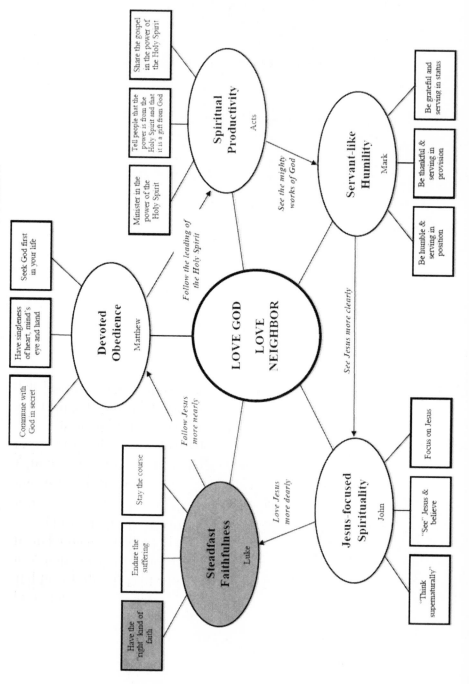

CHAPTER 7

Check Yourself:
The "Right Kind" of Faith

The "right kind of faith" is the first issue concerning faithfulness that is presented in Luke, chapter 9 (verses 1–17; 37–43a; 51–56). It is important for us to know what God says about having faith in Him because otherwise, we may end up with the "wrong kind of faith," and as a result, our faith in Him will be shaken.

Trust in the power of Jesus, minister to the sick and needy, and persevere.

Most of the Hebrew people at the time of Jesus had the wrong kind of faith. This wrong kind of faith was characterized mostly by the Jewish spiritual leaders who trusted in their own power to perform rites and rituals that would, in their mind, prove them to be faithful to God. This type of faith relied more on the traditions of men than on the Word of God, had as its purpose meeting the needs of the Jewish spiritual leaders by bringing glory to themselves, and was fairly easy to follow if you had the time (which most of the sick and needy did not have). Jesus, on the other hand, calls his twelve disciples together and gives them power and authority over demons, to heal diseases, to proclaim the kingdom of God, and to perform healing (vv. 1–2). Then, He tells them to take *nothing* for their journey (v. 3)! This will require a faith different from that of the Jewish spiritual leaders. The disciples' mission will mean not trusting in their own power, but trusting in the power of Jesus. This type of faith will rely on Jesus (the Word of God) rather than the traditions of men. It will have as its purpose helping the sick and needy in the power of Jesus, and giving glory to God rather than doing things that will bring glory to themselves. It would take a great deal of perseverance in the power of Jesus to overcome the obstacles in their path and will be much more difficult than doing a few rituals. We can see that the disciples have the "right kind of faith" because they "went throughout the villages, preaching the gospel and healing everywhere" (v. 6)! The disciples entrust themselves to the power of Jesus. Herod hears all about what is going on and is "perplexed" (vv. 6–7). He is perplexed because he is not ready to entrust himself to Jesus but is merely curious about whom He might be (vv. 7–8).

There are many today that are like Herod. They are curious about Jesus, but are not about to relinquish the trust that they have in themselves, others, or other things because they do not know who Jesus is. They obviously do not have the "right kind of faith." Also, there are those who profess to believe in God, like the Hebrew people of Jesus' day, but are caught up in rites and rituals that are the traditions of man. These people are not ready to relinquish the trust that they have in themselves because they are comfortable where they are. They do not have the "right kind of faith." However, those who are true disciples of Jesus have a type of faith which trusts in the power of Jesus. It is a type of faith that relies on Jesus (the Word of God), that helps the sick and needy in the power of Jesus, and perseveres in the power of Jesus during times of when obstacles seem to thwart our way. This kind of faith in Jesus will not be shaken.

Experiencing "trusting in the power of Jesus, ministering to the sick and needy, and persevering."

The day I placed my faith in Jesus was a dramatic one for me. I had long since given up on trusting my parents or others; I trusted in myself and my understanding of philosophy and psychology. Now, I had been raised in the church. I believed that there was a Jesus. I believed His teachings about helping other people. However, I did not have the *power* to help other people. I would *try* to help other people, but I did not have the power to go past the point of my own pain to help them. I was trying to help the sick and the needy, and I was persevering. However, I was ministering in my own power and not that of the power of Jesus. I had the wrong kind of faith. The day that I saw the power of Jesus exhibited in His crucifixion, I entrusted myself completely to Him. If I had trusted one hundred percent in philosophy or psychology that failed, I told myself that I must give the power of Jesus a chance. As a result, I trusted in the power of Jesus one hundred percent, and it worked! He has never failed me. Finally, I had come to the "right kind of faith"—trust in the power of Jesus, minister to the sick and needy, and persevere! The "right kind of faith," requires *all* three of these elements.

Don't miss the opportunity.

Subsequently, the disciples have another opportunity to entrust themselves to the power of Jesus; but they do not see the opportunity, nor do they respond well to Jesus' direction. The disciples tell Jesus to send the crowd away so that they can find food and lodging for themselves (vv. 12). They do not see the opportunity to meet the needs of those that are hungry. This is contrary to the purpose of the "right kind of faith" which is to meet the needs of the sick and needy. When directed by Jesus to feed the five thousand, they say that they are unable to do so (v. 13a) because they are thinking about trying to do it in their own power. They are not thinking about relying on the power of Jesus, the Word of God, which is the "right kind of faith." They do not try to feed the five thousand when the food resources were very small because they are thinking about the enormity of the problem. They are not thinking about persevering in the power of Jesus, which is the right kind of faith. A short period of time had elapsed since the disciples exhibited the "right kind of faith," and here they are exhibiting the wrong kind of faith—they are not seeing how they are able to meet the needs of the people by entrusting themselves to the power of Jesus.

How true that is for the disciples of Jesus today. We may entrust ourselves to the power of Jesus one time; but then another opportunity presents itself, and we do not even see it. The Holy Spirit may even prompt us to see the opportunity, but we revert back to our old ways of relying on our own power or the power of others. The opportunity begins to look more and more like an impossible task, and we question God about how we can do it. If we are doing this, we do not have the "right kind of faith," and our faith in Jesus may be shaken.

Experiencing "not missing the opportunity."

Now, I am a type "A" personality. I am up in the morning looking for tasks to accomplish. I cannot tell you, as a young Christian, how many times God presented opportunities for me to minister to others, and I did not see them because I was so focused on my "tasks." One time, I was going down in an elevator, and there was an elderly woman in the elevator as well. I could tell that she was distraught, and I thought about asking her if there was some problem. However, I had my tasks to accomplish, and so I said nothing and went on my way to accomplish my "tasks." Almost immediately, I said to myself, "Missed opportunity!" Each time something like this happened, I would ask God for forgiveness and pray that he would help me to see the opportunities in the future. Today, one of my prayers first thing every morning is that God would provide opportunities for me to minister to others, that He would give me "eyes" to see those opportunities, and that He would help me subject my flesh to the power of the Holy Spirit so that I would have the power to do the work of ministry for Him.

Don't try to do it in your own power.

Problems continue for the disciples when Jesus returns from the mountain after the transfiguration. Jesus finds a man with a son who is possessed with an evil spirit (vv. 38–39). The man tells Jesus that he begged His disciples to drive out the evil spirit but that they could not do it (v. 40). Jesus is very upset with His disciples (v. 41). They *do* see the opportunity to meet the needs of the boy with the evil spirit, which would be the purpose of the "right kind of faith." However, they rely on their own power to attempt to drive the spirit out. They do not rely on the power of Jesus, the Word of God, which is the right kind of faith. No amount of perseverance to work this miracle would have mattered if the disciples were not relying on the power of Jesus.

Here again, we disciples of Jesus today may see an opportunity to minister to the sick and needy, but we try to minister in our own power and not in the power of Jesus. This is a habit we must, with God's help, break. It is not having the "right kind of faith," and our faith in Jesus may be shaken.

Experiencing "not trying to do it in your own power."

In my days as a young Christian, this was a huge struggle. My first reaction most of the time in ministry was to think naturally instead of supernaturally and rely on my own power. I would try to help the sick and needy, and I would fail. Again, I would ask God for forgiveness and for help to think supernaturally. Today, I try to remember to pray before I become engaged in any form of ministry. I ask God to help me subject my flesh so that the power of the Holy Spirit can have its way to work.

Don't attempt to misuse the power.

James and John continue to have difficulty when they witness the unwelcoming attitude of the Samaritans (vv. 51–53). They ask Jesus if it is all right for *them* to "command fire to come down from heaven to consume them (the Samaritans)" (v. 54). Jesus rebukes His disciples! James and John want to destroy these people in dramatic fashion. Obviously, this is not the purpose of the "right kind of faith," which meets the *needs* of people. James and John also are suggesting to Jesus that *they* could bring fire down from heaven in *their own* power. Here, James and John are not thinking about relying on the power of Jesus, the Word of God. Jesus comments on the absurdity of their idea (vv. 55–56). Again, no amount of perseverance to overcome this obstacle, which would be the "right kind of faith," would have mattered if James and John were not focusing on meeting the needs of the Samaritans and relying on the power of Jesus.

Sometimes, disciples of Jesus today will attempt to use the power of God in inappropriate ways. Certainly, Jesus teaches us to pray for our enemies and not to attempt to use God's power to destroy them. There are many other ways that we may attempt to misuse God's power. When this happens, God will not allow His power to be used, and we may become disillusioned with God because He will not do what we want. Remember the line in a song that goes "Oh, Lord, won't you buy me a Mercedes Benz?" This is not having the "right kind of faith," and our faith in Jesus may be shaken.

Experiencing "not attempting to abuse the power."

Personally, I do not ever remember trying to misuse the power of God. Not that I can say that it has not happened or that it could happen in the future. I am in such awe of the power of God that I want to be sure how it is to be applied. Sometimes I think that I am not bold enough in its application.

Jesus, our example of the "right kind of faith."

Chapter 22 of Luke provides a view of the application of the concept of having the "right kind of faith" versus not having the "right kind of faith." By examining each of the people described in this chapter, it can be seen who is exhibiting the "right kind of faith."

There are many people described in Luke 22 who do not exhibit the "right kind of faith." The chief priests, the teachers of the law, the council of elders, and the temple guards show that they did not have the "right kind of faith." They are looking for a way to kill Jesus during Passover (v. 2). They give Judas money to betray Jesus (vv. 4–5). Jesus describes their condition as "the power of darkness" (v. 53). They ask Jesus if He is the Christ because they are in hopes that His answer will lead to His death (vv. 66–71). We can see these leaders are not relying on the power of Jesus, the Word of God, but are trusting and acting in their own power which Jesus describes as darkness. They are not concerned with meeting the needs of the sick and needy in the power of God, but only with killing Jesus. They certainly are persevering but are misusing the power that was given to them. These spiritual leaders do not have the "right kind of faith."

The guards obviously do not have the "right kind of faith," as they mock, beat, and insult Jesus (vv. 63–65). They certainly are not relying on the power of Jesus, the Word of God, nor meeting the needs of the sick and needy. They are misusing the power that was given to them.

Judas does not have the "right kind of faith." He allows Satan to enter Him (v. 3). He betrays Jesus for money (vv. 4, 6) and with a kiss (v. 48). Judas is not relying on the power of Jesus, the Word of God, but on His own power, the power of money, and the power of Satan. He is not interested in meeting the needs of the sick and needy but only in serving himself by obtaining money for the betrayal of Jesus. He is misusing the power that he has as a disciple of Jesus and has turned himself over to the power of Satan. Judas definitely does not have the "right kind of faith."

The other disciples do not go as far as Judas, but they also do not have the "right kind of faith." They discuss among themselves about which of them it might be who would betray Jesus (v. 23) and then dispute with each other about who is regarded to be the greatest (v. 24). Instead of watching to protect Jesus in the garden, they go to sleep from sorrow (v. 46a), and are warned by Jesus to pray so that they will not enter into temptation (v. 46b). They ask Jesus if they should strike with their swords, and one of them cuts off the ear of the high priest (vv. 49–50). The disciples are not relying on the power of Jesus, the Word of God, but are in great fear and are responding in their own power. They are not concerned about serving the sick and needy but are only concerned with preserving their own lives and positions. They are going to sleep because of their depression. The disciples do not have the "right kind of faith."

Peter is closer than most of the other disciples, but he also does not have the "right kind of faith." He publicly denies Jesus three times (vv. 57, 58, 60–62). Peter is not relying on the power of Jesus, the Word of God; but is relying on his own power in an attempt to stay alive. He is not concerned with serving the sick and needy, but is only concerned about his own survival. He certainly misses a great opportunity to serve. Peter does not have the "right kind of faith." (Jesus suggests that Peter will eventually have the "right kind of faith—v. 32)

Jesus stands alone in Luke 22 as the only one who has the "right kind of faith." Jesus, through the symbolism of the Passover sacrifice, describes to His disciples about His sacrifice for them (vv. 14–22). He prays to the Father, and the Father sends an angel to strengthen Him (vv. 39–44). Jesus allows Himself to be arrested (vv. 47–53). He allows Himself to be punished (vv. 63–65). He allows Himself to be condemned to death (vv. 66–71). Jesus is relying on the power of the Father and not just His own power. He is allowing His life to be sacrificed in order that the sick and needy can be "*saved*," and *He* is not about to miss the opportunity to do so. Wow, Jesus has the "right kind of faith"! What an example for us who are His disciples! What a contrast with those in this chapter that do not have the "right kind of faith"!

Summary.

Many things can be learned from these portions of the Gospel of Luke. People who trust in themselves, others, or other things do not rely on the power of Jesus, the Word of God; are not concerned with serving the sick and needy; and do not persevere in the power of Jesus when obstacles present themselves. These people rely on themselves, others, or other things in order to protect themselves and their interests. They are focused on selfish gain. They usually take the most expedient route, which may change from time to time as conditions dictate, in order to accomplish their ends. I call these "**rocky soil**" people the "**SHALLOW PEOPLE,**" they do not have the "right kind of faith," and their faith in Jesus will be shaken when times of trouble occur.

Conversely, people who have the "right kind of faith" trust totally in the power of Jesus. They rely on the power of Jesus, the Word of God; serve the sick and needy; and persevere in the power of Jesus when obstacles present themselves. They follow Jesus' example. Jesus *relied upon the Father's power* as He faced the cross. He was committed to *serve the sick and needy* by allowing Himself to be sacrificed in order that they could be saved spiritually. He *persevered* through His arrest, punishment, and condemnation to death and did not waver. We then, as disciples of Jesus, must examine ourselves. 2 Corinthians 13:5–6 states, "Examine yourselves to see whether you are in the faith; test yourselves. Do you not realize that Christ Jesus is in you—unless, of course, you fail the test? And I trust that you will discover that we have not failed the test." As disciples of Jesus, we must have the "right kind of faith," and our faith in Jesus will not be shaken. **The glorification of God and the satisfaction of our need for power come when we fully trust in the power of Jesus and persevere in the serving of the sick and needy. God will empower us through His Holy Spirit. We, then, will *not* be the "rocky soil," and our faith in Jesus will not be shaken but will be *steadfast*. We are loving God and loving our neighbor. Steadfast faithfulness in the form of having the "right kind of faith" is the "mind of Christ."**

> **Departing, they began going throughout the villages, preaching the gospel and healing everywhere. (Luke 9:6)**

Do we have more of the "right kind of faith?"
Are we following Jesus a little more nearly?
Let's go on!

FRAMEWORK FOR SPIRITUAL MATURITY

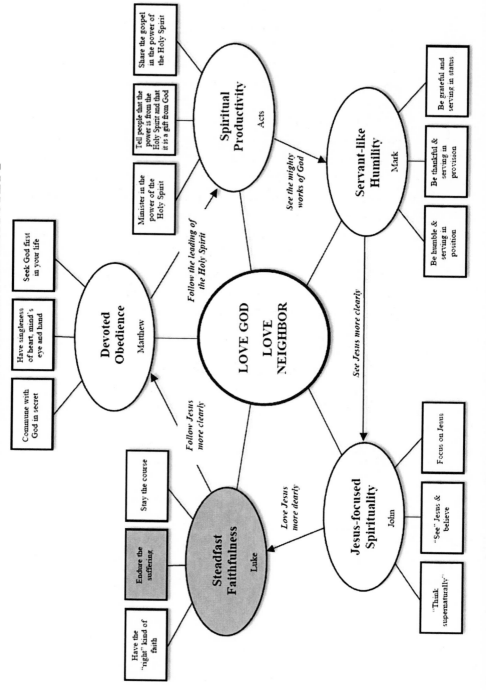

CHAPTER 8

Rejection Advice:
Endure the Suffering

The second issue concerning steadfast faithfulness is to "endure the suffering" and is found in Luke, chapter 9 (verses 18–27, 43b–45, and 57–61). If we are going to follow Jesus, we need to know that the journey will not be without suffering (I Peter 4:12–14).

Follow Jesus in spite of rejection and persecution.

Jesus asks His disciples who the crowds think He is (v. 18). They respond that some say John the Baptist, some say Elijah, and some say one of the old prophets has risen again (v.19). Jesus then asks them directly who the disciples think He is (v. 20a). Peter responds, "The Christ of God" (v. 20b). At that point, Jesus describes the rejection and suffering that will accompany the mission of the Christ—"The Son of Man must suffer many things and be rejected by the elders and chief priests and scribes, and he be killed (v. 22a). He also speaks of His deliverance—"and be raised up on the third day" (v. 22b). Jesus knows that He must be doing what the Father has planned for Him no matter what persecution faces Him. He knows that He must not fear man and be focused on His spiritual mission.

The disciples, I do not think, have any idea that the Christ is going to suffer and die. I believe that they think that the Christ will ride into Jerusalem on a white horse and drive out the Romans. They must be in shock at what Jesus has just said to them. Then Jesus says the following:

> **If anyone wishes to come after Me, he must deny himself, and take up his cross daily and follow Me For whoever wishes to save his life will lose it, but whoever loses his life for My sake, he is the one who will save it. For what is a man profited if he gains the whole world, and loses or forfeits himself? For whoever is ashamed of Me and My words, the Son of Man will be ashamed of him when He come in His glory, and the glory of the Father and of the holy angels. (vv. 23–26)**

If they want to follow Jesus, the disciples must not be worrying about themselves, but must be ready to experience the rejection and suffering that will accompany their mission for Him. An unwillingness to do this will have dire consequences.

Many people today believe that they are disciples of Christ. However, they are not able to place the mission to which Jesus has called them before self-interest. They resist becoming a "living sacrifice" (Rom. 12:1). They are not able to endure the suffering that accompanies their sacrifice, and their faith in Jesus may be shaken.

Experiencing" following Jesus in spite of rejection and persecution."

The lack of power to endure the personal sacrifice is what plagued my helping of others before I received Jesus. As I said before, I believed the teaching of Jesus concerning the helping of others but that I was unable, in my own power, to go past the point of my own pain in serving them. Certainly, this was something that I understood very well.

As I mentioned before, in the late 1960's to early 1970's Louise and I were providing a group home for teens who were experiencing difficulty in their lives This group home was in a subdivision in northern Virginia. As we attempted to minister to these young people, we experienced some persecution from a few of the members of the community (not all, thank God). As these people drove by in their cars, they would curse at the teens who were in the yard. Rumors were spread throughout the community that Louise was a blond hussy and that I was a wild man with long hair and a beard. I conducted a Bible study for local teens at the house on Wednesday afternoons. The rumor was that the only reason that the teens were coming was that we were giving out drugs. One woman, who was married to a staff person on the Un-American Activities Committee in Washington, was telling people that we were communists. We experienced a raid by the local police department. Then there was the day we took in an African-American girl. Shortly after, Louise found herself facing four women from the neighborhood at her door complaining about our action. We persevered through the rejection and persecution by means of the power of the Holy Spirit, and God blessed our ministry.

In the mid-1980's, I was an elder in a church in Rhode Island. The elder board of the church was working on a new direction to which they had come through prayer. All of the elders, I feel, had come under affliction by the evil one in attempt to distract us from our direction. Personally, I lost my job, I lost my house, and I lost my 25 year-old son who was killed in an automobile accident all within six months– Job? Many people suggested that I step away from the elder board for awhile to "recover". My response was that it was not time to back off and circle the wagons. No, it was time to advance and to serve God even more in the direction that He had called me! We are in a great spiritual battle! I was able to persevere through the affliction through the power of the Holy Spirit, as did the other elders; and God blessed the ministry of the church.

Follow Jesus in spite of the "lows" that might follow the "highs.

Jesus has just driven a powerful demon out of a boy and has healed the boy (v. 42). All are amazed at the greatness of God displayed through Jesus' healing of the boy (v. 43a). "All," most probably, included Jesus' disciples who were unable to drive out the demon. All are just marveling at all that Jesus is doing (v. 43b). Again, I am quite sure that Jesus' disciples are part of the group that is marveling. I imagine that this is quite a "high" for the disciples, as they were associated with the person who was the subject of all the marveling.

At the high point of all the marveling, Jesus tells His disciples that He will be betrayed and delivered into the hands of men (v. 44). Through this ominous prophecy, Jesus wanted to let His disciples know that even though He is experiencing success in His ministry at the moment, later down the road He also would experience low points in suffering. He tells the disciples to let His words sink into their ears (v. 44). In other words, Jesus is telling them not to forget what he is saying even though they might not understand at the moment.

If the disciples want to follow Jesus, they must know that there will be times of success in their ministry and their will be times of suffering. They should be ready when the times of suffering come and not let the suffering affect their faith in Jesus.

Many Christians today are "into" the highs of the faith. They love a meaningful worship service or an exciting retreat. However, sometimes, when they come down "off the mountain" to everyday life, they become discouraged, especially when confronted with suffering. As a result, their faith in Jesus may be shaken.

Experiencing "following Jesus in spite of the 'lows' that might follow the 'highs'."

I know a sister in the Lord that had significant difficulty with the highs and lows. She would experience a significant spiritual victory in her life only to have it followed by a significant suffering.

Satan is just waiting for an opportunity to discourage us, and what better time to do that than right after one of our spiritual highs. This sister and I had a conversation about this, and I reminded her not to let Satan steal the "joys" of her spiritual victories. I reminded her to be ready for the sufferings that might follow and to continue to give praise to Jesus for the victories. We, as disciples of Jesus, must be ready for the lows that might follow the highs of our spiritual walk and ministry. We must not let them shake our faith in Jesus! Jesus will empower us and deliver us!

Follow Jesus no matter what the conditions.

As Jesus is going along the road to Jerusalem with his disciples, someone (probably one of His disciples) told Jesus that he would follow Jesus wherever He went (v. 57). Jesus' response indicates that physical discomfort and suffering will accompany following Him, and He intimates that the person is probably not ready to go there (v. 58). Jesus tells another person (probably one of His disciples) to follow Him (v. 59a). The response of this person is that he has responsibilities to tend to before he will be able to follow Jesus (v. 59b). A third person (probably one of His disciples) tells Jesus that he will follow Him, but that he has some personal relationships that must be considered first (v. 61). In all of these scenarios, it is apparent that "the spirit is willing, but the flesh is weak" (Matt. 26:41).

Many Christians today mean well, but have not placed their trust fully in Jesus. So it seems that this is the problem with His disciples in the above scenarios. Their fear of physical and/or emotional pain may inhibit their ability to relinquish and fully trust in Jesus. Jesus calls them to action; but, to some, the idea of physical discomfort and suffering may prevent them from following Jesus. To others, the fear of appearing to be irresponsible in the worldly sense (not burying a father) prevents them from following Jesus. To still others the fear of appearing to be inconsiderate in the worldly sense (not saying goodbye) prevents them from following Him. To all of the above, the fear of suffering shakes their faith in Jesus and inhibits an immediate response on their part to follow Him

Experiencing "following Jesus no matter what the conditions."

As I mentioned before, Louise and I were called by the Lord to operate a group home for teenagers who were experiencing problems in life. We would have eight to twelve teens (boys and girls) at any given time living in our home. At that time, our three children were elementary school age. Both Louise's mother and my mother were upset with what we were doing. They were concerned that harm would come to their grandchildren from the teens in our home. Louise's mother would even send padlocks to us and tell us to put them on our bedroom doors. They both felt that we were being irresponsible and were not shy about sharing their feeling with us. We trust you fully, Jesus!

In 1972, Louise and I sensed very strongly that the Lord was calling us from ministry in Virginia to ministry in Rhode Island. During Christmas 1972, Louise and I traveled to Rhode Island to visit family and to consider what we felt was the Lord's calling. Louise went looking for a house. She found an elderly couple that wanted to move to a smaller house and to rent the one in which they were currently living. We needed a large house because we had seven children living with us at the time. I went looking for a job as a teacher and was promised such a job by a school superintendent. We both returned from our quests sure that Jesus wanted us to go to Rhode Island.

During Easter of 1973, Louise and I made another trip to Rhode Island to confirm a place to live and a job. Louise went to the elderly couple and found out that they had decided to stay in their house and not to rent it. I went to see the superintendent, and he told me that the mayor had frozen all hiring in the city. We both returned from our quests doubting that Jesus wanted us to go to Rhode Island.

Louise and I decided to spend the next day in prayer and consideration of what the Lord's will was in this matter. The next morning was cold, and I went out to warm up the car. I was reading Matthew 6, which is where I go when I am seeking the Lord's will. I was reading about how our Heavenly Father provides for the birds of the air, and how He will provide for us if we seek His kingdom and His righteousness. I looked up for a moment and saw Louise's grandmother throwing bread on the snow for the birds as she always did. Hello! When Louise came out, I told her that we must consider whether or not there were needs in Rhode Island that Jesus wanted us to meet. If we determined that there were needs, we needed to pray in order to see if God wanted us to meet those needs. After much prayer and consideration on that day, Louise and I decided to move to Rhode Island even though we had no house and no job.

In June of 1973, Louise and I, with seven children, readied ourselves for the trip to Rhode Island. With the help of Louise' cousin, Jack; his wife, Elaine; and a friend of theirs, Eddie; we loaded two U-Haul trucks and headed for Rhode Island—no house and no job. We trust you fully, Jesus!

In response to our sensing Jesus' love for us, Louise and I are compelled to serve Him in any way that He leads. In our lives, we believe that consideration of Jesus comes first. He comes first before our relationship with each other. He comes first before our relationship with our family. He comes first before our relationship with our friends. Some of our family and some of our friends sometimes are upset with us when we consider Jesus before them. They feel that we are being inconsiderate of them. We trust you fully, Jesus!

We, as disciples of Jesus, must not fear physical, emotional, and/or social suffering in our following of Jesus. We must trust Him fully, and He will empower us and deliver us!

Jesus, our example of how to "endure the suffering."

Chapter 23 of the book of Luke provides a view of how Jesus endured the suffering that accompanied His rejection and persecution. He endures the circumstances facing Him, the tendency to pull back from ministry, and the "low" that followed His "high."

Certainly, we see in Chapter 23 that neither Pilate nor Herod is interested in enduring any type of suffering. They pursue any politically expedient avenue to avoid rejection by the Jewish leaders.

We find Jesus to be in sharp contrast with Pilate and Herod. Jesus is rejected and persecuted by the chief priests and scribes (vv. 2, 18, 21, 23), by Herod (v. 11), by Pilate (vv. 24–25, by the "rulers" (v. 35), by the soldiers (vv. 36–37), and by one of the criminals on the cross next to Him (v. 39). He endures the suffering resulting from their rejection and persecution in spite of the circumstances He will encounter. Physically, He faces crucifixion, the worst torture known to man. Socially, His disciples abandon Him. Emotionally, God, the Father, turns His face away because Jesus has taken the sin of the world upon himself. Knowing all of this, Jesus is unequivocal in answering about whom He is (v. 3), and does not defend himself (v. 9). In taking this course of action, Jesus is well aware of the consequences. What is Jesus' response to the suffering that accompanies His rejection and persecution? He endures, perhaps even embraces, it in spite of all of the above circumstances.

Not only does Jesus endure the suffering, but He is actively ministering while it is happening. He warns the women following Him of the future suffering that they and their children will endure (vv. 27–31). He forgives those that are rejecting and persecuting Him by saying, "Father, forgive them; for they know not what they are doing" (v. 34). He spiritually ministers to one of the criminals being crucified with Him. When asked by the criminal if Jesus will remember him when He comes in His kingdom, Jesus says, "Truly I say to you, today you shall be with Me in paradise" (vv. 40–43).

Certainly, being on the cross is a very low point for Jesus. Only days before He entered Jerusalem hailed as the *King*. Now, He is being crucified like a criminal. The soldiers mock Jesus about His being the King of the Jews (vv. 36–38). The "other" criminal being crucified with Jesus mocks Jesus about being the Christ (v. 39). Then, Jesus dies on the cross (v. 44–46). It does not get any lower than this. However, even in this lowest of lows, Jesus is a testimony to God for those around Him. Jesus is a testimony to His trust in the Father by saying out loud, "Father, into Your hands I commit my spirit" (v. 46). Jesus is a testimony to a gentile non-believer, a centurion, who had seen the crucifixion. This centurion praises God and says,

"Certainly, this man was innocent" (v. 47). Jesus is a testimony to a Jewish seeker, Joseph of Arimathea. Joseph risks his position on the Council and perhaps his life by going to Pilate and asking for Jesus' body (vv. 50–53). His action can only be attributed to his belief in who Jesus is. Jesus is a testimony to the women who had come out of Galilee with Him. They perhaps are risking their lives by following Jesus' body to the tomb (v. 55). They have not given up their following of Jesus. Jesus, even at His lowest point, is a shining testimony of God the Father to those around Him.

Summary.

We can learn much from this portion of Luke's Gospel. People who cannot endure the suffering of their rejection and persecution for Jesus' sake will not be steadfast in their faith. When the time of tribulation comes upon them, they will fall away (Luke 8:13) and wilt like the plant in the rocky soil. These people will change their stand for Jesus in order to avoid the suffering that might come otherwise. I call these **"rocky soil"** people the **"SHALLOW PEOPLE,"** they cannot endure the suffering, and their faith in Jesus will be shaken.

On the other hand, those people who "endure the suffering" trust totally in the power and example of Jesus. They can face the suffering (physical, emotional, and/or social) that accompanies any circumstance of rejection and persecution; they are active in doing the Lord's work while in the midst of their suffering; and they are a testimony of God to all that are around them. These people "walk in the Spirit" (Gal. 5:16) and will be steadfast in their faith. **The glorification of God and the satisfaction of our need for power are set fully in trusting in the power of Jesus to endure *our* suffering. God will empower us with His Holy Spirit and deliver us. We, then, will not be the "rocky soil," and our faith in Jesus will not be shaken but will be *steadfast*. We are loving God and loving our neighbor. Steadfast faithfulness in the form of enduring the suffering is the "mind of Christ."**

And He was saying to them all, "If anyone wishes to come after me, he must deny himself, and take up his cross daily and follow Me. (Luke 9:23)

Are we enduring the suffering when it comes?
Are we following Jesus a little more nearly?
Let's go on!

FRAMEWORK FOR SPIRITUAL MATURITY

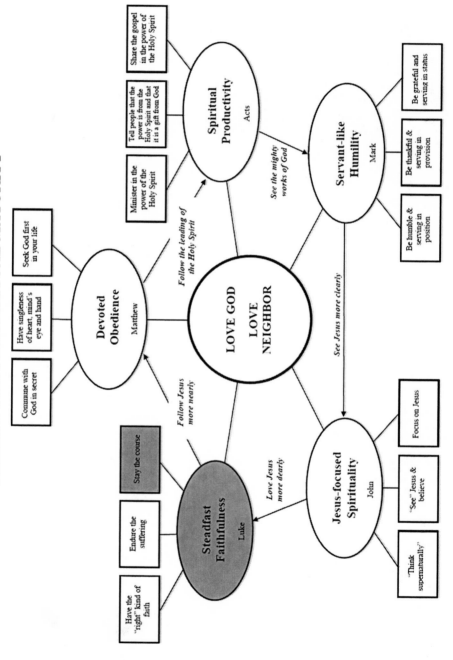

Finish Well:
Stay The Course

The third issue concerning steadfast faithfulness is "stay the course" and is found in Luke, chapter 9, verses 28–36; 46–50; 62. Following Jesus will not always be easy. We must not become weary but must press on with our focus on Jesus (Gal. 6:9–10, Heb. 12:1–3).

Only listen to Jesus.

Jesus takes Peter, James, and John up to the mountain to pray (v. 28). Jesus is transfigured and is talking with Elijah about what is going to happen in Jerusalem (vv. 29–31). Peter, James, and John see Jesus in his glory and also Elijah and Moses standing with Him (v. 32). As Elijah and Moses are about to leave, Peter suggests that three tabernacles should be made, one each for Jesus, Elijah, and Moses (v. 33). At this point a cloud forms, and God the Father speaks from the cloud saying, "This is my Son, *My* Chosen One; listen to Him" (vv. 34–35). When the voice had spoken, Elijah and Moses were gone; and Jesus was alone (v. 36).

The point being made to the disciples, here, is that it is Jesus, alone, with whom they should "tabernacle." God the Father tells the disciples that they are to listen only to Jesus and not Elijah, Moses, or anyone else.

Even today, people who claim to be disciples of Jesus "listen" to others. Some people are not satisfied with the Word of God and the Holy Spirit, but are looking for something else that they consider more exciting, emotional, intriguing, mystical, etc. Certainly, there is enough "stuff" out there to which they can listen, and it may cause them to stray from their complete faith in Jesus.

Experiencing "listening to Jesus."

When I first received Jesus, I wanted to learn as much as I could about what *Jesus* said and what *Jesus* did. I wanted to follow Jesus, and I needed to listen to *Him*. I read the Gospels over and over, especially the words in red letters. If you looked at the top edge of my Bible, you could see where the top of the pages in the Gospel books were darker than the top of the rest of the pages. I was totally committed. I listened to Jesus as I read the Gospels. I listened to Jesus in prayer through the Holy Spirit. I listened to Jesus as I attended to the preaching of the Word. I had no desire to listen to anyone else. I had to watch myself that I was not rude when other people were talking to me. Jesus, Jesus, Jesus! Talk to me Jesus! I'm listening!

If we are listening to Jesus alone, we will be less likely to stray in our faith in Him. As we listen and follow, Jesus will deliver us time and time again! Our faith in Jesus will become stronger and stronger.

Don't be distracted by the things of the "self."

An argument starts among the disciples about which of them might be the greatest (v. 46). Jesus knows what they are thinking in their heart (v. 47a). The thinking in their heart is all about themselves. It is pride, pure and simple. Jesus gives an object lesson by taking a child and telling the disciples that "receiving" that child is where their hearts should be (vv. 47a-48). Instead of being prideful, they should be humble in their position and be ready to receive the little children. By receiving the little children in Jesus' name, Jesus tells the disciples that they will be receiving Jesus; and by receiving Jesus, they also will be receiving God the Father (v. 48). Jesus instructs the disciples that the one who is the least humble and ministering to the needy among them is the one who is great (v. 48).

Some disciples of Jesus today get into disputes about who is the greatest and become jealous of one another wanting to be the greatest. This is a prideful attitude that becomes hurtful to others and destructive to the church, and may cause some to stray from their complete faith in Jesus.

Experiencing "not being distracted by the things of the "self.""

The area of ministry that I struggle with in the above manner is that of music. My desire is to use the music to praise God and to help others to praise God. However, once in a while, pride will raise its ugly head, and I will begin to think that what I am doing is pretty "great." When this happens, I am not humble; I am not praising God; and may not even be helping others to praise God.

We need to be humble in our ministry as disciples of Jesus. Pride will get us "off course" in our service to Jesus and to others. If we sense the pride creeping into our service, we need to ask for forgiveness, humble ourselves before the Lord, and return to a complete faith in Jesus. He will help us!

Don't look back!

One of the people who indicates a desire to follow Jesus tells Jesus that he first must say goodbye to those at home. Jesus has an incredibly direct response to the suggestion—"no one, after putting his hand to the plow and looking back, is fit for the kingdom of God." (v. 62).

If a farmer looks back as he is plowing, the plow will go off its course and the furrow will not be straight. My great uncle, Wall, was a farmer. When he started to plow a furrow, he would pick out something like a tree on which to focus and begin to plow. He would stay focused on the tree, not looking back, until he reached it. His furrow was straight. Jesus is telling the would-be follower that he must no longer look back and trust in the things of the past or his "plow" will go off course. Instead, he must keep his focus forward on Jesus (like the tree on which my uncle focused) and completely trust in Him. If he does this, his "plow" will stay on course and his furrow will be straight. The consequence to the follower for not keeping his focus on Jesus and trusting in Him completely is that he will not be "fit for the Kingdom of God." When a plow goes off course, the furrow is not straight. I believe that Jesus is saying that all the furrows in the Kingdom of God must be straight; and for that to happen, disciples need to have their focus on Him.

Today, some would-be followers of Jesus "look back" and trust in the things with which they are familiar such as people, possessions, money, etc. When the "plow" of their life goes off course and the "furrows" of their life are crooked, they have a difficult time understanding what has gone wrong, and some of them even blame God. All of this may shake their faith in Jesus.

Experiencing "not looking back"

When it comes to the big things in life such as dealing with tragedy, big decisions about direction in life, teaching the Word of God, etc; I seem to be able to keep my focus forward on Jesus, and I am trusting completely in Him. However, when it comes to the little things in life, I have more of a struggle. I think, somehow, that Jesus should not be bothered with the little things in life and that I should be taking care of the little things. Wrong! Daily, I am learning to focus on Jesus to help more and more with the little things, as well as the big things.

We need to keep our focus on and trust in Jesus all of the time. We must not look back and trust in the things familiar to us in the past. If we feel that our "plow" is going off course or that our "furrow" is beginning to look crooked, we need to ask Jesus for forgiveness and get our focus and trust back on Him. He will help us!

Examples of how to "stay the course."

The characters depicted in Chapter 24 of the Gospel of Luke provide a good example of how to "stay the course." They are to listen to Jesus, only; be humble; and look forward with a focus on Jesus.

The women come to the tomb looking for Jesus, but they do not find Him in the tomb (vv. 1–3). When the two men that appear speak, they remind the women of what Jesus has said to them—"The Son of man must be delivered into the hands of sinful men, and be crucified, and the third day rise again" (vv. 4–7). The women listen to Jesus because they remember His words (v. 8). They not only remember His words, but they trust in His words and go to tell the disciples (v. 9). These women are a good example of how to "stay the course" in that they listen and trust in the words of Jesus, they are humble, and they are looking forward with their focus on Jesus.

Peter must have listened to Jesus and remembered what he said because he runs to the tomb to check it out himself (v. 12). Peter marvels at what has happened because the words that Jesus spoke about himself were true (v.12). Peter tells the other disciples (v. 34). Peter is a good example of how to stay the course because he listened and trusted in the words of Jesus, he is humble, and he is looking forward with his focus on Jesus.

The other disciples, however, do not listen and trust in the words of Jesus, they are not humble, and they are not looking forward with their focus on Jesus. The entire group feels that what the women said is "nonsense" and refuses to believe them (v. 11). They must not have listened to Jesus. Two of the disciples leave Jerusalem and are on their way to Emmaus (v. 13). They certainly are not staying the course. However, after Jesus speaks to them at length, they do listen to Him and return to Jerusalem to tell the other disciples (vv. 14–35). The other disciples, who are gathered listening to the two that were on their way to Emmaus, are frightened by Jesus' appearance in their midst (v. 36, 37). They think that He is a spirit (v. 37). They really do not believe Jesus' words from before, or they would not have been frightened. They are not humble, and they are not looking forward with their focus on Jesus. The disciples are still not staying the course.

Jesus reassures the disciples that it is He and shows them evidence of that (vv. 38–43). Then, He reminds them of the words that He had spoken to them when they were first with Him (v. 44) and opens their minds so that they can understand the Scriptures (vv. 44–47). Finally, Jesus reminds His disciples that they are witnesses to the truth about

Him and that He will send the Holy Spirit upon them (vv. 48–49). Jesus blesses them and ascends into heaven in their presence (v. 50). It seems that, at this point, the disciples are "listening to Jesus only," are humble, and looking forward with their focus on Jesus; and as a result, it appears that they are prepared to "stay the course."

Summary.

We can learn much from this portion of Luke's Gospel. Some people are not staying the course because they refuse to listen to Jesus only, are prideful, and are looking back. They will not be steadfast in their faith. When time of tribulation comes upon them, they will fall away and wilt like the plant in the rocky soil. They will change their stand for Jesus because they are not focusing on the direction provided by Him. I call these **"rocky soil"** people the **"SHALLOW PEOPLE"** because they cannot stay the course.

On the other hand, those people who "stay the course" trust totally in the power and example of Jesus. They listen to Jesus only, are humble, and are focused forward on Jesus. These people will be steadfast in their faith. **The glorification of God and satisfaction of our need for power come when we trust in the power of Jesus and stay the course. God will empower us with His Holy Spirit and will deliver us. We, then, will not be the "rocky soil," and our faith in Jesus will not be shaken but will be steadfast. We are loving God and loving our neighbor. Steadfast faithfulness in the form of staying the course is the "mind of Christ."**

> **But Jesus said to him, "No one, after putting his hand to the plow and looking back, is fit for the kingdom of God." (Luke 9:62)**

Are we staying the course more?
Are we following Jesus a little more nearly?
Let's go on!

Summary
Section III

All of the concepts concerning steadfast faithfulness that we have seen in Chapter 9 are best summarized in the "Parable of the Friend at Midnight:"

> **Suppose one of you has a friend, and goes to him at midnight and says to him, "Friend, lend me three loaves; for a friend of mine has come to me from a journey, and I have nothing to set before him"; and from inside he answers and says, "Do not bother me; the door is already been shut and my children and I are in bed; I cannot get up and give you anything." I tell you even though he will not get up and give him anything because he is his friend, yet because of his persistence he will get up and give him as much as he needs.(Luke 11:5–8)**

Suppose one of *our* friends comes to *us* at 11:30 PM and is need of food after a long trip. What do we do? If we have the "right kind of faith," we will rely on the Word of God. The Word of God shows us right here in Luke 9 that we are to help the sick and needy; and so, if we have the "right kind of faith," we will seek to meet our friend's need. Now, we do not have any bread in our house, but we could bake some. Well, how long would that take? Our friend is very hungry after his trip and needs to eat right away! Are we going to attempt to meet his need in our own power by baking the bread? That would not be the "right kind of faith." Perhaps, because it is, after all, after the late news, we could chastise our friend for coming so late and send him packing. This would be a misuse of our power, and we would not be exhibiting the "right kind of faith." So, we decide to get help in order to meet our friend's need of hunger and go down the road to a friend of ours that we know always has plenty of bread.

So, we knock on our friend's door. It is now midnight. We share our story with our friend and ask him for three loaves of bread. Our friend seems a bit bothered by our intrusion and tells us that he has locked his door, that he and his children have gone to bed, and that he is not about to get up and give us anything. Are we going to "endure the suffering?" Are we going to follow Jesus in spite of rejection? We were kind of excited to think that we would be able to get bread from our friend, but now, we are discouraged because it looks like that is not going to happen. Are we going to follow Jesus in spite of the "lows" that follow the "highs." If we are going to "endure the suffering," then we need to follow Jesus no matter what the conditions! So, we "endure the suffering" and keep knocking.

Well, there is no change in the response from our friend about getting up and giving us some bread. Shall we give up? What did Jesus say? Are we going to listen to Him only? Should we be embarrassed about how all of this looks to the neighbors who are looking out of their windows? Should we go back home and bake some bread? No indeed, we need to "stay the course" and keep knocking and knocking and knocking!

Well, what do you know; our friend is getting up, opening the door, and giving us as much bread as we need. He says that the reason that he got up and gave us the bread was not because of the fact that we were his friends. No, indeed, he said he got up and gave us the bread because of our shameless persistence. Perhaps it was our steadfast faith in our friend, exhibited in our shameless persistence, which caused our friend to respond to us with such abundant graciousness. **God is trying to increase the faith of believers through His Word and His Holy Spirit so that their faith can become steadfast. In this way they, through trust, can fully experience the power of Jesus (the Holy Spirit) in their lives!** Where are we in all of this? Do we have the "right kind of faith?" Do we "endure the suffering?" Do we "stay the course?" Are we the rocky soil or not the rocky soil? Do we have the "mind of Christ?"

The glorification of God and the satisfaction of our need for a sense of power come through trusting in the ultimate power,

the power of Jesus. We need to have the "right kind of faith," "endure the suffering," and "stay the course." If we do, we will have steadfast faithfulness and will *not* be the "rocky soil." We will be loving God and loving our neighbor. This is the "mind of Christ" concerning steadfast faithfulness.

> Now after this the Lord appointed seventy others, and sent them in pairs ahead of Him to every city and place where He himself was going to come. And He was saying to them, "The harvest is plentiful, but the laborers are few; therefore beseech the Lord of the harvest to send out laborers into the harvest. Go; behold, I send you out as lambs in the midst of wolves. Carry no money belt, no bag, no shoes; and greet no one on the way. (Luke 10:1–4)

Are we following Jesus a little more nearly?
Are we following Him nearly enough to be obedient to Him?
Let's go on!

Note: If you want to pursue the theme of "steadfast faithfulness" further in the Gospel of Luke, turn to Appendix VIII-C for a study outline. The outline provides for a macro study (based on a micro study) of the scripture and is written in an application format.

FRAMEWORK FOR SPIRITUAL MATURITY

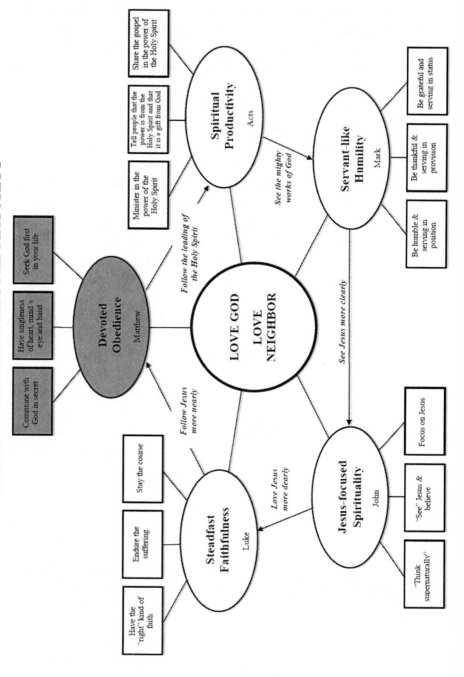

SECTION IV

Devoted Obedience

A farmer went out to sow his seed...Other seed fell among thorns, which grew up and choked the plants...The one who received the seed that fell among the thorns is the man who hears the word, but the worries of this life and the deceitfulness of wealth choke it, making it unfruitful. (Matt. 13:3b; 7; 22)

Now, if we are humble and find that our sense of worth comes from appropriating the love and acceptance of Jesus, if we have been spiritually transformed so that we possess the Holy Spirit and are truly free to choose the way of Jesus, and if we have steadfast faith in Jesus and fully submit and entrust ourselves to His power; then we should, because of our sense of God's love and power in our lives, be devotedly obedient to His will. However, the Parable of the Sower tells us that some people, who are in a position to be obedient, are not so because they are distracted by the worries of the world and the deceitfulness of wealth (Matt. 13:22). The seed that falls on the thorny ground, penetrates the soil, germinates, and grows to be a full plant. However, the thorns that grow up around the plant choke it out (Matt. 13:22). Jesus explains to His disciples that the "thorny-ground" person hears God's Word, but that the worries of the world and deceitfulness of wealth choke the Word. As a result, the plant does not bear any fruit (Matt. 13:22). This suggests to me the issue of disobedience to God. In my reading in the Gospels, I determined that the theme of the Gospel of Matthew is obedience and more specifically an obedience that is motivated by devotion.

Thinking back to my understanding of human intrinsic needs, the need related to devoted obedience is security. We need to know that someone or something will provide for our physiological needs, i.e., food, clothing, shelter, etc. Knowing that these things will be provided gives us a sense of security. We might, at some level, understand that God provides everything; but our flesh is weak, and we begin to worry about whether or not our needs will be met. As a result, we may seek to rely on other sources of provision in our lives. In addition, in our seeking other sources of provision, we may become distracted into accumulating more provision than we really need in hopes of increasing our sense of security. The focus of our life and our time, then, will be on worry and the accumulation of wealth and will leave little or no time to do the work to which the Lord has called us. How can we begin to be obedient to God when we are spending all of our time worrying about our security in the world and our accumulating wealth, which we think might increase the level of our security? In God's eyes, this is disobedience. We must trust (goes back to faith) that God will meet all of our physiological needs. Our focus and time needs to be on determining what God's will is for our life and then on doing it. We will certainly need the Word of God to accomplish this. If this, then, is the direction of our life, we will be obedient; and God will provide for all of our needs. However, if we are like the "thorny soil," we will be disobedient to God, will not be doing the work to which He has called us, and will be unproductive for God. I call the **"thorny soil"** people the **"UNPRODUCTIVE PEOPLE."** Jesus says that the Word of God in these people will be choked out and that these people will be unfruitful for God (Matt.13:22). How can the Word be fruitful in a person's life if it has been choked out? On the other hand, if we do not allow the worries of the world and the deceitfulness of wealth to choke out the Word of God in our lives, and if we are being **obedient** to Jesus through His Word, we *will* be fruitful for God. He will meet all of our **physiological needs**, and we will have an incredible sense of **security**, even our **eternal security!**

Chapter 6 of the Gospel of Matthew provides an insightful presentation concerning man's disobedience and reveals the "mind of Christ" concerning devoted obedience. In Section IV of this book, the three *process*-issues that cause disobedience will be explored. In the next three chapters, we will examine each of these three issues and how Jesus provides a way for us to deal with them.

FRAMEWORK FOR SPIRITUAL MATURITY

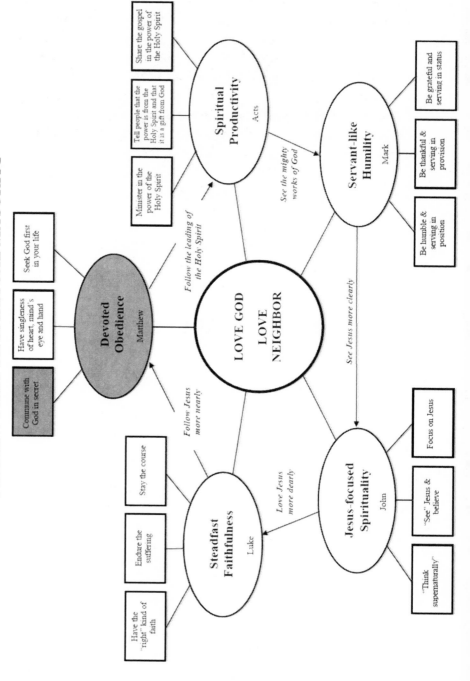

CHAPTER 10

Stay Tuned:
Commune with God in Secret

"Communing with God in secret" is the first issue concerning the process of obedience and is presented in Matthew, chapter 6, (verses 1–15). To commune means to converse intimately. God desires to have an ongoing intimate conversation with us. We can have this conversation, Jesus instructs, by giving, praying, and fasting. In order that the conversation be intimate, Jesus says that the giving, praying, and fasting must be done in secret.

Give in Secret.

Jesus tells the people to whom he is speaking that they should not be "practicing their righteousness before men" because their Father in heaven will not be pleased, and He will not reward them for their actions (v. 1). Jesus gives an example of this "practicing righteousness before men" in that hypocrites in the synagogues and streets try to draw attention to themselves when in the act of giving. (Remember from Section III that the focus of our faith should be ministering to the sick and needy.) Jesus says that in giving in this way, these people have their reward (v. 2) It is a worldly reward and one that comes from the hypocrisy of giving not to serve others, but giving in order to solicit praises for themselves. Jesus instructs those listening concerning the right way to give. He says that when we give to the poor, we should do it in *secret* (v. 3). By doing this, Jesus says, the Father will be pleased and will reward us (v. 4). Why is it that he will not reward us when we give in public and will reward us when we give in private? I think it is because of the reason behind our giving. When we give in public, it could be that we are giving in order to solicit praise from others. Here, there is possible gain for us; there is no pure sacrifice; and this could result in hypocrisy. However, when we give in private, there is nothing worldly in it for us. It is a pure sacrifice of what God has provided for us. It is clear that we are only doing it out of obedience to God, and God will reward us secretly. How will He reward us? We will need to wait until chapter 12 in order to find out more specifically.

I also believe that "giving in secret" is a sign to the Father that we are serious about wanting to have a relationship with Him, a relationship in which we are humble and obedient. I feel that this is the reason that Matthew lists "giving" first before "praying" and "fasting."

One day, I was just beginning a Bible study class at my church on this portion of scripture when about thirty people from the nearby homeless shelter unexpectedly came into the room. I thought to myself, "How am I going to teach these people about giving? They have nothing to give." I said to the Lord, "Lord, please help me to see what to do here!" What immediately came into my mind was the word, "forgiving." "Thank you, Lord," I said. If we have no material possessions, we certainly can give our mercy, our forgiveness. So I proceeded with the study with this concept included. One of the homeless people even provided an example for the class! In addition, all of this reinforced my understanding about "giving" coming before "praying" and "fasting." We also see this later in Matthew 6 when Jesus warns the people that if we do not forgive others "first," He will not answer our prayers for forgiveness. Again, in Matthew 5 (vv. 24–25) Jesus instructs the people to be reconciled (forgiveness) to others "first" before bringing their gifts to the altar.

Today, we see many people in the secular world and in the church who give to the poor publicly. It is not to say that what is given will not help those who receive it. However, the Father will not be pleased and will not reward those people if the giving is self-serving, is not a pure sacrifice, and is not done purely out of obedience to Him. Jesus says in Matthew 7 (vv. 21–23) that He will not acknowledge those things that we do for Him unless they are in His will. In addition, if we give to the poor privately and are not the object of praise by other people; then, perhaps, God will get the praise and glory! Is this not as it should be?

Experiencing "giving in secret."

I was convicted at some point in my spiritual journey that the best way to give financially in secret to the poor is to give to the church to which I belonged, and to encourage the church to give to the poor. In this way, my giving is in secret; and if the poor respond with praise, it is for the church. The church is the "bride of Christ," and this would provide an opportunity for members of the church to tell the poor that the gift is from God and that Jesus is both the reason for the giving and the ultimate gift, Himself, from God. Praise and glory be to God! This does not preclude us from financially giving directly to those in need, especially if it is an emergency situation, nor does it preclude us from giving of our time, our love, and our spiritual gifts. However, we just need to be sure to let those, to whom we have given, know where the praise and glory belongs.

Pray in secret.

Jesus continues His discourse on communing with God in secret by turning to prayer. He says that the hypocrites just love to pray in public so that they may be seen by others (v. 5). Here, the "practicing of their righteousness before men" is in the form of prayer. Again, Jesus states that praying in this manner results in a worldly reward and one that comes from the hypocrisy of praying not to be heard by God, but to solicit praise from other people. Jesus instructs those listening about the right way to pray. He says to go into your inner room, close your door, and pray to our Father who is in secret (v. 6). Wow, He is pretty specific about how private our prayer should be. If we pray to our Father in secret, He will reward us (v. 6). Why will He reward us if we pray in secret? I believe that when we are praying in secret, there is no worldly gain for us; it is a humble sacrifice of our position, and it is clearly only a result of obedience to Him. How will He reward us? Again, we will need to wait until we get to chapter 12.

Jesus continues His instruction about prayer by telling those listening that they should not pray using meaningless repetition (v. 7). Here is a presumption of thinking that God will hear us if we keep saying it over again when in fact our Father knows what we need even before we ask it (v. 8).

Then Jesus gives us a format for prayer. First, we need to acknowledge who it is that is holy—our heavenly Father (v. 9). Next, we need to acknowledge whose kingdom is to come and whose will is to be done—our heavenly Father (v. 10). Then we ask Him for our daily bread, the forgiveness of our sins, and leading of us not into temptation but delivering us from evil (vv. 11–13a). Finally, we acknowledge again whose kingdom it is—our Father's, who has the power—our Father, and who should get all the glory—our Father (v. 13b). Then there is a footnote: If we want our sins to be forgiven, it is mandatory that we forgive the sins of others (vv. 14–15).

Many of those who profess to be believers today do not spend very much time in private prayer. They may say grace at the table, attend to corporate prayer in the worship service, and participate in group prayer in a Sunday school class, ABF, or fellowship group. However, they do not take the time to pray privately. It is not to say that these types of public prayer are inappropriate. However, the Father most of all desires them to pray to Him in secret and will not reward them unless they are obedient to Him. Some who do pray privately may have prescribed prayers that they repeat over and over (v.7). Jesus says not to be like these people because the Father knows what we need before we ask Him (v. 8). Some may not spend some of their private prayer following the format that Jesus provided. We need to be obedient to the words of Jesus concerning prayer.

Experiencing "praying in secret."

My prayer life is an ever-developing process. Today, I begin my day by privately praying in the format that Jesus provided. I note at the beginning of the prayer that it is the Father's kingdom that is to come, not mine, and that it is the Father's will that it is to be done, not mine. It is a time for me to humble myself before the Father and acknowledge His holiness and His rightful position.

When I think about His provision of our "daily bread," I consider the manna that was provided to the Israelites in the desert (Exod. 16:4–5). It lasted for only one day—except for the Sabbath (Exod. 16:5). I pray for physiological provision (such as safety, the accomplishment of routine chores of the day, financial provision for food, shelter, healing, etc.) for the day, only. I pray for the provision of spiritual bread—the Bread of Life, Jesus (the Word of God). I ask for the help of the Holy Spirit in understanding the Word and its application. I meditate on the scripture that says that the Father provides for the birds of the air, and if so, will certainly provide for me (Matt. 6:26).

When it comes to asking for forgiveness, I start by meditating on the body and blood of Jesus. I thank God for the body of Jesus that absorbed the punishment for my sin. I thank God for the shedding of the blood of Jesus that resulted in the forgiveness of my sin. Praise be to God! I am so grateful. I confess my sins of commission and my sins of omission and ask for forgiveness in the name of Jesus. I meditate on the scripture that suggests that my continued sinning crucifies Jesus again and puts Him to an open shame (Heb. 6:6). I ask for help from the Holy Spirit to help me not to sin as it is not what I desire. I pray for those people with whom I am having difficulty and express my forgiveness toward them.

Then, I ask for deliverance from temptation and evil. I meditate on the scriptures that describe how God delivered Job (Job 42:10–17), Jesus (Mark 16:1–7), Peter (Acts 12), Paul (Acts 16:19–40), and other people of faith (such as those described in Hebrews 11). I ask for deliverance for myself, my entire family, my spiritual family, and those that I feel may be under persecution or affliction.

Finally, I again acknowledge God's position in the kingdom, His power, and all the glory that is due Him. Praise be to God! Then, I pray that he will provide opportunities to minister, that He will give me "eyes" to see those opportunities, and that He will help me to subject my flesh to His Holy Spirit so that I will be able to minister in His will and power. I am in prayer all day long talking with God about what it is that He wants me to do and how He wants me to do it. I end the day by thanking Him for each specific blessing of the day.

Fast in secret.

Jesus concludes his discourse on "communing in secret" with the practice of fasting. He says that the hypocrites neglect their appearance and put on a gloomy face when they are fasting so that they will be noticed by others (v. 16a). Here, the "practicing of righteousness before men" is done in the form of fasting. Again, He says that fasting in this manner results in a worldly reward and one that stems from hypocrisy (v. 16b), in which one is not listening to God, but is soliciting praise from other people. Jesus instructs the people about the right way to fast. He tells them to freshen up their appearance so that their fasting will not be noticed by others (v. 17a). If we fast in secret, our Father will reward us in secret (v. 17b). He will reward us because our fasting in secret can be of no worldly gain to us, is a pure sacrifice of our serving (to God and not ourselves), and it clearly accomplished only as a result of obedience to Him. How will He reward us? Again, we will have to wait until chapter 12.

Fasting is basically the abstinence from partaking of food for a period of time. During the period of time that we are fasting, we are better able to focus and concentrate on God by denying ourselves the things which gratify our flesh. We are in a better position to hear what God is saying to us. Praying is a good time to *talk* to God. Fasting is a good time to *listen* to God. Although abstaining from food is still a good way to put away the distractions of the flesh, in today's world fasting also might be turning off the television, the computer, the cell phone, etc. Many people, who profess to be believers today, do not even consider the act of fasting. One wonders if they can hear what God is saying to them.

Experiencing "fasting in secret."
•

I fast often in the sense of "getting away" from the distractions of everyday life in a "retreat" mode. Sometimes, it takes me three days before I can begin to "listen" to God most effectively. In addition, I have fasted in the sense of not sleeping, either by staying up late or waking up in the middle of the night and not going back to sleep. I have been able to "listen" to the Lord clearly in both of these types of fasting. Also, I believe that the fasting needs to be done concurrently with meditating on the Word of God.

Examples of "communing with God in secret."

Chapter 26 of Matthew provides a contrast of those who are "communing with God in secret" and those who are not.

In verses 1–25, we find the chief priests, scribes, and elders showing that they are not "communing with God in secret" about their *giving*. Instead, they are communing with each other in secret about how they can *take* and kill Jesus and maintain the security of their positions (vv. 3–6). The disciples are not "communing with God in secret" about *giving* in their indignant response to the woman who anoints Jesus with perfume (vv. 7–13). They suggest that the money could be used for the poor; but given Jesus' response, they were probably considering *taking* the money for the group's purse and thereby enhancing the security of the group. In addition, their confusion about whether or not they would be the one to betray Jesus speaks to their insecurity even in their relationship with Jesus (vv. 20–22). Judas is not "communing with God in secret" about *giving,* but is communing with the chief priests concerning *taking* money for betraying Jesus (vv. 14–16, 23–26), Judas is focused on his own financial security. Only the woman appears to be "communing with God in secret" about her *giving*. She does not seem worried or insecure about giving something of hers to Jesus that is of great value. It seems that she is "giving in secret" even though there are people around. She is not trying to impress anyone, draw attention to her-self, nor solicit praise from those present. In fact, she is berated by the disciples for her action. It seems that she is being obedient to God in anointing Jesus with the perfume in order to prepare His body for burial (vv. 6–7). Jesus is clearly pleased by the gift and states at least one of the rewards that she will receive (vv. 12–13).

In verses 26–46, we see that the disciples are not "communing with God in secret" concerning their prayer. Jesus instructs them to keep watch and pray so that they may not enter into temptation while he goes to pray (vv. 41, 44). Each time Jesus comes back He finds his disciples *not* in prayer but sleeping (vv. 40, 43, & 45). Luke 22:45 indicates that the reason for the disciples "sleeping" is "sorrow." The disciples are most probably worried and depressed about what Jesus had just shared with them and its possible impact on their own personal security. Jesus, on the other hand, goes to the garden at Gethsemane and "communes with the Father in secret" by praying (vv. 36–39, 42, and 44). He is making sure of God's will concerning the giving of His life through crucifixion, and we can sense His desire to be obedient to the Father—"Your will be done" (v. 42). Does this remind us of a piece of the format for prayer that Jesus gave in Matthew 6:9–13?

In verses 47–75, we see that there are a whole host of people who are not "communing with God in secret" through fasting. Is Judas fasting and listening to God when he decides to betray Jesus (vv. 47–50)? No, he is thinking about what he might get with the money he will make. Is the disciple who cut off the ear of the high priest's slave fasting and listening to God (v. 51)? No, he is trying to defend Jesus (and himself as well). Have those in the crowds been fasting and listening to God when they demand Jesus' be arrested as one would a robber (v. 55)? No, they are all interested in pleasing the religious leaders. Are the disciples fasting and listening to God when they leave Jesus and run away (v. 56)? No, they are only interested in saving their own skins. Is Peter fasting and listening to God when he denies Jesus three times (vv. 69–75)? No, he is only interested in warming himself by the fire and saving his own skin. None of these people are "communing with God in secret" by fasting, and they are not listening to God. Only Jesus who is "communing with God in secret" through fasting (listening) knows exactly what God's will is, and He does it. Jesus has, at His disposal, twelve thousand angels to protect him (v. 53), but does not use them to serve Himself. He is obedient in His service to the Father, and allows His capture (vv. 47–56), His unfair trial (vv. 57–64), and His death sentence (vv. 65–68).

Summary.

Some people who profess to believe do not take time to meditate on the Word of God and to commune with God in secret. This is because they are worried about their own provision. Instead of waiting on God, they go forth, worrisome, seeking to provide wealth for themselves. Also, in an attempt to seek security in their relationship with God; they give, pray, and fast. However, they may give, pray, and fast *in public* so that those around them will praise them for their "godly" work. There is no humility; there is no pure sacrifice, there is no communion with God; and there is no obedience to God. These people have no idea what it is that God wants them to do and how He wants them to do it. The worries of the world and the deceitfulness of wealth choke them out like the plant on the **"thorny soil."** As a result, they are **spiritually unproductive** because they are distracted from God by worry, wealth, and the things of the world. I call these **"thorny soil"** people the **"UNPRODUCTIVE PEOPLE."**

On the other hand, those who "commune with God in secret" do not put the seeking of their own personal security before their obedience to God. They are humble and willing to sacrifice in a pure manner apart from the eyes of men. They give in secret, pray in secret, and fast in secret; and they trust in God for their security and reward. These people are devoted in their obedience to God. **Glorification of God and the satisfaction of our need for security come from our obedience to God through communing with Him in secret. God will provide! We, then, are *not* the "thorny soil." We are loving God and loving our neighbor. Devoted obedience in the form of communing with God in secret is the "mind of Christ."**

And your Father who sees what is done in secret will reward you. (Matt. 6:4b, 6b, 18b)

Are we communing more with God in secret?
Are we following the leading of the Holy Spirit?
Let's go on!

FRAMEWORK FOR SPIRITUAL MATURITY

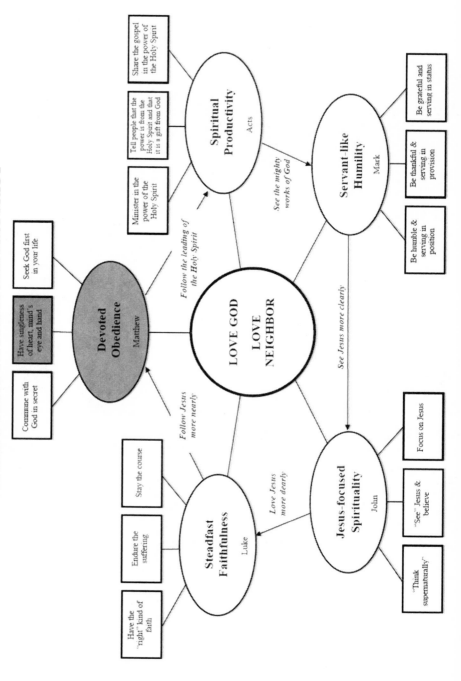

CHAPTER 11

Totally Committed: Have Singleness of Heart, Eye, and Hand

Singleness of heart, eye, and hand is the second issue concerning obedience and is presented in Matthew 6:19–24. Singleness suggests *integrity* in that there is *oneness* present in *all* aspects of our lives.

Singleness of the heart.

Jesus tells the people that it is not wise to store up "treasures on earth" because rust and moth will destroy them and thieves will break in and steal them (v. 19). These earthly treasures are the material things and the material wealth of the world. However, Jesus tells the people to store up "treasures in heaven" because rust and moth will not destroy them and thieves cannot break in and steal them (v. 20). These treasures are the things done in obedience to God. The type of treasures we spend time storing up will depend on which one we love the most (v. 21). Do we love the material things and wealth of the world, or do we love God? Where are our hearts?

I feel that what is in our hearts is our desire—what is it that we want? Many of those who profess to be believers today spend their time in an attempt to gain more wealth and possessions such as clothes, houses, cars, boats, electronic paraphernalia, etc. Many possessions and much wealth tend to give them an illusion that their sense of security is increased. They spend little time doing the things that God has called them to do such as ministering to the sick and needy and sharing the Gospel message. Certainly, if we are giving, praying, and fasting in secret; God has "spoken" to us, and we know what it is that he wants us to do. The question is whether or not we will be obedient to His will, and this is a decision of the heart. Now, we know the desire of God's heart. He loved the world so much that He allowed the sacrifice of His Son, Jesus, in order to take away our sins (John 3:16). Do our hearts truly sense this love of God the Father? We also know the desire of Jesus' heart. He willingly allowed Himself to be sacrificed in His obedience to the Father and in His compassion for us (Matt. 26). Do our hearts truly sense the love of Jesus? We also know that we are able to love with our hearts because God first loved us (1 John 4:19). What should be the desire of our hearts, then, to this incredible love from God the Father and Jesus? Should we not want to love them? If we love them, what should that love look like? Jesus says in John 14:13, "If you love me, keep my commandments." Jesus is looking for an obedience of the heart, a devoted obedience. Where is the desire of our hearts? What do we really want?

Experiencing "singleness of heart."

On the day I received Jesus as my Savior, I was so overwhelmed by who Jesus really was, and what He had accomplished on the cross. I can remember thinking to myself about my past seeking for the truth about living life. I had tried philosophy and had given that one hundred percent. I had tried psychology and had given that one hundred percent. Neither had worked. If I had given philosophy and psychology one hundred percent, why should I not give Jesus a one hundred percent try? I did. Everything became about Jesus. Into the Gospels I went. Jesus said to do this. I tried to do what Jesus said. Jesus did that. I tried to do what Jesus did. Did I make mistakes? Yes, I did. What did I do? I asked for forgiveness and the wisdom and power of the Holy Spirit, and then I tried again. However, through all of this early time in my spiritual growth, one thing was very clear to me. My heart was for Jesus. My heart was for Jesus. My heart was for Jesus. Slowly, but surely, I became more and more obedient to God. Now, I am later in my spiritual growth, and do you know what? My heart is for Jesus. My heart is for Jesus. My heart is for Jesus!

Singleness of the eye.

Jesus tells the people that the eye is the lamp of the body (v. 22). If the eye is clear, Jesus says; then the whole body will be full of light (v. 22). Jesus is the Light; and if we can keep our eye clear, the Light will fill our whole body. We can be full of Jesus, the Light. However, if the eye is bad (in the sense of evil), Jesus says; then the whole body will be full of darkness (v. 23). I think what Jesus is saying here is that we need to fill ourselves with Him through our eye which He, Himself, has cleared. If we do this, we will see God's perspective of righteousness; and our thinking and our intentions will be stayed on righteousness. However, if we allow the darkness of sin to cloud and darken our eye, we will not see God's perspective of righteousness, and our thinking and intentions will be on sin.

Many of those who profess to be believers today have a problem with maintaining God's perspective of righteousness by not keeping their eye clear. As a result, their thinking and intentions become sinful. This is especially true for those coming from a particular habitual sin. They stop the sin for a period of time, but they do not allow Jesus to fill them with His light. After a period of time of trying to stay away from their habitual sin, they go back to it. This reminds me of the story Jesus told in Matthew 12:43–45. Here, the unclean spirit goes out of a man; the man cleans up his house, but he leaves it empty. The unclean spirit returns, finds the house empty, and goes and brings seven spirits worse than himself to live in the house. The man's state is worse than before. It seems that this type of people seem to gain a temporary comfort and security in their old habits. Others just allow the specks of sin to collect in their eye and darken; and over a period of time, they lose God's perspective on righteousness. How can these people even begin to be obedient to God when they do not maintain a clear eye and keep a focus on what God's righteousness is? What becomes of their thinking and their intentions? Are *we* maintaining a clear eye that can keep a focus on God's righteousness? Does our thinking and intentions reflect God's righteousness and His will?

Experiencing singleness of the eye.

Receiving Jesus as my Savior was such a dramatic event for me. I had strived for acceptance throughout my whole life and never had truly experienced it. On this day of redemption for me I understood that Jesus died to take away all of my sins; and if I believed in Him that way, God would ACCEPT me. What amazing grace! Jesus cleared up my eye and my whole body was filled with His light. This was so dramatic for me, and I experienced a great sense of freedom. There was no way that I was ever going back. Well, what if I sinned again, and I did. The first chapter of I John talks about walking "in the light." In verse 8, it says that if we say that we have no sin, we are deceiving ourselves and the truth is not in us. However, it says in verse 9 that if we confess our sins, God is faithful and righteous to forgive us our sins and to cleanse us from all unrighteousness. Okay, I have got it! Jesus has cleared my eye and filled me with His light. I try to do what the Light, Jesus, tells me to do because that is where my heart is. However, the flesh is weak; and I sin. I realize that I have a speck in my clear eye, and that speck casts a shadow in my body. This is sort of like developing a cataract. Time for emergency surgery! Quick, now, I repentantly confess that sin to God and ask forgiveness in the name of Jesus! My eye is clear again, and there is no shadow in my body. The surgery is successful. Amazing grace, again; praise be to God! We must be diligent in this practice of clearing the eye so that we do not lose sight of the righteousness of God and are able to maintain righteous thinking and intentions.

Singleness of the hand.

Jesus tells the people that they cannot serve two masters (v. 6:24). He says that by trying to serve both masters, they will either hate one and love the other, or be devoted to one and despise the other (v. 24). In short, they will be constantly conflicted in their service. Jesus goes on to identify the two basic masters as God and wealth, and specifically states that there is no way that they can serve both (v. 24).

It is our hand with which we serve. It is our hand that does the doing. What are we choosing to do? Many of those who profess to be believers today try to serve both God and wealth. In this way, they feel that they can provide for all of their security needs. They may have been serving wealth for part of their life and then profess to believe in Jesus. These people might begin to serve Jesus but cannot give up on trying to accumulate wealth. Others might have grown up in the church believing that they were serving Jesus; but as they became adults, their focus shifted more to the accumulation of wealth. "You know, I want to serve Jesus," but "show me the money." Jesus says that we cannot serve both God and wealth. If we try to do so, we will be constantly conflicted. This reminds me of a story Jesus told in Matthew 9:17. Jesus says that you can't put new wine into old wineskins because the new wine will ferment and explode the rigid old wineskins. What he is saying is that we can't put our new life with Jesus in our old life with the world. Which are *we* choosing to serve? What are the actions of *our* hands?

Experiencing singleness of the hand.

In serving Jesus, Louise and I both believe that we need to be serving the sick and needy and to be sharing the Gospel message; making money is not the primary consideration. As a result, we feel that any of our possessions or money belongs to Jesus, and we need to be on the lookout for how *He* wants us to use them. We feel that any living places that we have, should be made available to people in need and to our brothers and sisters in Christ. We feel that any vehicles that we have, should be made available to people in need and to our brothers and sister in Christ. We feel that any food that we have, should be made available to people in need and to our brothers and sister in Christ. We feel that any money that we have, should be made available to people in need and to our brothers and sister in Christ. Compared to me, Louise is way ahead of the curve in this matter. One day I came home, and Louise literally had emptied our refrigerator and given the food to a needy family. Another day I came home, and she had given our dining room table and chairs to a family in need. In another instance, she had given our bed to another family in need. As mentioned before, at one point in our life Louise and I were providing a group home for teens, and it took $1,500 a month beyond our own resources to operate it. If we know what God wants us to do, then we should just do it. We constantly need to check ourselves in order that we are not deceived about the singleness of our hands, and that our singleness truly is for serving God and not wealth.

Examples of singleness of heart, eye, and hand.

Chapter 27 of Mathew provides a contrast of those who have a "singleness of heart, eye, and hand" for God and those that do not.

In verses 1–11, we can see examples of the "singleness of heart." The chief priests and the elders have a singleness of heart, but their singleness is not on God. The desire of their heart is to put Jesus to death (v. 1), and they refuse to assume any responsibility for Jesus' betrayal (vv. 4, 6–10). The singleness of their hearts is on evil and their own security. We can see that Judas has a divided heart. On the one hand, his "treasure" was money. He betrays Jesus for thirty pieces of silver to provide for his own security. On the other hand, he is a disciple of Jesus and must have some feeling for Him. Judas seems to have reflected on the desire of his heart and noted the division. He feels remorse for what he has done, returns the money to the chief priests and elders, and hangs himself (vv. 3–5). We can see in Judas the problem of a divided heart, and we also can see the consequence of such division—the exploding wineskin. Jesus admits to Pilate that He is the King of the Jews (v. 11). Jesus knows by this admission that His death will be sealed, but he does so in obedience to the Father. Serving the Father is the desire of Jesus' heart, and Jesus' heart is single on the Father.

In verses 12–14, we can see examples of the "singleness of the eye." The chief priests and elders have a singleness of the eye, but again their singleness is not on God. The intention of their eye is on darkness and evil. They make many *false* accusations against Jesus (vv. 12–14). This is not of God and is all about *unrighteousness* and an attempt to provide for their personal security. Jesus has an eye that is clear and single on the Father, and Jesus feels quite secure in the Father's hands. He knows what righteousness is; He is it! As a result, there is no need for Him to respond to the accusations of the chief priests and elders.

In verses 15–66, we can see examples of the "singleness of the hand." Pilate and Pilate's wife seem to know that Jesus is righteous and should be released (vv. 19, 23). However, knowing what is right to do, Pilate, instead does what is wrong and orders Jesus to be crucified. Pilate does what is politically expedient for his own security and does not have a singleness of hand for God of any kind. The soldiers have a singleness of hand to serve only themselves. They use Jesus as a means for their entertainment and their provision (vv. 27–37). Simon, the Cyrene, has a singleness to serve Jesus by carrying the cross, but his singleness is as a result of coercion (v. 32). It is hard to tell whether or not he has a singleness of hand for God because his act is not voluntary. The robbers that are crucified with Jesus and the crowds that pass by have a singleness of hand in serving themselves. They are attempting to justify their insulting behavior toward Jesus within the security of a mob (vv. 38–44). They certainly do not have a singleness of hand for God. Jesus, in contrast to all of the above, has a singleness of hand in serving the Father. In His quote of scripture (Ps. 22) we can see this singleness of Jesus' service to the Father, and again, His confidence in placing His life in the Father's hands. In verses 51–53, we see the result of Jesus' obedience and singleness of hand to the Father. The veil of the temple is torn in two symbolizing the new access for the people to God through the crucifixion of Jesus (v. 51). In addition, many bodies of the saints are resurrected and appear in Jerusalem showing Jesus' power over the grave (vv. 52–53). Another result is that Jesus, in His singleness of hand, is a testimony to non-believers. The centurion and those others who were guarding

Jesus believe that Jesus truly is the Son of God (v. 54). Wow, Jesus certainly was spiritually productive! Some of the women who serve Jesus have a singleness of hand toward Him. They still continue to follow Him even after His death, most probably at great risk to their own lives (vv. 55–56, 61). Joseph of Arimathea has a singleness of hand in serving Jesus in that he asks Pilate for Jesus' body and lays Him in his own tomb (vv. 58–60). Joseph does this at great risk to his position and to his very life. Finally, the chief priests and Pharisees exhibit their singleness of hand to serve themselves, and not God, by convincing Pilate to guard Jesus' tomb (vv. 62–66). Here, the chief priests and Pharisees go to great lengths in an attempt to provide for their own security.

Summary.

Some people are not single in their heart, their eye, and their hand toward God because their singleness is on their own personal security. The desire of their heart is on the things of the world; their eye and whole body are dark with sin, and the action of their hand is unrighteousness. These people have not been communing with God in secret; their hearts, eyes, and hands are not focused on God; and all of this is disobedience to God. (see Appendix X, "Cycle of Disobedience" ff for a visual representation of this.) The worries of the world and deceitfulness of riches choke these people out like the plant on the **"thorny soil"** in the Parable of the Sower. They are distracted from God by the things of the world and are spiritually unproductive. I call these people the **"UNPRODUCTIVE PEOPLE"** because they do not have their heart, eye, and hand single on God; and as a result, they bear no fruit for God.

Conversely, those who have their heart, eye, and hand on God do not put their own personal security before their obedience to God. The desire of their hearts is to love God and to obey His commandments. Their eyes are clear and their thinking and intentions are righteous. The service of their hand is placed in God's hand and is responsive to His direction through the Holy Spirit. These people trust in God fully for their security and are obedient to Him.

They are a testimony of God to those around them concerning the fact that Jesus is the Son of God, that Jesus has provided access to God the Father through His death on the cross, that Jesus has power over death and the grave, and that they are followers of Jesus. (see Appendix X, "Cycle of Obedience" ff for a visual representation of this.) **Glorification of God and the satisfaction of our need for security come from our obedience to God in the singleness of our heart, eye, and hand. God will provide! We, then, are not the "thorny soil." We are loving God and loving our neighbor. This is the 'mind of Christ' concerning singleness of heart, eye, and hand.**

> **Where your treasure is, there your heart will be also...The eye is the lamp of the body; so then if your eye is clear, your whole body will be full of light...You cannot serve God and wealth. (Matt. 6:21–24)**

Do we have more of a singleness of heart,
eye, and hand toward God?
Are we following the leading of the Holy Spirit?
Let's go on!

FRAMEWORK FOR SPIRITUAL MATURITY

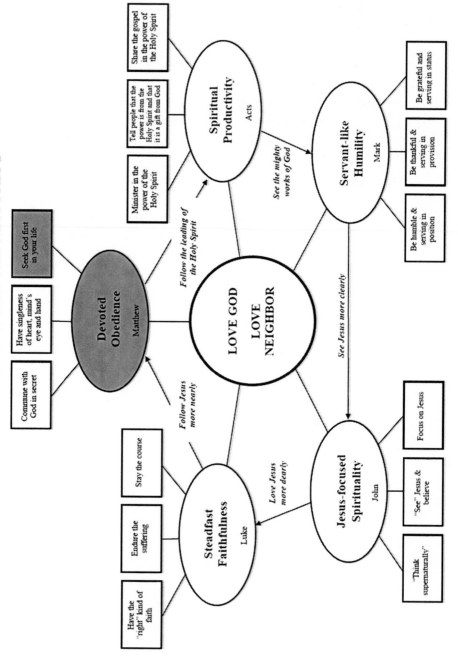

CHAPTER 12

Numero Uno:
Seek God First in Your Life

Seeking God first in your life is the third issue concerning obedience and is presented in Matthew 6:25–34. From the beginning of the day to the end, seeking God should be primary!

Seeking first personal security, the absence of pain, and pleasure.

Jesus tells the people not to worry about their life, i.e., eating and drinking, or their body, clothing (v. 25a) He then asks them if life is more than food; and the body, more than clothing (v. 25b). He is asking them to think about whether there is more to life than just eating and more to the body than just clothing it. He tells them that birds do no work, and yet our heavenly Father feeds them (v. 26a). He then asks them if they are worth more than the birds (v. 26b). Jesus is suggesting, here, that if God takes care of the birds, He certainly will take care of them. Jesus questions them next about whether any of them, by worrying, can add time to their life (v. 27). The answer is obvious to all—no one. Jesus asks them why they worry about clothing (v. 28a). Then He tells them that lilies do no work, but God clothes them more beautiful than Solomon in all his glory (vv. 38b-29). Jesus, as He did with the bird analogy, asks the people that if God provides beautiful clothing for the grass, He most certainly will provide beautiful clothing for them (v. 30). With this understanding of God's provision, Jesus instructs the people not to worry about food, drink, or clothing (v. 31). He reminds them that the non-believers are eagerly seeking after all those things, but believers need not worry about it because God knows that they have need of all those things (v. 32).

Harkening back to the Parable of the Sower, the thorns of the "thorny soil" are the worries of this life and the deceitfulness of wealth (Matt. 13:22) both of which choke out the Word of God. In fact in verses 23–32, Jesus is telling the people not to seek the "thorns." He is telling them not to rely on worry about their personal security or survival related to hunger, thirst, or nakedness or on their wealth. He is telling them not to rely on their wealth nor worry because their heavenly Father already knows that they need all of these things. Then we, as believers, need to know that we should not be seeking the "thorns" related to reliance on wealth or worry about personal security! Finally, Jesus tells them not to worry even about the next day. Jesus is telling them to take life one day at a time! This reminds me of God's instructions to the Israelites in the wilderness about His provision of the "manna" (Exod. 16:4).

Seeking first His kingdom and His righteousness.

After Jesus tells the people that their heavenly Father is aware of all of their needs (32), He tells them to seek God's kingdom and God's righteousness first in their life (v. 33a). If they do, Jesus says that their heavenly Father will meet all of their needs related to food, drink, and clothing (33b) and, by extension, all of their needs. Remember that in Chapter 10, we saw that God would reward giving, praying, and fasting in secret (being obedient to Him). Well, here we see some of the rewards!

What does it mean to seek first His righteousness? It means to do what is right according to God's perspective and not that ourselves or the world. What does it mean to seek first His kingdom? It means to participate in and to build up the things of God's kingdom and not our kingdoms or the kingdoms of the world. We, as believers, need to be seeking God's will in our life and then doing it. This is being obedient to God. If we want to have our needs met, we should be focused not on meeting our needs but doing God's will first in our life.

Experiencing seeking first His kingdom and His righteousness.

When I was a high-school basketball coach it was a real ego trip for me. I had a lot of pride of position. I had so much pride that I resigned my position shortly after receiving Jesus as my Savior. Coaching had become a right hand of prideful sin that needed to be cut off (Matt. 5:30). Two years after my resignation, the new coach came to me to ask me to coach the JV team. He could find no one to coach the team and practice was to start the next day. After prayer, I told him that I would help him under one condition. If Jesus wanted me to do something else for Him during practice time or games; Jesus would come first, and I would not be able to execute my coaching duties. He agreed because he was desperate, but it worked out. When I needed to do something for Jesus first, he covered my coaching duties.

Remember the story back in Chapter 9 in which Louise and I moved from Virginia back to Rhode Island? It was our trusting in Jesus and our meditation on this passage in Matthew 6 that determined our course. We were not seeking first to meet our own needs of security, but were seeking first God's kingdom, and His righteousness in the power of the Holy Spirit. As a result, He met all of our needs abundantly in Rhode Island.

Remember the story in Chapter 6 where I described the importance of my focus on Jesus at the time of my son's death? It was my focus on Jesus, my trust in Jesus, and my meditation on this passage in Matthew 6 that caused me to seek God's will in continuing to minister to my family and my church family (I was an elder) during this difficult time. I was not to seek how to meet my own needs of security, but was to seek God's will in how to continue to meet the needs of others. This I was able to do with the help of the power of the Holy Spirit. Now, while I miss my son very much, the Lord has provided me with *many* spiritual sons to more than fill that void. As we continue to seek Him first, He continues to meet all of our needs abundantly. What a great and gracious Father we have!

Examples of seeking first God's kingdom and His righteousness.

Chapter 28 of Matthew shows a vivid contrast between those who are seeking personal security through reliance on worry and wealth and those who are seeking first the kingdom of God and His righteousness.

The two Mary's continue to seek Jesus by coming to His grave (v. 1) Even though they know Jesus is dead, they are not concerned about meeting their own needs of security but continue to seek Him and to do what is right for Him. Angels appear to the women, tell them that Jesus is risen from the dead, and that they will see Him, and instruct them to go and to tell the disciples (vv. 2–7). The women go to tell the disciples (v. 8). The women are obedient. They are not concerned with meeting their own needs but are seeking first to do the things that will build the kingdom of God. Jesus meets the women on the way, and they worship Him (v. 9). He instructs them to tell the disciples to meet Him in Galilee, and they will see Him there (v. 10). How Jesus blesses the women because of their obedience!

Conversely, when the chief priests and elders receive the report from the soldiers about what had happened, they bribe the soldiers to tell everyone that Jesus' disciples stole the body (vv. 11–15). None of the chief priests, the elders, or the soldiers is seeking the kingdom of God or His righteousness. They are being totally disobedient and seeking to meet their own needs of security by means of their wealth.

The eleven disciples proceed to Galilee (v. 16). The disciples seem to be seeking Jesus first and not being concerned about their own needs. When the disciples see Jesus, they worship Him (v. 17a). However, some were doubtful (v. 17b). It appears that some of the disciples were concerned more about meeting their own needs of security through their worry than being totally obedient to Jesus. Jesus instructs them to make disciples of all nations, baptizing them, and teaching them to observe all that He had commanded them (vv. 19–20a). *This* is what it means to seek first the kingdom of God and His righteousness. Jesus reaffirms His authority in heaven and earth and reminds His disciples that he is with them always (vv. 18a, 20b). Jesus senses the doubters and speaks in this manner to reassure them that He will meet all their needs if they are obedient to Him and put Him first in their life.

Summary.

Some people today who profess to be believers are not seeking first the kingdom of God and His righteousness. They are consumed with meeting their needs of security in their own way and in their own power. The worries of this life and the deceitfulness of wealth choke them out like the plant on the **"thorny soil"** in the Parable of the Sower. These people are distracted from God by the things of the world and are spiritually unproductive. I call these **"thorny soil"** people the **"UNPRODUCTIVE PEOPLE."**

On the other hand, those that seek God first in their life, do not rely on worry or wealth for their security. These people trust in God fully for their security and are obedient to Him. They are committed to doing what is right according to Jesus. They are committed to the building of His kingdom by making disciples. **The glorification of God and the satisfaction of our need for security come from our obedience to God in seeking first the kingdom of God and His righteousness. God will provide! We, then, are not the "thorny soil." We are loving God and loving our neighbor. This is the "mind of Christ" concerning seeking first the kingdom of God and His righteousness.**

> **But seek first His kingdom and His righteousness, and all things will be added unto you. (Matt. 6:33)**

JOHN WEDLOCK

Are we seeking first the kingdom of God
and His righteousness more?
Are we following the leading of the Holy Spirit?
Let's go on!

Section IV
Summary

The results concerning devoted obedience that we have seen in Section IV are best illustrated in the Parable of the "House Built on a Rock:"

Therefore everyone who hears these words of mine and acts on them maybe compared to a wise man who built his house on the rock. And the rain fell, and the floods came, and the winds blew and slammed against that house; and yet it did not fall, for it had been founded on the rock. Everyone who hears these words of Mine and does not act on them, will be like a foolish man who built his house on the sand. The rain fell, and the floods came, and the winds blew and slammed against that house; and it fell— and great was its fall. (Matt. 7:24–27)

On which type of ground are we going to build our house? Jesus is stating here that there are only two choices. One choice is to hear Jesus' words and not to put them into practice. This represents the house (life) that is built on the sand (provision of the world), and its end is destruction. The other choice is *to hear Jesus' words and to put them into practice.* This represents the house (life) that is built on the rock (provision of Jesus), and its end is *secure.* Some people may think that they can build their house half on the sand and half on the rock. This is not what Jesus is saying. To be totally secure, the house must be built totally on the Rock (Jesus)!

God is trying to increase the obedience of believers through His Word and His Holy Spirit so that their obedience can be one of uncompromising devotion. In this way, through God's provision, they can glorify God by their actions and fully experience the security of God in their lives! Where are we in all of this? Are we communing with God in secret? Do we have singleness of heart, eye, and hand toward Jesus? Are we seeking God first in our lives? Are we the "thorny soil" or not the "thorny soil?" Do we have the "mind of Christ?"

The glorification of God and the satisfaction of our need for security come through our total reliance on the provision of God. We need to commune with God in secret, have singleness of heart, eye, and hand, and seek God first in our lives. If we do this, we have devoted obedience and are not the "thorny soil." We are loving God and loving our neighbor. This is the mind of Christ concerning devoted obedience to God.

> **Therefore everyone who hears these words of mine and acts on them, may be compared to a wise man who built his house on the rock. (Matt. 7:24)**

Are we being more devotedly obedient to God?
Are we following the Holy Spirit enough to be productive for Jesus?
Let's go on!

Note: If you want to pursue the theme of "devoted obedience" further in the Gospel of Matthew, turn to Appendix VIII- D for a study outline. The outline provides for a macro study (based on a micro study) of the scripture and is written in an application format.

FRAMEWORK FOR SPIRITUAL MATURITY

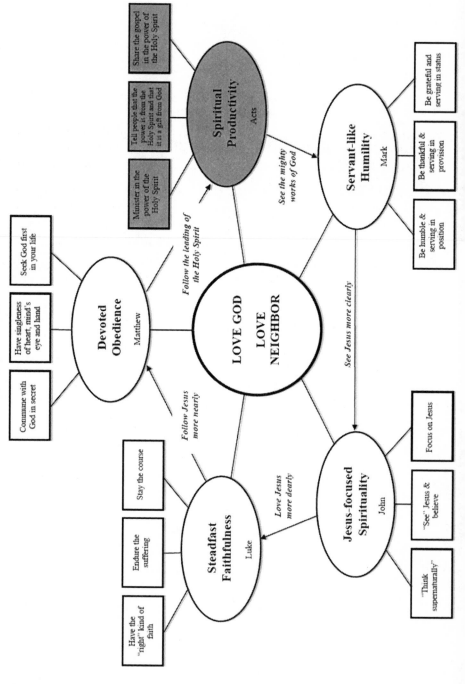

SECTION V

Spiritual Productivity

The sower went out to sow his seed...Other seed fell into the good soil, and grew up, and produced a crop a hundred times as great... But the seed in the good soil, these are the ones who have heard the word in an honest; and good heart, and hold it fast, and bear fruit with perseverance. (Luke 8:5, 8, 15)

Now, if we are humble and find that our sense of worth comes from appropriating the love and acceptance of Jesus, if we have been spiritually transformed so that we possess the Holy Spirit and are truly free to choose the way of Jesus, if we have steadfast faith in Jesus and fully submit and entrust ourselves to His power, if we are devotedly obedient to God through the working of the Holy Spirit in our lives and through trusting in God's constant provision for our security; then we should, through the power of the Holy Spirit, be spiritually productive. The Parable of the Sower tells us that some people are spiritually productive. The seed falls on the good ground, penetrates the soil, germinates, grows into a full plant, and bears fruit. Jesus explains to His disciples that the **"good soil"** person hears God's word, keeps it, and with perseverance bears fruit thirty, sixty, and one hundred times. This suggests to me spiritual productivity. I call these **"good soil"** people the **"PRODUCTIVE PEOPLE."** In my reading in the Gospels, I determined that the theme of the Book of Acts relates to spiritual productivity by the working of the Holy Spirit through believers.

Thinking back to my understanding of human intrinsic needs, the need that relates to spiritual productivity is meaning. We need to feel that we are productive as a part of something larger than ourselves and that we are contributing to the whole. In this age, the "whole" on earth related to God is the Body of Christ, the church. When someone has faith in Jesus, that person receives the Holy Spirit. Jesus provides believers with spiritual gifts of the Holy Spirit in order to minister within the Body of Christ.

> **For just as we have many members in one body and all the members do not have the same function, so we who are many, are one body in Christ, and individually members one of another. Since we have gifts that differ according to the grace given to us, each of us to exercise accordingly. (Rom. 12:4–6a) But to each one is given the manifestation of the Spirit for the common good…And the same Spirit works these things, distributing to each one individually as He wills…For even as the body is one and yet has many members, and all the members of the body, though they are many, are one body, so also is Christ…For the body is not one members, but many…But now God has placed the members, each one of them, in the body, just as He desired…But now there are many members, but one body…Now you are Christ's body, and individually members of it. (1 Cor. 12:7, 12, 14, 18, 20, and 27)**

If we are the **"good soil,"** we will be productively **ministering in the power of the Holy Spirit** and exercising the gifts of the Spirit to others (I call the **"good soil"** people the **"productive people"**). As I said earlier, Jesus says that the Word of God in these people will be fruitful thirty, sixty, and one hundred times. In addition, we will have a **purpose**/mission within the Body of Christ that will give us a great sense of **meaning**.

Chapter 3 of the Book of Acts reveals the "mind of Christ" concerning spiritual productivity. In Section V of this book, the three step process concerning spiritual productivity will be examined. In the next three chapters, we will look at each of these steps and how the Holy Spirit provides for us to carry them out.

FRAMEWORK FOR SPIRITUAL MATURITY

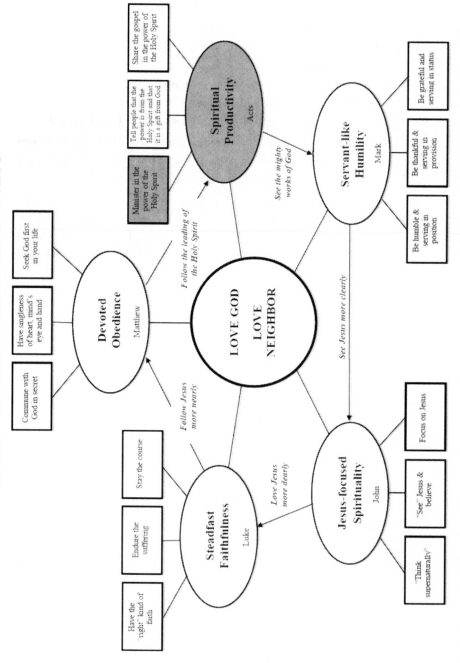

CHAPTER 13

Just Do It:
Minister to the Needy in the Power
of Name of Jesus, Holy Spirit

"Ministering to the needy in the power of the name of Jesus, Holy Spirit" is the first step in spiritual productivity and is presented in Acts, chapter 3, verses 1–10.

Discern the need.

Peter and John are going up to the temple to pray (v. 1). On the way they encounter a man, lame from birth, who begs them to give him money (vv. 2–3). Peter and John fix their gaze on him and tell him to look at them (v. 4). The man gives his attention to them thinking that they are going to give him some money (v. 5). Peter says to the man that he has no silver or gold to give him, but that what he will give the man will be in name of Jesus the Nazarene (v. 6). Peter instructs the man to walk (v. 6). Even though Peter and John are on their way to something very important (going to the temple to pray), they stop, interrupt their important business, and give attention to man who is in need. We need to note that Peter and John do not automatically give the man that which he was asking. Instead, they focus on him, attempting to discern what it is that he really needs. Will a little money really help him? He still will be lame

155

and not at all be able to provide for himself. Peter decides to give him the ability to walk through the power in the name of Jesus, Holy Spirit. (I believe that Peter is invoking the presence and power of the name of Jesus through the power of the Holy Spirit)

In this day, we find people who do not even stop their busy lives in order to meet the needs of the needy. It reminds me of the Levite and the priest in the parable of the "Good Samaritan" (Luke 10:30–37). Seeing the beaten man by the side of the road, they passed by on the other side. This is not so with Peter and John here. Like the "Good Samaritan" in the parable, Peter and John *stop* to help the lame man.

Some people might stop and give to the needy, but never discern the true need. They never take the time to connect with those who are in need. Connecting would take more time out of their task-oriented day. It would mean loving and involving themselves with other people. It would mean observing and interpreting behavior to best know how to help them. Other people do not discern a true need because they are uncomfortable with the physical, mental, or spiritual condition of those in need. Certainly, this is a possibility for the Levite and the priest. However, this does not deter Peter and John. They engage themselves with the lame man in order to determine the best way to help him. Like the "Good Samaritan," Peter and John take the time to connect with the lame man and are not "turned off" by his condition.

Finally, some people do not understand that, in discerning the need, we should be considering long-term solutions wherever possible. Peter and John just did not want to give the lame man a short-term fix—money. They wanted to provide a more long-term solution—the ability to walk. Like the "good Samaritan," Peter and John consider a long-term solution for the lame man. There are many needy around us, and they are "lame" in various ways. In the discerning of their lameness, we should be considering the best solution for healing their lameness and be helping them to "walk."

Experiencing "discerning the need."

I mentioned previously about the day I was going down an elevator with an elderly woman. I was on my way to "accomplish" something, but noticed that the woman seemed to be troubled. I purposely did not engage her because I knew that it would delay me. I just closed my eyes and "walked on by." The Holy Spirit really leaned on me after that incident. I was totally convicted that it was a sin of omission. I asked the Lord for forgiveness and committed myself to be more aware and open to those in need around me. My prayer each morning is that the Lord would provide opportunities for me to minister to the needy and that he would give me eyes to see those opportunities.

One day, when Louise and I were visiting a very poor widow, a Cadillac drove up in front of the widow's tarpaper shack. Two women, "dressed to the nines," stepped out carrying a basket of food for the widow. They came to the door and knocked. The widow went to the door, and the women gave her the basket of food. The widow thanked them and asked them if they would like to come in for a cup of tea. We could see that the women were taken aback and uncomfortable by the invitation, and they left hurriedly. The widow closed the door and said to us, "Let's pray for those two women." More than the food, this widow needed to have an opportunity to serve and have fellowship, but the two women were repulsed by the living conditions and were unable to discern the widow's true need.

In my involvement with churches today, I see that they do a fairly good job of meeting the immediate needs of their congregation and surrounding community, but I feel that they fall short in meeting the long-term needs—helping the "lame" to "walk."

My hero in this area of discerning needs is my wife, Louise. Wherever we are, she is discerning the needs of the people around her. She absolutely has a spiritual gift. If we are in a restaurant, she quickly discerns the needs of the waitress. If we are traveling, she discerns the needs of the housekeepers and other help in the hotel. If we go to a supermarket, she is discerning the needs of those in the market, both the help and the customers. No matter what the group of people surrounding her, she is constantly discerning needs.

One night, she received a telephone call. It was a wrong number, but Louise discerned that the lady who called was in distress. She spent at least two hours on the phone with the lady, listening to her problems, and suggesting ways of healing, including Jesus. She even discerns needs over the telephone!

When I was a high-school teacher, I began to talk to students individually about their needs. I found that I was not able to spend enough time talking to them in the school setting to make a difference in their lives. As a result, I helped to set up a drop-in center that was open in the evenings. Even conversations at the drop-in center were not enough to meet the needs of some of the more troubled young people and those from dysfunctional families. Louise and I began to take some of the young people into our home in order that they could be exposed to a functional family setting. We discerned, with some youth, that talking was not enough; they needed to *see* and *experience* appropriate family relationships. This was the way of meeting their true needs in order that they could successfully return home or go out on their own.

Meet the need.

Peter seizes the man by the right hand and raises him up, and immediately, his feet and ankles are strengthened (v. 7). With a leap, the man stands up, begins to walk, enters the temple with Peter and John, and walks, leaps, and praises God (v. 8). Peter and John not only discern the true need of the lame man, but they *meet* that need in the power of the Holy Spirit. (See James 2:14–17)

When we, as believers, discern a need in a "lame" person, we should not stop there. We should move to meet that need in the best way possible—through the power of the Holy Spirit. We must be careful not to attempt to meet the need in our own power because we will fail and any glory that could have gone to God will be lost on us.

Experiencing "meeting the need."

Again, my hero in this area is Louise. As I mentioned before, there is no hesitation on her part to act to meet the needs of a "lame" person ("Singleness of hand" portion of Chapter 11). She is acting in the power of the Holy Spirit to meet the needs. When people are having physical problems and/or emergencies, she jumps right in to minister to them. Even when women ask her to help them with problems in their lives, she pinpoints the issues with incredible accuracy and provides direction based on scripture.

To the wonder and amazement of those watching

Now, all the people see the man, who was lame, walking and praising God (v. 9). Everyone is taking note of him because they remembered when he used to be at the temple gate begging for money (v. 10a). They were all filled with *wonder* and *amazement* at what had happened to him (v. 10b). All the people are amazed that Peter and John heal the man who was lame from birth.

Even today, when we minister to the "lame" in the power of the Holy Spirit, and people see the results of our ministry, they are amazed. They are amazed that we stopped our busy lives for a moment to meet someone else's need, that we accurately discerned the need, and that we sought the best possible solution available to meet the need. They are amazed that we took of our time and resources to meet the need. They are amazed at the response of the person whose need was met.

Experiencing "to the wonder and amazement of those watching."

At one time, I was teaching a Bible study at a thrift store. There was a homeless man who would come faithfully to the study every week. One day, we were studying this portion of scripture (Acts 3). In the midst of our discussion, he began to tell a story about two elderly church ladies. He said that once a week these ladies would make a bunch of sandwiches and take them to a nearby park where there were homeless men. He said it was *amazing* to see these two elderly ladies giving out the sandwiches to, what he called, a bunch of "winos." He said the women should have been afraid but were not. They told him they were doing it because it was what Jesus wanted.

He just went on and on about his *amazement* with the ministry of these two elderly women.

Examples of "ministering in the power of the Holy Spirit."

Chapter 28 of Acts provides an example for us about ministering to the needy in the power of the Holy Spirit.

In verses 1–10, the Apostle Paul is delivered from the storm at sea and finds himself on Malta (v. 1). There, he is bitten by a viper (vv. 2–3). However, he survives to the amazement of all (vv. 4–6). The "leading man" on the island is a man named Publius (v. 7). Paul learns that the father of Publius is very ill, and Paul heals him (v. 8). Notice that Paul prays before he heals the father (v. 8). This, I believe, indicates Paul is seeking the power of the Holy Spirit, in his ministry to the father. After Paul heals the father, the rest of the people on the island who have diseases come to Paul to be cured (v. 9). The people on the island honored Paul and his companions with many marks of respect and supplied them with all they needed to continue their sail (v. 10). The people of the island are amazed at Paul's ministry to them. Now, what we should observe, here, is that Paul is a Roman prisoner. He has just survived a horrendous storm at sea and a bite from a venomous snake. Is he concerned about his own needs? No, he has a purpose/mission. What *is* Paul doing? He is ministering to the needy in the power of the Holy Spirit!

In verses 11–15, Paul is received by the brethren in Rome and is encouraged in his ministry by those brethren. In verses 16–23, Paul attempts to minister in the power of the Holy Spirit, to the Jews in Rome, but they reject what Paul has to say (vv. 24a, 29). However, Paul perseveres and tells the Jews that the salvation of God has been sent to the Gentiles and that they will listen (vv. 24b-29). In verses 30–31, Paul ministers to all that come to him. Again, we should observe that Paul is a Roman prisoner. Is he concerned that he is on house arrest with a Roman soldier assigned to guard him? What *is* Paul doing? He is ministering to the needy in the power of the Holy Spirit!

Summary.

Some people minister to others in the power of their own name and spirit, most of the time for selfish or prideful reasons. These may not be seeking meaning within the whole but want control and power for themselves. Others, indeed, may be seeking meaning as part of a whole in the natural world. The results of these types of ministry are usually temporary and unsuccessful.

Conversely, those who minister to others in the power of the name of Jesus are lead by the Holy Spirit and are provided gifts of the Spirit in order to accomplish the ministry. They discern the need and meet the need to the amazement of those watching. They see the mighty works of God being accomplished through themselves and through collaboration with other believers. They sense a **purpose/mission** within the Body of Christ. These people are productive in their spirituality; they are the **"good soil."** I call these people the **"PRODUCTIVE PEOPLE." The glorification of God and the satisfaction of our need for meaning come from our ministering to others in the power of the Holy Spirit. We are in awe of the productive power of the Holy Spirit working through us. We, then, are the "good soil." We are loving God and loving our neighbor. Spiritual productivity in the form of ministering in the power of the Holy Spirit is the "mind of Christ"**

> **But Peter said, "I do not posses silver and gold, but what I do have I give to you; in the name of Jesus Christ the Nazarene—walk!" And seizing him by the right hand, he raised him up; and immediately his feet and his ankles were strengthened. (Acts 3:6–7)**

Are we ministering in the power of the Holy Spirit?
Are we humbled by the mighty works of God that we see?
Let's go on!

FRAMEWORK FOR SPIRITUAL MATURITY

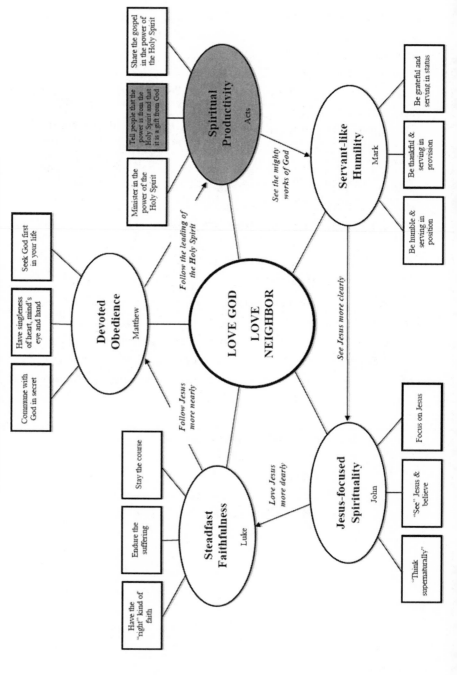

Consider the Source: Humbly Explain About the Source of Power to Those Who are "Amazed"

"Humbly explaining about the source of the power to those who are amazed" is the second step in spiritual productivity and is present in Acts, chapter 3, verses 11–16.

Ministry is not accomplished in our own power and piety.

While the man is clinging to Peter and John, all the people run to Peter and John full of amazement (v. 11). When Peter sees all the people coming in amazement, he gives a disclaimer about the source of the power that has amazed them. He tells them that the power to cause the lame man to walk *did not* come from his or John's power or piety (v. 12).

Sometimes, we, as believers, minister in the power of the Holy Spirit, and are surprised by the amazed reaction of those around us. This reaction may come from those to whom we are ministering and/or those who are witnessing our ministry. They may be amazed at our motivation to do the ministry and/or the effect of the ministry itself. We need to understand that the working of the power of the Holy

Spirit *will amaze*, and we need to be prepared to give the disclaimer that Peter gives. We need to state that it is not because of our own power or our own "religiousness" that the ministry is accomplished. We need to do this immediately so that no thought will enter their minds that will give any glory to us for either the motivation to do the ministry or the effect of the ministry itself.

Experiencing explaining that the "ministry is not accomplished in our power and piety."

Immediately after receiving Jesus as my Savior and Lord, I began, for the first time, to minister to others in the power of the Holy Spirit and not in my own power or self-righteousness. I *was* surprised by the amazement of those to whom I ministered and to those who witnessed the ministry. I must admit that I did not know exactly what to do with the amazed reactions. This may have been due to some residual pride that I had not dealt with completely. However, I began to realize, through Scripture and the leading of the Holy Spirit, that this was a key piece of our testimony to those to whom we are ministering and those who witness our ministry. I began to respond to the reaction by extending my right arm above my head and pointing the index finger of my right hand upwards. This motion has become my first response. It seems to get attention, stops the discussion, and begins to give me the chance to explain that it is not through my own power or piety that the ministry was motivated and effective.

The effect of the ministry is accomplished through the power of the name of Jesus, Holy Spirit.

Peter explains to the "men of Israel" that it is on the basis of Peter's faith in the name of Jesus, Holy Spirit, that the lame man was healed (vv. 13–16a). Peter goes on to explain that it is on the basis of faith in His name that the name of Jesus has given the man perfect health (v. 16b).

After we give the disclaimer that the power behind our ministry is not our own power or our own piety, we then need to explain the actual source of the power. We need to share that the power is in the name of Jesus that comes in the form of the Holy Spirit.

Experiencing explaining "the effect of the ministry is accomplished through the power of the name of Jesus, Holy Spirit."

One morning, I observed a young man approach a pastor after the worship service. The young man had been moved by the pastor's sermon and shared that with the pastor. The pastor stood there seemly dumbstruck by the young man's comments. He raised both hands in the air, told the young man that he did not know how to respond to the comments, and walked away. What a missed opportunity for the pastor to explain the source of the power that had made his sermon so moving and to give glory to God.

After giving the disclaimer about the fact that the ministry that I do is not done in my own power or piety, I try quickly to expand my explanation to include comments about the truth that the power comes from the Holy Spirit. Sometimes it is received, and sometimes it is not.

Example of "explaining the source of the power."

Chapter 27 of Acts provides an example for us about explaining that the source of the power for ministry comes from the Holy Spirit.

Paul is a Roman prisoner and is being transported by ship to Rome (vv. 1–2a). The trip goes slowly, and the ship finally puts in at Fair Havens (vv. 2b-8). However, to continue the voyage will be dangerous because of the storms prevalent at that time of the year (v. 9a). Paul boldly admonishes the crew that to continue the voyage would certainly result in "damage and great loss, not only of the cargo, and the ship, but also of our lives" (vv. 9b-10). However, the centurion (the Roman officer in charge) is more persuaded by the pilot and the captain of the ship than Paul (v. 11). Notice at this point that the centurion is not listening to the prisoner, Paul, but is listening to the experienced seamen, the pilot, and the captain. The ship puts to sea and soon encounters a fierce storm (vv. 12–17). The storm violently tosses the ship to the point that the crew jettisons the cargo and then even the ship's tackle (vv. 18–19). The storm rolls on for many days and all hope of being saved is abandoned (v. 20). After they had gone for a long time without food, Paul stands up in the midst of all and tells them that they should have listened to his advice not to sail (v.21). Paul tells them that an angel of God told him that there would be no loss of life and that Paul would stand before Caesar (vv. 21–24). Paul tells all of them to keep up their courage because he believes in God and that things will turn out exactly as he was told (v. 25). Also, he tells them that the ship must run aground on an island (v. 26). Finally, the ship is driven aground, and they throw out anchors to hold the ship (vv. 27–29). Some of the sailors try to sneak away from the ship using the ship's boat (v.30). Paul warns the centurion and the soldiers that the sailors must remain on the ship or else they, themselves, will not be saved (v. 31). The soldiers cut the lines from the ship's boat and let it fall away (v. 32). Notice how the centurion seems to be listening to Paul more than he was before. It had been fourteen days since anyone had had any food (v. 33). Paul encourages them to eat in order that they might survive, telling them that not a hair on their head will perish (v. 34). Paul gives thanks to God, breaks bread, and begins to eat (v. 35). They are all encouraged and begin to eat themselves (v. 36). Notice that all are now listening to Paul. After the 276 persons aboard the ship have eaten, they are encouraged enough to get back to work to save the ship (vv. 37–38). They sight the land, pull the anchors up, and let the sea drive the ship ashore (vv. 39–40). However, the ship strikes a reef and begins to break apart (v. 41). The soldiers' plan was to kill the prisoners so that none would be able to swim away and escape (v. 42). We need to note here that Roman soldiers were never to allow their prisoners to escape on punishment of death. The centurion, wanting to be sure that Paul survives, keeps the soldiers from killing the prisoners and orders everyone to swim to shore (vv. 43–44a). Note that the centurion is *really* relying on Paul at this point. Everyone is brought to land safely (v. 44b).

Paul ministers to the centurion before the trip, but the centurion rejects his ministry because he feels that he is in control. Then, in the midst of the storm, Paul ministers to all on board the ship by bringing them the encouraging message that an angel from God told him that no one would perish. Paul explains clearly that this message is not from him but from God. He is indicating that God is the source of the power to provide for them. When some of the sailors try to sneak away, Paul ministers to the centurion and the soldiers by warning them not to let the sailors leave the ship. Here, the centurion listens to Paul and receives Paul's ministry. The centurion is not as certain about himself as he was before. Paul ministers to all on board again by encouraging them to eat and to continue to try to save the ship. However, before Paul eats; he gives thanks to God in front of all. Again, Paul is indicating that the source of the power of all provision is God. Finally, the centurion prevents the soldiers from killing the prisoners, including Paul, because he believes that Paul's God can provide for *him*. How right he is!

Sometimes, when we minister to others in the power of the Holy Spirit, our ministry is rejected, especially by proud people. When people's circumstances become dire, they sometimes are more willing to receive our ministry. Like Paul, we need to be sure to explain to the people who receive our ministry that the power behind the provision is from God. Then, they also may be willing to allow the power of God to come to them through Jesus, and we need to be ready to tell them all about it!

Summary.

Some people who minister to others in the power of the Holy Spirit do not openly give glory to God and allow those to whom they minister, and those watching, to believe that it is due to their *own* power and piety that the ministry took place. This is not giving glory to God and is disobedience to Him.

On the other hand, those who minister in the power of the Holy Spirit, are quick to tell those who are "amazed" that the power which caused the motivation and/or effect of that ministry is from the Holy Spirit. They sense a **purpose**/mission within the Body of Christ. These people are productive in their spirituality; they are the "good soil." I call these people the **"PRODUCTIVE PEOPLE."** The glorification of God and the satisfaction of our need for meaning come from our explaining to those that are "amazed" that our ministry to others is done in the power of the Holy Spirit. We give all the glory to God in our explanation of the source of the power. We, then, are the "good soil." We are loving God and loving our neighbor. Spiritual productivity in the form of explaining that the Holy Spirit is the source of the power in our ministry is the "mind of Christ."

> Men of Israel, why are you amazed at this, or why do you gaze at us, as if by our own power or piety we had made him walk? The God of Abraham, Isaac and Jacob, the God of our fathers, has glorified His servant Jesus. (Acts 3:12b-13a)

Are we ministering in the power of the Holy Spirit?
Are we explaining that the source of the power
of our ministry is the Holy Spirit?
Let's go on!

FRAMEWORK FOR SPIRITUAL MATURITY

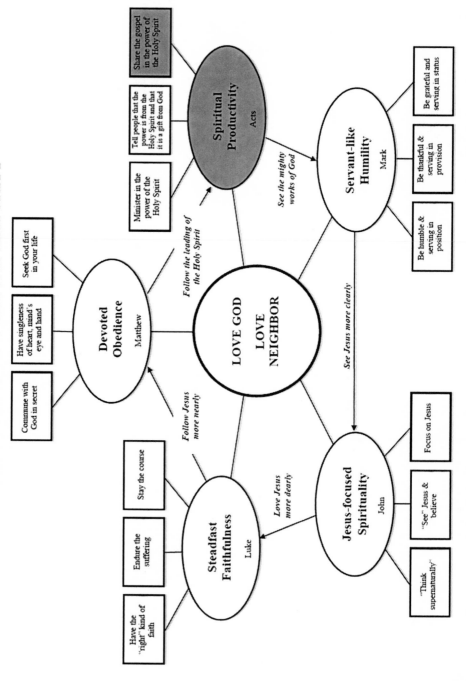

CHAPTER 15

I Love to Tell the Story: Share About Jesus

"Sharing about Jesus with those that are amazed" is the third step in spiritual productivity as presented in Acts, chapter 3, verses 17–26.

Share that the prophecy concerning the Christ is fulfilled in Jesus.

Peter boldly speaks to the people and tells them that God has already announced that His Christ would suffer (vv. 17–18a). (We can see this clearly in the 53rd chapter of the prophet Isaiah.) Here, Peter is confirming to the people the prophecies that describe the nature of the suffering the Messiah would experience. Peter goes on to say that these prophecies are fulfilled in Jesus (v. 18b). Certainly, Peter is considering his audience whom he knows is aware of both the prophecies and the suffering of Jesus, which they had witnessed some fifty days prior.

Today, when we share about Jesus with non-believers, sometimes we do not share about the prophecies related to His ministry. Certainly, those to whom Peter was speaking were aware of the prophecies and would have made an immediate connection. A present-day non-believer, however, would be unaware of these prophecies and would not be making any connection. As a result, many believers today feel that it is not necessary to include this piece of information in their sharing about Jesus.

However, it is my feeling that it *is* important to share this piece of information. If we do not, it might give the non-believer the impression that Jesus' ministry and His suffering were some kind of impromptu acts by God. We want to ensure that a non-believer understands that Jesus' ministry and suffering was a planned act by God going back to the beginning of time.

Experiencing "sharing that the prophecy concerning the Christ is fulfilled in Jesus."

When I "share" about Jesus with people, I like to do so in the context of John 3. I have already written about this in Chapter 5, but bear with me while I share it again.

In John 3:14, Jesus states, "As Moses lifted up the serpent in the wilderness, even so must the Son of Man be lifted up." Jesus is referring back to a time when the Israelites were in the wilderness after their exodus from Egypt (Num. 21). The Israelites became impatient with their journey, and they complained about God and Moses (Num.21:4–5). God sent fiery serpents that bit the Israelites, and those that were bitten *died* (Num. 21:6). As a result, the Israelites came to Moses, confessed their sin, and asked Moses to intercede with God to remove the serpents from among them (Num. 21:7a). Moses interceded for them (Num. 21:7b). God responded by telling Moses to make a fiery serpent out of brass and to put it on a pole (Num. 21:8a). God also told Moses to inform the Israelites that everyone that had been bitten would *live* if they looked upon the bronze serpent on the pole (Num. 21:8b). So, Moses made a bronze serpent and set it on a pole. If a serpent bit anyone and that person looked to the bronze serpent, he *lived* (Num. 21:9).

Jesus' Old Testament reference here is a prophetic analogy of what will happen to Him. He will be lifted up to suffer and die on a cross. Rhetorically, I ask people with whom I am sharing, "Where are we in all of this?" I tell them that we have all been bitten by the serpent (Satan) in the Garden of Eden (Gen. 1:26–3:24). We all have inherited sin from the original sin of Adam and Eve. In addition, we have all sinned on our own as well (Rom. 3:23). We are like the Israelites—bitten by the serpent and *dying*. At the moment of our birth, we are *dying*! We need the intercession of God!

Share that they need to repent and turn back to God so that their sins may be wiped away in order that times of refreshing may come from the presence of the Lord and that He may send Jesus, the Christ, preached to them.

As a result of the fact that Jesus is the Messiah (v. 18), Peter exhorts the crowd to repent of their sins so that their sins can be wiped away (v. 19a). He tells them that if their sins are wiped away, times of refreshing will come from the presence of the God and that He will send Jesus, the Christ, to them (vv. 19b-21).

Certainly, we, as believers, must share with non-believers that they must repent of their sins before God. If they do, we can promise them that God will revive them from their deadly state with the presence of His Holy Spirit and will send Jesus, the Savior, to them.

Experiencing "sharing that they need to repent and turn back to God so that their sins may be wiped away in order that times of refreshing may come from the presence of the Lord and that He may send Jesus, the Christ, preached to them."

When I am "sharing about Jesus" with people, I tell them that they need to repent of their sins before God and ask for His forgiveness. I tell them that *I* do not need to know anything about their sins and that they just need to move forward to see and believe in Jesus.

In John 3:15–16, Jesus says, "so the whoever believes in Him will have eternal life. For God so loved the world that He gave His only begotten Son, that whoever believes in Him shall not perish, but have eternal life." In the context of what Jesus has just said about the Israelites and their need to look at the serpent on the pole, I believe that Jesus is making an analogy to the people to whom He is speaking and their need to look at Him on the cross. Jesus is saying to the people that if they look at Him on the cross and believe in Him, they will have eternal life. Jesus will take the punishment for their sin upon Himself, and they will not *die*; they will *live*. Now, Jesus says that the people need to believe in Him. What does that mean more specifically? I feel that the Apostle John goes on in the following nine chapters to describe what believing in Jesus means.

In order to see and believe in Jesus, we need to see and believe that He is Lord, Source of the Holy Spirit, Christ, one sent by God, Savior, Prophet, Miraculous Healer (John 4); One sent by God, the Father (John 5); the Bread of Life (John 6); Source of the "Living Water"—Holy Spirit (John 7); Light of the World—the truth about sin, that it can be forgiven (John 8); Light of the World—the truth about sin, that it can be healed (John 9); the Door of the Sheep/the Great Shepherd (John 10); the Resurrection and the Life (John 11); and the King (John 12).

I believe that when we first see and believe in Jesus that we see and believe in at least one of the above ways. On the day that I saw and believed in Jesus, I saw and believed in Him as the "Source of the Living Water." It was His power that humbled me before Him, and I was in total awe of Him! Then, my belief in all of the other areas followed. My wife, Louise, first saw and believed in Him as the "Light of the World—truth that frees us from all the lies and all our sin" and the "Door of the Sheep" and "the Great Shepherd." My brother, Bruce, saw and believed in Him first as the "Bread of Life." When I am "sharing about Jesus" with people, I ask them if they see and believe in Jesus in one or more of the above ways and encourage them to pursue their beliefs in all of the ways in which we can believe in Jesus.

Share that they need to listen to Jesus.

Peter reminds the people that Moses told them that God would raise up a prophet from among them and that they should "give heed to everything He says to you" (v. 22). Peter goes on to say that every soul that does not heed that prophet will be destroyed (v. 23). In addition, he tells them that all the prophets, beginning with Samuel, announced what would happen. Peter reminds them further that they are the "sons of the prophets" and the covenant that God made with Abraham and that in Abraham's "seed all the families of the earth shall be blessed" (v. 25a). Peter tells the people that God has raised up His Servant (Jesus) and sent Him to bless them first by "turning every one of them from their wicked ways" (v. 26).

Now, we can see that Jesus comes first to the people of Israel, but we can see that He came also so that "all the families of the earth shall be blessed." By this, I feel that God means that the Gentiles will also partake of the blessing of Jesus, and that blessing is turning every one of *us* from our wicked ways. Praise God! Now, our response needs to be that we give "heed" to everything Jesus says to us. We need to listen to Jesus!

Experiencing "sharing that they need to listen to Jesus."

I tell people, with whom I am sharing Jesus, that John the Baptist really gives a great narrative on "listening" to Jesus. John is explaining to his disciples why they should not listen to him anymore but now should listen to Jesus. You give a listen:

> **"He who comes from above is above all, he who is of the earth is from the earth and speaks of the earth. He who comes from heaven is above all. What He has seen and heard, of that He testifies; and no one receives His testimony. He who has received His testimony has set his seal to this, that God is true. For He whom God has sent speaks the words of God; for He gives the Spirit without measure. The Father loves the Son and has given all things into His hand. He who believes in the Son has eternal life, but he who does not obey the Son will not see life, but the wrath of God abides on him." (John 3:31–36)**

Wow, *that* says it all! We need to listen to Jesus! How do we do that more specifically? I feel that the Apostle John goes on to describe this in chapters 13–17 of his Gospel. I believe John is telling us to get our *focus* on Jesus.

I share with people that in order to listen and obey Jesus, we need to *focus* on Him. We need to focus on Jesus as the "Master washing His disciples' feet—servant-like humility (John 13); the Way, the Truth, and the Light—Jesus-focused spirituality (John 14), the True Vine—steadfast faithfulness (John 15), the Sender of the Holy Spirit—devoted obedience (John 16), and the Great Unifier—spiritual productivity (John 17). Notice how the focus on Jesus relates to the themes of the Gospels. How do we listen to Jesus? We read, meditate upon, and understand the Gospels with the help of the Holy Spirit!

"Example of "sharing about Jesus."

Chapter 26 provides an example for us concerning sharing about Jesus.

Paul is permitted by King Agrippa to speak (v.1). Paul boldly begs Agrippa to listen to him patiently (vv. 1–3). Paul starts by stating his position as a Pharisee for the hope of Israel, which includes the belief in resurrection (vv. 4–8). He recounts his zeal in persecuting followers of Jesus (vv. 9–11). He tells of his personal encounter with Jesus in which he is instructed by Jesus to open the eyes of the Jews and Gentiles about Jesus, the Savior (vv. 12–18). Paul gives testimony about his obedience to Jesus in telling the Jews and Gentiles about Jesus that they might turn from darkness to light and from the dominion of Satan to God, and that they might receive forgiveness of sins and an inheritance among those who have been sanctified by faith in Jesus (vv. 19–21). Finally, Paul shares that the Christ was to suffer, and that by His resurrection from the dead, He would be the first to proclaim light both to the Jewish people and to the Gentiles (v. 23). Festus responds by saying that Paul is mad and Agrippa laughs Paul off (vv. 24–32).

We need to be more like Paul—ready to share about Jesus. We need to be ready to recount our sinful condition. We need to share about our personal encounter and relationship with Jesus. We need to tell about Jesus' call in our life. Finally, we need to share that through Jesus' suffering and resurrection He has brought salvation to the people of the world who believe in Him!

Summary.

Certainly, we can see that Peter was committed to share about Jesus with those that were amazed. We see that the Apostle Paul was of the same mind. In Romans 10:13–15, the Apostle Paul states as follows:

> **"for 'whoever will call on the name of the Lord will be saved'. How then will they call on Him to whom they have not believed? How will they believe in Him whom they have not heard? And how will they hear without a preacher? How will they preach unless they are sent."**

How are the non-believers going to call on the name of Jesus unless they have heard about Him? They cannot! Even in the Old Testament, God spoke about this concept to the people of Israel through Isaiah the Prophet:

> **"Thus says the Lord, the King of Israel and His Redeemer, the Lord of hosts. I am the first and I am the last, and there is no God besides Me. Who is like Me? Let him proclaim and declare it; yes, let him recount it to me in order, from the time that I established the ancient nation, let them declare to them the things that are coming and the events that are going to take place. Do not tremble and do not be afraid; have I not long since announced it? And you**

are My witnesses. Is there any God besides Me, or is there any other Rock? I know of none. (Isa. 44:6–8)

Jesus, himself, speaks to His disciples in Mathew 28:18b-20:

"All authority has been given Me in heaven and on earth. Go therefore and make disciples of all the nations, baptizing them in the name of the Father and the Son and the Holy Spirit, teaching them to observe all that I commanded you and lo, I am with you always, even to the end of the age."

Jesus speaks to His disciples again in Acts 1:8:

"but you will receive power when the Holy Spirit has come upon you; and you shall be My witnesses both in Jerusalem, and in all Judea and Samaria, and even to the remotest part of the earth."

Paul specifies that it is a preacher that will share about Jesus. The word that Paul uses for preacher is defined in the Greek as a herald or one who proclaims the truth (the Gospel). God, speaking through Isaiah the Prophet, also speaks of proclaiming and declaring. Jesus, in Matthew 28:18–20, speaks of teaching. I believe that the preacher/herald/one-who-proclaims/declarer/teacher refers to the role of the evangelist and pastor/teacher described in Ephesians 4:11 and the teacher described in 1 Corinthians 12:28. The evangelist and pastor/teacher are gifts from Christ. The teacher is gifted by the Holy Spirit. Not everyone is going to have the gift of evangelism, pastor/teacher, or teacher; but those to whom it is given must exercise the gift if they wish to be spiritually productive.

God, speaking through Isaiah the Prophet, also indicates that the people of Israel are His witnesses. The word, witness, in the

Hebrew means a witness in the sense of one who has a testimony. Jesus, in Acts 1:8, commands his disciples to be witnesses throughout the world. The word, witness, in the Greek means a witness in the sense of a judicial hearing, which suggests that he/she would have a testimony. A testimony would come from one's providing evidence about something or someone. For Christians, it is giving evidence about the presence of Jesus in our lives and our personal relationship with Him.

Providing testimony about Jesus to another could consist of such things as our conversion (Acts 26:1–23), the great works of God in our life (Mark 5:19–20, John 9:17–34), our giving answer to whomever asks about our reason to hope (1 Pet. 3:15), the constraint in our life (2 Cor. 5:14), our sanctification (1 Cor. 1:30), the presence of the Holy Spirit (John 3:8, Acts 9:3, Acts 16:9, 1 Pet. 1:2), our confidence about our resurrection (2 Cor. 4:14), our devotion to Christ (Phil. 3:4–14), and the hope of the crown of righteous (2 Tim. 4:7–8) just to mention a few.

At *all* times, we need to be ready to share about Jesus. We need to be His witnesses and give testimony about him. If called, we need to evangelize, preach, or teach about Jesus. We need to tell them that the prophecy concerning the Christ is fulfilled in Jesus. We need to tell them, as a result, that they need to repent of their sins so that they can be revived by the Holy Spirit and that they may receive Jesus, the Christ, sent to them by God, the Father. Finally, we need to tell them that they need to listen to Jesus. I call these **"good soil"** people who persevere in doing all of this sharing about Jesus the **"PRODUCTIVE PEOPLE."**

The glorification of God and the satisfaction of our need for meaning come from our sharing about Jesus so that others, too, can receive Jesus, the Christ, as their Savior and Lord. In doing this we sense purpose/mission within the Body of Christ. We persevere in sharing about Jesus. We, then, are the "good soil." We are loving God and loving our neighbor. Spiritual productivity in the form of sharing about Jesus is the "mind of Christ."

Therefore repent and return, so that your sins may be wiped away, in order that times of refreshing may come from the presence of the Lord; and that He may send Jesus, the Christ appointed for you. (Matt. 3:19–20)

Are we sharing about Jesus?
Are we humbled by the mighty works of God that we see?
Let's go on!

Section V
Summary

We have seen so far the spiritual productivity of Peter and Paul. So let us summarize this section by looking at the spiritual productivity of Philip as described in Acts 8.

Philip has a great ministry going on in Samaria (vv. 6–8). However, Philip receives instructions from an angel of the Lord to leave his great ministry in Samaria and to go to a desert road that goes to Gaza (v. 26). What is on a desert road? There is sand, rocks, and maybe a few snakes. On the surface, this would not appear to be a great place to minister. However, Philip is obedient to the Lord, perseveres, and goes (v. 27a). On the road, Philip finds a powerful Ethiopian (nation in Africa) leader who is returning to Ethiopia after worshipping God in Jerusalem (v. 27b). The leader is sitting in his chariot reading the prophet, Isaiah (v. 28), and The Holy Spirit instructs Philip to go to the chariot (v. 29). Philip responds to the Holy Spirit by *boldly* approaching the chariot and asking the leader if he understands what he is reading (v. 30). Certainly, Philip is **ministering in the power of the Holy Spirit**, to one who is spiritually needy. The leader must be **amazed** at Philip's offer to help him and invites Philip into the chariot (v. 31). The leader asks Philip to explain a passage in Isaiah 53 that describes the Messiah (vv. 32–34). (This reminds me of the Romans 10:13–15 scripture that we saw in the summary of chapter 15). Then Philip, boldly exercising the spiritual gift of teaching, begins from the Scripture passage to **share Jesus** with the leader (v. 35). How, possibly did the Gospel message first reach Africa? Was it possibly because of the ministry of the Holy Spirit through a follower of Jesus on a *desert road*?

Here it is! We need to follow the leading of the Holy Spirit and persevere no matter what the circumstances seem to be! We need to boldly minister in the power of the Holy Spirit! We need to exercise the gifts of the Holy Spirit! We need to boldly share about Jesus! (see Appendix XI, "Spiritual Productivity," for a visual overview of all of this.)

God is calling his people to ministry through His Word and His Holy Spirit so that His Gospel message will be spread to all nations. In this way, through God's provision, His people can fully experience meaning in their lives! Where are we in all of this? Are we ministering in the power of the Holy Spirit? Are we sharing with those that are "amazed" that the motivation and effect of our ministry comes from the power of the Holy Spirit? Are we sharing about Jesus? Are we the "good soil?" Do we have the "mind of Christ?"

The glorification of God and the satisfaction of our need for meaning come through our serving God within the unity of the Body of Christ. We need to minister in the power of the Holy Spirit, explain the source of the power to those who are amazed, and share about Jesus. If we persevere in doing this, we are spiritually productive and are the "good soil." We are loving God and loving our neighbor. This is the "mind of Christ" concerning spiritual productivity.

Are we humbled by the mighty works of God that we see?
Do we see Jesus a little more clearly?
Let's go on!

Note: If you want to pursue the theme of "spiritual productivity" further in the Book of Acts, turn to Appendix VIII-E for a study outline. The outline provides for a macro study (based on a micro study) of the scripture and is written in an application format.

Appendix XI, "Spiritual Productivity," provides a visual overview of the relationships among the processes related to "spiritual productivity " found in the Book of Acts.

Also, Appendix XII, "Framework for Spiritual Community," provides a visual representation of how a spiritual community should function.

EPILOGUE

Spiraling Out of Control (Of Ourselves): Around The "Framework" Again And Again

"He (Jesus) must increase, but I must decrease."
(John 3:30)

Now, if we are humble and find that our sense of worth comes from appropriating the love and acceptance of Jesus, if we have been spiritually transformed so that we possess the Holy Spirit and are truly free to choose the way of Jesus, if we have steadfast faith in Jesus and fully submit and entrust ourselves to His power, if we are devotedly obedient to God through the working of the Holy Spirit in our lives and through trusting in God's constant provision for our security, and if we boldly persevere in our mission of ministering to others in the power of the Holy Spirit, explaining that the source of the power *is* the Holy Spirit, and sharing about Jesus; then we *will be humbled* by the **mighty works of God**. The more we are humbled; the more we will see Jesus clearly. As a result, we will begin another journey around the "Framework of Spiritual Maturity." This process will be on going until we go to glory!

This reminds me of a verse from the old hymn, "Deeper, Deeper":

Deeper, deeper, blessed Holy Spirit,
Take me deeper still,
Till my life is wholly lost in Jesus
And His perfect will.

CHAPTER 16

The Choice:
Standing Around or Being
Witnesses for Jesus

"...you will receive power when the Holy
Spirit has come upon you and you shall be
My witnesses both in Jerusalem, and all Judea
and Samaria, and even to the remotest part of
the earth. And after He had said these things,
He was lifted up while they were looking on,
and a cloud received Him out of their sight.
And as they were gazing intently into the sky
while He was going, two men in white clothing stood beside them. They also said, "Men
of Galilee, why do you stand looking into the
sky? This Jesus, who has been taken up from
you into heaven, will come in just the same
way as you have watched Him go into heaven."
(Acts 1:9–11)

I believe that the "two men in white" are telling the "men of Galilee"
that it is time to stop standing around because there is much work
to do until Jesus comes again. Where are we in this passage? Are we
standing around or are we at work as an active witness for Jesus? The

"Framework for Spiritual Maturity" can be a useful tool for us in our becoming a more active and more effective witness for Jesus. The following are ways that I have found this "framework" to be helpful to me and others in our spiritual walk:

Discern self: examine yourself "Test yourselves to see if you are in the faith; examine yourselves!" (2 Cor. 13:5).

Where are we on our spiritual journey?

If we are going to be a better witness for Jesus, we first need to identify where we are in our spiritual walk. One of the ways to do this is to see where we are relative to the five themes of the Gospels in the "framework." Are we at "servant-like humility," "Jesus-focused spirituality," "steadfast faithfulness," "devoted obedience," or "spiritual productivity?" Now, sometimes, we may be dealing with more than one area, but we usually can determine in which area we are the most.

Even though we may be the good soil, we still have our flesh, which may allow pieces of the not-so-good soil to creep in along the edges. I have to be ever diligent in my self-examination to be aware of such encroachments, ask God for forgiveness, and seek His help in dealing with the encroachments. One of the best ways that I have found to do this is to study the Gospels in the "framework," one-on-one, with other another man. This provides a consistent way for me to be in constant self-examination. Men with whom I study express their thanks to me for meeting with them, but I quickly return the thanks and tell them that our study together helps *me* to stay the course for the Lord.

What do we need to study and apply in order to grow spiritually?

Once we determine "where we are," we need to study the Gospel that applies to "where we are." I have provided study guides based on the themes (Appendix VIII) and have written them in an application format. These guides are by no means cast in stone. I am continually refining them. Once we finish studying the Gospel, "where we are," we can move on to the next. At some time we may want to go back and visit the Gospel studies in the "framework" that were skipped. If we want to approach the Gospel studies more as a "student," we might decide to start at the beginning. Both ways work; it depends on the individual.

Again, one of the best ways that I have found to grow spiritually is to study the Gospels in the "framework," one-on-one with another man. As we study, I am always learning new things that help me to grow spiritually, and it provides a way for me to do this on a consistent basis. I am so thankful for the men with whom I meet.

How do we expand our testimony?

As we do the Gospel studies, we need to expand and hone our testimony about our relationship with Jesus. In each of the chapters of this book, there are subsections that are entitled "Experiencing...." In these subsections, I have shared stories about *my* relationship with Jesus, and these are *my* testimony. As we all do the studies, we need to be filling in the "Experiencing..." subsections with our *own* stories (This also applies in doing the Gospel book studies). In this way, we will be able to expand *our* testimony for Jesus.

One of the best ways that I have found to expand my testimony is to be aware of the Lord's work in my life experiences, to be able to categorize them according to where they fit into the "framework," and to be ready to share them in conversation or teaching. Again, one of the best ways that I have found to hone my testimony about my relationship with Jesus is to share them one-on-one with other men. This provides a way for me to share on a consistent basis and helps me to remember the stories.

Discern others: guard your heart—"But false teachers also arose among the people, just as there will also be false teachers among you..." (1 Pet. 2:1a); "Do not give what is holy to dogs, and do not throw your pearls before swine, or they will trample them under their feet, and turn and tear you to pieces" (Matt. 7:6).

How can we be aware of false teachers?

As we listen to preachers, teachers, or people we meet in passing, as we read spiritual books, or as we listen to spiritual music; we can use the themes in the "framework" as means to evaluate their interpretation of the Gospels. As we listen to someone teaching in the Gospels, we need to see if the person's interpretation fits within the theme, the sub-theme, and the study outline for the particular passage. If it does not, we need to ask the person to explain further his/her interpretation. Also, we need to observe spiritual teachers and see if their behavior is consistent with the themes of the "framework."

I constantly use the "framework" when I am listening to Biblical teaching (Old Testament as well as New Testament), reading spiritual books, listening to spiritual music, or having a spiritual conversation with someone. I have used the framework for observing the behavior of spiritual leaders, and I have personally observed, on more than one occasion, the immense destructive effect of a false teacher.

> **Why do you yourselves transgress the commandment of God for the sake of tradition?...You hypocrites, rightly did Isaiah prophesy of you: "This people honors Me with their lips, but their heart is far away from Me. But in vain do they worship Me, teaching as doctrines the precepts of men." (Matt. 15:3b, 7–9)**

Not only has the "framework" helped me to separate true from false teaching and living, but it has helped to increase my faith as I see the "themes" showing up in the "true" teaching and living of spiritual leaders. Praise the Lord!

How can we protect ourselves?

As we share about Jesus, we may not be received. Just look what happened to Paul in the Book of Acts. He was beaten and imprisoned because of his sharing about Jesus. Here, we can use the "framework" to help us to see who these types of people are. They are the "wayside soil," the "hard people." The seed does not penetrate this soil; the Word does not penetrate these people. If we are sharing about Jesus and see that we are not being received, we need to stop sharing; and we need to move on to someone else that *will* receive us (Matt. 10:14).

I have experienced trying to share about Jesus with "wayside soil," "hard people." It took me a while to understand about protecting myself. I would linger too long with the "hard people" that refused to receive the Word and felt that I would be giving up too soon if I did not continue. In addition, I would become more and more depressed that these people would not accept my sharing. The result of my continuing to share was that the "hard people" became even harder and I became even more depressed. The scriptures in the previous paragraph helped me to understand how to deal better with the "hard people." I also began to understand that the convicting of other people about their sin and Jesus was not my job, but the job of the Holy Spirit (Titus 3:4–5). If I discontinue a relationship with a "hard person," I continue to pray for him and inform him that if he ever wants to get serious about Jesus to give me a call.

Discern others: make disciples—"Go therefore and make disciples of all nations" (Matt. 28:19a).

How can we improve our relationships with others?

As we interact with other people, we can use our understanding of the Parable of the Sower and be discerning about what type of "soil" they are. Once we do that (we are not judging), we can have a better understanding of their behavior and the intrinsic needs that they are attempting to meet. (see Appendices IV-VII) With this better understanding, we should more easily be able to develop patience with them. In addition, we should be able to establish more appropriate boundaries in our relationships with them and be better able to help them if they need it.

Before I was a believer, I was a perfectionist. I was very intolerant of those who were not. I just could not understand why people could not or would not do their best. After I became a believer, I was intolerant of non-believers who were not perfectionists *and* believers who were not following Jesus as closely as they might. I just could not understand why they could not or would not do their best, and I was quick to tell them so. Understandably my relationships with others were a bit strained to say the least. I was of no help to others but rather left a wake of destruction in my path! Louise tried to explain all of this to me, but to no avail. As I grew spiritually and understood the "framework" more, it was becoming clearer to me the possible reasons for the behavior of others. As my understanding grew, so did my tolerance and patience. The Beatitudes (Matt. 5:3–12) helped as well. All of this enabled me to establish appropriate boundaries in my relationships. If I discerned that someone was a "hard person," I understood that he/she was selfishly and pridefully caught up in things of the world, sin, and/or Satan and was not interested in seeking another direction. (Also, see above, "How can we protect ourselves") If I discerned that someone was a "shallow person," I understood that he/she was seeking power in multiple places other than just faith in Jesus and that he/she would be inconsistent in their faith and commitment to anything. If I discerned that someone was an "unproductive person," I understood that he/she was distracted by the "worry of the world and the deceitfulness of wealth" in his/her seeking of personal security and was being disobedient to God. If I discerned that someone was a "productive person," I understood that he/she was ministering in the power of the Holy Spirit, and I could see the fruits of the Spirit and the gifts of the Spirit manifest in him/her. The understanding of all of the above caused me to become more patient in my relationship with others (Again, the Beatitudes helped as well) and to establish more effective and stable boundaries with others. Not only that, but I began to see ways in which I could help others! Oh, my!

...first take the log out of your own eye, and then you will see clearly to take the speck outof your brother's eye. (Matt. 7:5)

How can we witness and evangelize?

When we are in conversation with people, we can ask the questions found in Appendix X, "Framework for Discipleship" ("What are you doing?," "What do you want?," "What are you thinking?," or "What are the results of what you are doing?") Usually, during the conversation around these questions, the people will begin to share their needs. After listening very carefully, we can begin to share about how Jesus has met our needs (witness). Then, we can share with them about how they can receive Jesus as their Savior, and how He will meet their needs as well (evangelize). We can use the explanation in Chapter 5 (John 3) of this book to help them to understand this. We need to understand that the *conversion* of people is not done by us but by the Holy Spirit (Titus 3:4–5).

Remember the hymn that goes—"I love to tell the story, t'will be my theme in glory, to tell the old, old story of Jesus and His love." I love to tell the story about Jesus and His love—not only at Calvary, but in my conversion, and my moment by moment walk with Him. I can be in conversations with people about the weather, sports, family, etc., and I am OK with it, *BUT* just give me an opening to tell a story about Jesus and His love and have a conversation about that. I come alive! I love to tell the stories! Jesus saved me! Jesus humbles me! Jesus loves me! Jesus heals me! Jesus teaches me! Jesus is my example! Jesus gives me the words to say! Jesus walks with me! Jesus guides me! Jesus empowers me! Jesus protects me! Jesus delivers me! Jesus uses me in His service! If I find out that the other person has not received Jesus as his personal Savior and discern his receptiveness through the convicting power of the Holy Spirit, I will share how he can receive Jesus using the explanation in Chapter 5 (John 3) of this book to help him to understand.

How can we help others to identify their place in their spiritual journey?

When we invite someone to do a Bible study with us and they agree to do so, we can begin with a study of the following:

- ○ The Parable of the Sower (see Appendix I)
- ○ The themes of the Gospels and their relationship to the Parable of the Sower
  (see Appendix II)
- ○ The progressive relationship among the soils in the Parable of the Sower and the related themes of the Gospels and Acts (see Appendix III)
- ○ Man's behavior motivated by his attempt to meet his basic intrinsic needs
  (see Appendix IV)
- ○ The connection between man's basic intrinsic needs and each of the paired themes of the Parable of the Sower and the Gospel books and Acts.
  (see Appendices V and VI)
- ○ Connection among the themes of each of the soils in the Parable of the Sower, the themes of the Gospel books and Acts, and man's intrinsic needs (see Appendix VII)

Then we can give the person a copy of the introduction of this book as a review of the above study and provide a copy of the "Framework of Spiritual Maturity—Overview" (see Appendix XIII) for the next study. (At this point we need to confirm with them that they still want to continue with the study.)

Next, we can study the "Framework for Spiritual Maturity, Appendix III) and the five major theme studies that are in this book (Mark 10, John 3, Luke 9, Matthew 6, and Acts 3). We also can make the study outlines for these chapters in Appendix VIII available to the person that we have invited. As I mentioned before, we need to be able to have our *own* stories, as much as possible, when it comes to the "experiencing…" portions of the study. After studying the five chapters (usually in five separate meetings), we can ask them where they think they are on the framework. Almost always they will be able to self-identify. Also, it would be necessary for us, in our discernment, to be in agreement with their assessment.

If people are non-believers or new believers, they usually self-identify as needing to start studies about servant-like humility (Mark) or Jesus-focused spirituality (John). If the person has a serious pride problem, we would probably start with servant-like humility (Mark) because his pride would keep him from seeing Jesus. If the person is humble, we might start with Jesus-focused spirituality (John). If the people are believers, they usually would self-identify as needing to start studies about steadfast faithfulness (Luke) or devoted obedience (Matthew). If the person has a faith issue, we usually would start with steadfast faithfulness (Luke). If the person has an obedience problem, we would usually start with devoted obedience (Matthew). I have never started in Acts with anyone, not to say that it could not happen.

How can we disciple others?

Once people identify where they are in the "Framework for Spiritual Maturity," we can ask them if they would be interested in doing the Bible book study that applies (see previous paragraph). If they agree, we can begin the book study using the study outlines in Appendix VIII. (Study outlines for teachers and "non-students" would be those with the final part of the sentences completed; study outlines for "students" would be those with the final part of the sentences blank.) As this is more of a macro Bible study, each chapter study can be done in one to one and a half hours (there are exceptions). Each chapter study should be accompanied by a discussion about the application of the Word to one's life, and accountability for that application should be ongoing. Once the first book study is done, we can move on to the next book study in the "framework." At any time, people may want to go back and do a book study that came before the one on which they self-identified in the "framework." Also, some may be more inclined to be "students" and will want to start at the beginning. This process is continued until Acts 28 is completed; this may take three to five years to complete. I do not usually disclose the projected time frame up front. I have noticed that the one being discipled really begins to become *very* serious about his spiritual walk somewhere during the study of Matthew. I generally use the "Framework for Discipleship" (Appendix X ff) as a guideline for discipling.

When you find someone who self-identifies at the "Matthew" level and who desires to teach or disciple others, you can pair him with another who is at the same level; and they can be Bible-study partners using the study outlines for Mark, John, and Luke. When the Lord leads them, they can begin to be on the lookout for someone to disciple or for a group to teach.

I feel that discipling should be gender specific—older men teaching younger men; older women teaching younger women. I usually meet with guys one-on-one and sometimes one-on-two or one-on-three if the two or three are in the same place spiritually. With the work schedule of most men and women today, it is impossible for some to commit to a weekly small-group meeting. I have some men with whom I meet who do not know their work schedule from week to week. However, if we are meeting one-on-one, we can easily schedule a time. I meet with the men weekly before work in the morning, between the end of work in the afternoon and dinner, in the evening, and/or sometimes on Saturday morning. We meet mostly at coffee shops, but also at their homes, my home, church, etc. We sometimes have met by cell phone or Skype if the distances are great. I feel that the smaller the group, the more personal the conversation can be and the more effective the accountability can be. I find that a person will grow at least three times faster in a one-on-one setting than in a small-group setting. As a result, I feel that one-on-one discipling is the most effective and the most efficient.

While meeting with someone, I feel that it is necessary to help them develop outcome processes that will make them more effective disciples of Jesus. These processes are learning to be a self-directed learner, a knowledgeable communicator, a wise choice-maker, a reflective self-evaluator, and a continuous improver, and together they form the "Framework for an Effective Disciple (see Appendix XIV). This framework overlays the "Framework for Spiritual Maturity" and the "Framework for Discipleship," and it represents the outcomes of one's following these two frameworks.

During the discipling process, there will be times of counseling. When we counsel, we can use the "Framework for Discipleship" (Appendix X) as a process. We need to listen and observe very carefully and attempt to identify specific needs. Then, we need to connect the specific needs to the larger basic intrinsic need. The "Needs Matrix" (Appendix VII) can lead us to match the Gospel(s) that is/are applicable. Next, we can go to the specific study outline in Appendix VIII that applies, and we can choose the portions of scripture that are specifically applicable for counsel. One example of this is when a brother came to me in his suffering. He shared with me about his suffering, and I listened intently. After he was done sharing, I expressed my empathy with his situation. He expressed concern about his ability to continue to deal with the suffering, which was an issue of faith. I offered to share some Scripture with him that I thought might help. He agreed that this would be a good idea. Using the "framework," I went to the section that I thought applied to this situation—"Endure the Suffering" part of "Steadfast Faithfulness." Using the study guide, I was able I was able to narrow the focus to scripture that applied to his situation. He was encouraged by the Word, and we prayed together that his faith would be increased, and that the Holy Spirit would comfort and sustain him through the trial.

In the discipling process, we should be modeling what we are teaching. We should walk the talk. We should share where we are struggling in our walk, and explain how we are dealing with it. For those whom we disciple, it will be easier for them if they can see the Word in action. Let us be "doers of the Word" (James 1:22–25), and let us "walk in the Spirit" (Gal. 5:25)!

"All authority has been given to me in heaven and on earth. Go therefore and make disciples of all nations, baptizing them in the name of

the Father and the Son and the Holy Spirit, teaching them to observe all that I commanded you; and lo, I am with you always even to the end of the age." (Matt. 28:19–20)

Appendix I
Parable of the Sower

Matthew 13:3–8, 18–32; Mark 4:3–20; Luke 8:4–15

"And he (Jesus) said to them (his disciples), know you not this parable? And how then will you know all parables?' (Mark 4:13)

Symbolism: Sower = Jesus   seed = the Word of God
                soils = people of the world   birds = Satan

Response to the sowing of the seed:

Wayside soil -They hear the Word and do not understand it.
Rocky soil -   They hear the Word and immediately receive it with joy.
Thorny soil - They hear the Word and go on their way.
Good soil -   They hear the Word with an honest and good heart, accept it, understand it, and hold it fast.

Result of responding to the sowing of the seed:

Wayside soil – Satan takes the Word out of their heart lest they believe and be saved.

Rocky soil—They have no root in themselves and last awhile; but when troubles or persecution arise because of the Word, they fall away.

Thorny soil—The worries of the world, the worries of this life, the riches of this life, the deceitfulness of wealth, the desire for other things, and the pleasures of this life choke the Word; and they become unfruitful.

Good soil—They bear fruit manifold with perseverance.

Lesson: We are to hear the Word with an honest and good heart, accept it, understand it, and hold it fast that we believe unto salvation and that we bear much fruit, with perseverance, to the glory of God!

Appendix II
Themes of the Gospels

GOSPEL	THEME	PARABLE OF THE SOWER
MARK	Servant-like humility	Wayside soil—selfish pride
JOHN	Jesus-focused spirituality	Transformation from natural focus
LUKE	Steadfast faithfulness	Rocky soil—unfaithfulness
MATTHEW	Devoted obedience	Thorny soil—disobedience
ACTS	Spiritual productivity	Good soil

Appendix III
FRAMEWORK FOR SPIRITUAL MATURITY

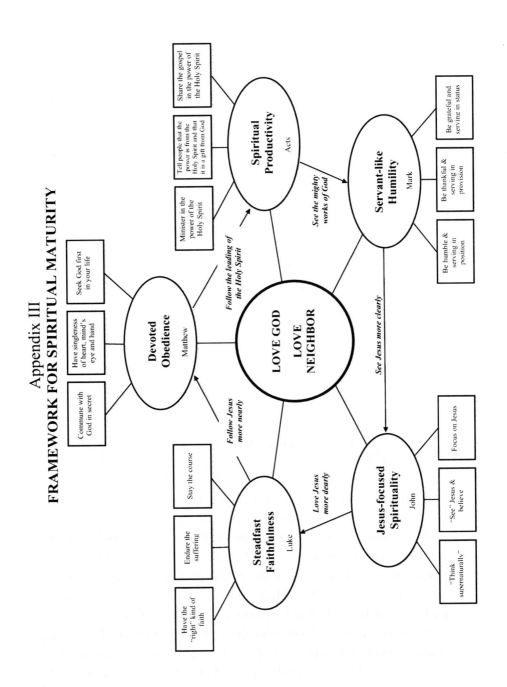

Appendix IV
Basic Human Needs

In 1985, William Glasser wrote a book entitled *Control Theory*[1], in which he identified five basic human needs—survival and repro-duction, belonging, power, freedom, and fun. [2]He suggested that these needs are intrinsic and are as a result of evolution. He also said that we create pictures in our heads that illustrate the optimum meet-ing of these five basic needs:

> We develop the pictures in our heads—the specific pictures that we believe will satisfy our built-in needs. At the time we are conceived, the requirement that we satisfy our basic needs is built into our genetic instructions, but when we are born, we have not the slightest idea of what these needs are or how to fulfill them. To satisfy them, even before birth, we begin to create what is best described as a picture album in our heads and begin to fill it with detailed pictures of what we want. Our whole lives will be spent enlarging these albums… Your picture album— in which you find love, worth, success, fun, and freedom—is the world you would like to live in, where somehow or other all your desires, even conflicting ones, are satisfied. (Glasser, 1985)

Glasser goes on to describe what he thinks causes human behavior:

> Living creatures are never stuck. If we can't get what we want with what we know, we will cre-ate new behaviors that may be more effective.

---

[1]   Glasser, William (1985)., Harper and Row, New York

[2]   Sigmund Freud also held this view. Freud, Sigmund (1915, 1957), "Instincts and Their Vicissitudes.", 14, 117–140, Hogwarth Press, London.

> But old or new, all our behavior is our constant
> attempt to reduce the difference between what
> we want (the pictures in our heads) and what we
> have (the way we see the situations in the world).
> (Glasser 1985)

In 1998, Glasser changed the name of his theory from "control theory" to "choice theory." [3]In addition, he redefined the five basic intrinsic needs as survival, love/loving sex/belonging, power, freedom, and fun. Finally, he provided some examples that help to understand his theory.

> If you get up in the morning and feel miserable, you can be sure that one or more of the five basic needs is not satisfied to the extent you would like to satisfy that need or needs. For example, if you wake up with the flu, the pain tells you that your need to survive is being threatened by an infection. If you awaken lonely because your last child has just left for college, your need for love and belonging is acutely unsatisfied. If you are up for a promotion at work and you will get the news today, your edginess is your way of dealing with this possible loss of power. If you get the promotion, you will feel good; if not, you will feel worse than you feel right now. If you have been counting on being free to go on a family vacation and discover that the dog is missing, you are angry because you are not at liberty to leave until you find him. If you are scheduled to have fun playing tennis, but it's starting to rain, you don't have to wonder if your need for fun is frustrated; your disappointment tells you immediately that it is. (Glasser, 1998)

Glasser goes on to explain that the pictures in our mind that depict the best ways to satisfy one or more of our basic needs become collectively our "quality world":

> As we attempt to satisfy needs, we are continu-
> ally creating and re-creating our quality worlds.

3   Glasser, William (1998)., Harper and Row, New York

> If I want a lot of power, I may put politics into
> my quality world. If survival is all I want, I may
> make Ebenezer Scrooge my role model. If free-
> dom dominates the pictures in my quality world,
> I may buy a small sailboat and blissfully sail the
> sea alone. (Glasser, 1998)

I am in agreement with most of what Glasser says. However, there are some areas where I differ. First of all, I felt that I needed to clarify for myself the differences between an intrinsic need and what satisfies an intrinsic need. In doing so, I determined that Glasser's survival need is part of a larger need for security, pleasure, and the absence of pain. The security need is satisfied by the provision of "things," such as shelter, that allow us to survive. The pleasure need is satisfied by the provision of 'things," such as music, that please our senses—smell, taste, hearing, sight, and touch. The absence of pain is satisfied by the provision of things, such as medication, that reduce the amount of physical and mental pain. [4]Provision of the "things" that meet our needs increases our sense of security.

Next, I determined that the "love/loving sex/belonging" need is not a need at all, but rather, a way in which to *satisfy* the need of worth. I believe that we all have a need to feel a sense of worth and that the way in which this need is satisfied is through love and accep-tance. I feel that Glasser's loving-sex need is part of the larger con-cept of love that satisfies the need of worth. In addition, I feel that Glasser's belonging need [5]is part of the deeper means of acceptance that also satisfies the need of worth. Experiencing love and accep-tance from others increases our sense of worth.

---

[4] Sigmund Freud also identified this need. Freud, Sigmund (1895, 1950, 1966), "Project for a Scientific Psychology." Standard Edition, 1, 295–391. Hogwarth Press, London

[5] Erich Fromm also identified belonging as a need. Fromm, Erich (1955)., Holt, Rinehart and Winston, New York

I determined that the way in which the need of freedom [6]is satisfied is through the amount of choice that we have. The greater the choice available to us; the greater the sense of freedom we have.

I feel that the way in which the need for power [7]is satisfied is through trust. We all need power in order to accomplish things in life, and we place our trust in the source of power that we feel will work the best for us. Placing our trust in this given source of power will increase our own personal sense of power.

Glasser's "fun" need, I feel, is part of the pleasure component of the need for security and part of a larger need for joy. I believe that the more that all of our needs can be satisfied, the deeper our joy will be. Fun, I feel, can contribute to our sense of joy but is short-lived and temporary.

To Glasser's five needs I have added a sixth—the need for meaning. Some feel that "meaning" is part of the concept of "power," but I feel that it is separate. [8]Power creates a sense of personal competence while meaning, I believe, suggests a sense of being part of and contributing to something larger than our own personal lives. Determining and fulfilling our purpose in contributing to a larger "whole" increases our sense of meaning.

Finally, I firmly believe that, contrary to Glasser, that the intrinsic needs existing within us are not as a result of evolution but as a result of the creation of God.

The **best** way to attempt to satisfy our needs is to be seeking to have the "mind of Christ" (1 Cor. 2:16), the one who created us. The "mind of Christ" is the quality world already established by the Creator. The seeking of God first in our life results in the satisfaction of all our needs. The Creator of man is, indeed, the only one through which man can truly and ultimately satisfy his intrinsic needs. Why do we continually create and recreate our "quality worlds" exclusive

---

[6]   Erich Fromm also identified freedom as a need. Fromm, Erich (1955)., Holt, Rinehart and Winston, New York.

[7]   Alfred Adler also identified power as a need. Adler, Alfred (1927, 1954)., Fawcett, New York

[8]   Victor Frankl also identified meaning as a need. Frankl, Victor E. (1963). Man's Search for Meaning, Washington Square, New York

of the "mind of Christ" and attempt to satisfy our needs in all the wrong places? We should be satisfying our needs by continually creating and recreating our quality worlds to be more like the "mind of Christ."

Appendix V
Intrinsic Needs, Gospel Themes, Parable of the Sower

NEED		*GOSPEL THEME*	*PARABLE OF THE SOWER*
WORTH	Mark	Servant-like humility	Wayside soil—selfish pride
FREEDOM	John	Jesus-focused spirituality	Transformation from natural focus
POWER	Luke	Steadfast faithfulness	Rocky soil—unfaithfulness
SECURITY	Matthew	Devoted obedience	Thorny soil—disobedience
MEANING	Acts	Spiritual productivity	Good soil— manifold spiritual productivity

Appendix VI
Basic Intrinsic Needs

The progressive relationship of intrinsic is based on the type of relationship in which we find ourselves. These needs can be categorized by type, and I would suggest the following levels that are based on Stephen Covey's hierarchy of needs[9].

LEVEL OF NEED	NEED	WAY IN WHICH NEED IS SATISFIED
Personal	Security	*Physiological provision*—But seek first His kingdom and His righteousness and all these things will be added to you. (Matt. 6:33)
Interpersonal	Worth	*Love and acceptance*—For God so loved the world, that He gave His only begotten Son, that whoever believes in Him shall not perish, but have eternal life. (John 3:16)
Managerial	Freedom	*Choice*—It was for freedom that Christ set us free; therefore keep standing firm and do not be subject to a yoke of slavery. (Galatians 5:1)
	Power	*Trust* —That He would grant you, according to the riches of His glory, to be strengthened with power through His Spirit in the inner man. (Eph.3:16)

[9] Covey, Stephen (1989). The Seven Habits of Effective People. Simon and Shuster, New York

Organizational	Meaning	
		Purpose—Go therefore and make disciples of all the nations, baptizing them in the name of the Father and the Son and the Holy Spirit, teaching them to observe all that I have commanded you; and lo, I am with you always, even to the end of the age. (Matt. 28:19–20)
NA	Joy	*Meeting of all the above needs*—Until now you have asked nothing in My name: ask and you will receive, so that your joy may be made full. (John 16:24)

Appendix VII
Theme Matrix

SOIL IN THE PARABLE OF THE SOWER	GOSPEL THEME	RELATIONSHIP	NEED	WAY NEED IS MET OR SATISFIED	MAN'S WAY*		GOD'S WAY*
Thorny (Unproductive)	Matthew	Personal	Security	Provision	Self-Provision Disobedience to God	C	Devoted Obedience to God: God's Provision
Wayside (Hard)	Mark	Interpersonal	Worth	Love and Acceptance	Selfish Pride	H	Servant-like Humility
Transformation from Bad Soil to Good Soil (Saved)	John	Managerial	Freedom	Choice	Natural Focus (Sin)	O	Jesus-Focused Spirituality (Sin/Not Sin)
Rocky (Shallow)	Luke		Power	Trust	Faith in Self and/or Other Things	I	Steadfast Faith in God
Good (Productive)	Acts	Organizational	Meaning	Purpose in the Whole	Productivity in the Natural Realm	C	Spiritual Productivity
N/A (Joyful)	N/A	All	Joy	Meeting all of the Above Needs	Loving Pleasure	E	All of the Above

*See Scripture Reference for "Choice" (over)

SCRIPTURE REFERENCE FOR "CHOICE"

NEED	MAN'S WAY		GOD'S WAY
Security	Mark 4:18–19; Mark 10:17–22	C	Matthew 6:24–33; Ephesians 6:10–14; Luke 11:5–8; John 3:16: John 5:16; Matthew 5:6
Worth	Mark 4:15; Mark 10:2–5; Mark 12;38; Mark 12: 41–44	H	Mark 10: 13–16; Mark 10:46–52; John 3:16; Romans 3:21–26; Matthew 5:3
Freedom	Romans 5:12; Ephesians 2:2–3; James 1:14–15; James 4:1–3; John 3:19–20	O	Romans 2:4; John 8:31–36; John 3:10–15; Romans 5:6–11; 1John: 1:5–9; Galatians 5:1
Power	Ephesians 2:9; Matthew 12:43–45; Proverbs 3:5–8; Luke 18:28–29; Mark 10:21–26; Luke 8:22–24; Mark 8:15; Mark 9:14–19	I	Ephesians 2:8; Matthew 4:1–11; Proverbs 3:5–8; Luke 8:25; Mark 10:27; Luke 18:30; Mark 8:15; Matthew 9:20–29
Meaning	Acts 5:1–11; Acts 6:1; Acts 8:18–24; Acts 9:1–2	C	Acts 4:32–37; Acts 6:2–7; Acts 4:18–20; Acts 8:14–17,25; Acts 9:3–22; John 8:8; Acts 8:4–8,26–40; Acts 10:1–21,44–48; Acts 16:6–7,8–10; I Corinthians 12:14–27
Joy	Proverbs 21:17; Titus 3:3; 2Timothy 3:1–4; Luke 8:14	E	Ecclesiastes 2:26 (Security); Isaiah 29:19 (Worth); Isaiah 12 (Freedom); Romans 15:13 (Power); Luke 1:46–49 (Meaning); John 3:29 & John 15:11 & John 16:24 & 1 John 1:3–4 (Full); James 1:2 & Luke 6:22–23 (Persecution); Luke 16:22 (Cannot Lose)

Appendix VIII
Gospel Study Outlines

Note: If copies of the study guides are to be used as handouts, it is recommended that they be enlarged to 8 ½ X 11.

Appendix VIII - A
The Gospel of Mark
Servant-like Humility

SERVANT-LIKE HUMILITY—THE GOSPEL OF MARK

MAJOR THEMES

Being humble in position and serving is...

not exhibited by the Pharisees/Jewish men in sending their wives away for no just cause with "writs of divorcement." (10:1–12, Deut. 24:1–4)

exhibited by Jesus in allowing the children to come to Him and in blessing them. (10:13–16)

Being thankful for provision and serving is...

not exhibited by the rich young ruler when told by Jesus to sell all his possessions and give them to the poor. (10:17–31)

exhibited by Jesus in describing His suffering, death, and waiting on the Father to raise Him from the dead. (10:32–34)

Being grateful for status and serving is...

not exhibited by the presumptuous behavior of James and John asking Jesus to sit them next to Him in heaven. (10:35–41)

exhibited by Jesus in telling His disciples that He did not come to earth to *be served* but *to serve* by giving His life as a ransom for many. (10:42–45)

Humility in position, thankfulness in provision, and gratefulness in status is…

> not exhibited by the disciples nor the crowd by keeping Bartimaeus away from Jesus and from not being able to "see" Jesus clearly (Son of David = Messiah). (10:46–52)

> exhibited by Bartimaeus the beggar who is humbled by his circumstances and "sees" Jesus clearly (Son of David = Messiah). (10:46–52)

BE HUMBLE - WE NEED TO UNDERSTAND THAT JESUS, IN HIS POSITION AS THE SON OF GOD,...

has chosen to use the power of His authority to...

> baptize with the Holy Spirit. (1:1–8)
>
> be pleasing to the Father. (1:9–11)
>
> resist the temptation of Satan. (1:12–13)
>
> preach the gospel of God. (1:14–15)
>
> draw disciples to himself. (1:16–20)
>
> teach and act with that authority, drive out demons, and heal diseases. (1:21–39)
>
> touch and heal a *leper*! (1:40–45)

desires to use the power of His authority to help change man's life by...

> forgiving sins. (2:1–12)
>
> ministering to sinners. (2:13–17)
>
> being the incarnation of the Day of Atonement. (2:18–20, Heb.9, I John 1:9)
>
> being the "new wine" which must be placed in new wineskins. (2:21–22)
>
> meeting man's needs. (2:23–28)

makes His power and authority available...

> *all* of the time, even on the Sabbath. (3:1–12).

through His disciples. (3:13–19)

even though it may be misinterpreted by friends and misrepresented by enemies. (vv. 3:20–30)

to those who do the will of God. 3:31–35)

BE THANKFUL - WE NEED TO UNDERSTAND THAT IN JESUS' PROVISION OF...

His word, we must...

> hear it, accept it, and be spiritually productive. (4:1–20)

> be a growing light to the world. (4:21–25)

> sow the seed, and God will work the miracle. (4:26–29, John 4:35–38)

> recognize that the Kingdom of God will start small and grow great. (4:30–32)

> know that He will explain the parables to His disciples. (4:33–34)

> trust in it, even in dire circumstances. (4:35–41)

His physical healing for us, we must *come to Jesus...*

> be healed, and tell others. (5:1–20)

> reach out and touch Jesus, and be healed. (5:25–34)

> ask Jesus, and find healing. (5:21–24, 35–43)

His miracles, we must...

> honor and believe in Him. (6:1–6)

> appropriate His power to meet the needs of others. (6:7–13)

> not destroy the provision of His miracles. (6:14–29)

not be blind to and miss opportunities to appropriate His power to meet the needs of others. (6:30–44)

be in prayer in our ministry to others. (6:45–46)

be open to their limitless nature. (6:47–52)

understand that His power is available to meet the needs of *any* others—whether Jew, Gentile, or anyone. (6:53–56)

His commandments, we must…

not neglect them for the traditions of men. (7:1–8)

not twist them for our own benefit. (7:9–13)

recognize that what defiles man (keeping him from following God's commandments) is not what goes into a man but what comes out from his heart. (7:14–23)

understand that they are available to everyone. (7:24–30)

let Jesus heal our deafness so that we can hear them clearly. (7:31–37)

His leadership, we must…

have compassion, give thanks, and serve others in the power of Jesus. (8:1–10)

beware of the false direction (which appeals to your natural pride) of spiritual and political leaders. (8:11–21)

persist in allowing Jesus to "grow us" in order that we can see Him more and more clearly. (8:22–26) see and acknowledge that He is the Christ. (8:27–30)

set our minds on God's (supernatural) interests. (8:31–33).

deny ourselves, take up our cross, and follow Him. (8:34–38).

His power, we must…

see the Kingdom of God in its power coming on us. (9:1)

commune with and listen to Jesus, *alone*. (9:2–13).

rely on His power (through prayer) and not our own (9:14–29)

observe Jesus' reliance on the Father's power as an example to us. (9:30–32)

use the power to be a servant of all, especially young believers. (9:33–37)

not hinder others from exercising God's power. (9:38–41)

cut out those things that cause us to stumble and may cause other believers to stumble. (9:42–48)

use God's power to be preserved and at peace with each other. (9:49–50)

BE GRATEFUL - WE SHOULD NOT BE PRESUMPTUOUS ABOUT...

His authority...

>   as the Messiah. (11:1–10)

>   over His "house" and all things. (11:11–26)

>   by questioning it. (11:27–33)

His provision for His people...

>   nationally. (12:1–12)

>   supernaturally. (12:13–17)

>   eternally. (12:18–27)

>   theologically. (12:28–37)

>   who are humble and give out of their need. (12:38–44).

the future and...

>   not rely on the accomplishment of men. (13:1–2)

>   beware of false messiahs and teachers and not be in fear of wars and natural disasters. (13:3–8)

>   stand firm and be prepared for persecution. (13:9–13)

>   not follow false Christs and false prophets. (13:14–23)

>   be prepared for His second coming. (13:24–27)

not think that we might know the exact timing of future events events. (13:28–32)

work at our assigned tasks and be alert for His second coming. (13:33–37)

MODELING SERVANT-LIKE HUMILITY

Who is not modeling "being humble in position and serving?" (14)

Chief priests/scribes/elders/council/officers—are seeking how to seize Jesus by stealth and kill Him (vv. 1–2); are glad that Judas wants to betray Jesus and offer Judas money to do so (vv. 10–11); send a crowd to seize Jesus (vv. 43–46, 53); and try to obtain false testimony against Jesus, accuse Him of blasphemy, condemned Him to be deserving of death, and spit on Him and beat Him (vv. 55–65)

Judas—goes to the chief priests to betray Jesus in exchange for money (vv. 10–11), is identified by Jesus as His betrayer (vv. 17–21), and betrays Jesus with a kiss (vv. 41–46)

Disciples—are indignant with and scold the woman who anoints Jesus (vv. 3–5), do not stay awake and keep watch (vv. 32–42), and leave Jesus and flee (vv. 50–52)

Peter—boasts that he will not fall away (vv. 29–31), cuts off the ear of the high priest's slave (v. 47), follows Jesus at a distance and warms himself by the fire (v. 54), and denies Jesus three times and weeps (vv. 66–72)

Who is modeling "being humble in position and serving?" (14)

Jesus—allows the woman to anoint His body (vv. 3–9), provides a place for He and His disciples to eat the Passover (12–16), provides a symbolic remembrance of His sacrifice for His disciples (vv. 22–25), prays to the Father (vv. 35–36, 39, 41), submits to the fulfillment of prophecy (vv. 48–49), does not respond to the false accusations against Him (vv. 60–61a), and does respond affirmatively to the question about His being the Christ (61b-62)

Who is not modeling "being thankful for provision and serving?" (15)

> **Chief priests elders/scribes/council**—deliver Jesus to Pilate because of envy (vv. 1, 10), accuse Jesus falsely (3), stir up the crowd to release Barabbas instead of Jesus (v11), and mock Jesus on the cross (vv. 31–32a)

> **Pilate**—chooses to please the crowd by having Jesus scourged and by handing Him over to be crucified (vv. 4–15)

> **The crowd**—asks Pilate to release Barabbas and to crucify Jesus (vv. 8–14) and hurls abuse at Jesus on the cross (29–30)

> **The soldiers**—mock Jesus (vv. 16–20), force a passerby to bear Jesus' cross (v. 21), crucify Jesus and cast lots for His garments (vv. 22–26), and crucify two robbers with Him (v. 27)

> **Robbers** crucified with Jesus—insult Jesus (v. 32b)

Who is modeling "being thankful for provision and serving?" (15)

> **Jesus**—responds to Pilate as to who He is (v. 2) and allows Himself to be scourged and crucified (vv. 15–39, Ps. 22)

> **The "women"**—look on from a distance (vv. 40–41) and look on to see where Jesus is buried (v. 47)

> **Joseph of Arimathea**—asks Pilate for Jesus' body, wraps Him in a linen cloth, lays Him in a tomb, and rolls a stone against the entrance (vv. 42–46)

Who is not modeling "being grateful for status and serving?" (16)

Mary, Mary, and Salome—do not tell the disciples what they saw at the tomb (vv. 7–8)

The disciples—do not listen to Mary Magdalene or the "two walking" about their seeing Jesus (vv. 9–14)

Who is modeling "being grateful for status and serving?" (16)

Mary, Mary, and Salome—go to the sepulcher (vv. 1–6)

Mary Magdalene—tells the disciples that Jesus is alive (vv. 9–11)

The "two walking"—tell the disciples that they have seen Jesus (vv. 12–13)

The disciples—respond to Jesus' directions (vv. 15–20)

SERVANT-LIKE HUMILITY—THE GOSPEL OF MARK

MAJOR THEMES

Being humble and serving in position is...

(10:1–12) _____

_____

_____

(10:13–16) _____

_____

Being thankful and serving in provision is...

(10:17–31) _____

_____

_____

(10:32–34) _____

_____

_____

Being grateful, not presuming to be served, and serving is ...

(10:35–41) _____

_____

(10:42–45) _____

_____

_____

_____

Humility in position, provision, and service is...

(10:46–52) _____

_____

_____

_____

(10:46–52) _____

_____

_____

_____

BE HUMBLE - WE NEED TO UNDERSTAND THAT JESUS, IN HIS POSITION AS THE SON OF GOD...

has chosen to use the power of His authority to...

(1:1–8) _____

(1:9–11) _____

(1:12–13) _____

(1:14–15) _____

(1:16–20) _____

(1:21–39) _____

_____

(1:40–45) _____

desires to use the power of His authority to help change man's life by...

(2:1–12) _____

(2:13–17) _____

(2:18–20) _____

(2:21–22) _____

_____

(2:23–28) _____

makes His power and authority available…

(3:1–12) _____

(3:13–19) _____

(3:20–30) _____

_____

(3:31–35) _____

BE THANKFUL - WE NEED TO UNDERSTAND THAT IN JESUS' PROVISION OF...

His word, we must...

(4:1–20) _____

(4:1–25) _____

(4:26–29, Jn. 4:35–38) _____

(4:30–32) _____

_____

(4:33–34) _____

_____

(4:35–41) _____

His physical healing, we must...

(5:1:20) _____

(5:25–34) _____

(5:21–24, 35–43) _____

His miracles, we must...

(6:1–6) _____

(6:7–13) _____

_____

(6:14–29) _____

(6:30–44) _____

_____

_____

(6:45–46) _____

(6:47–52) _____

(6:53–56) _____

_____

His commandments, we must...

(7:1–8) _____

(7:9–13) _____

(7:14–23) _____

_____

_____

(7:24–30) _____

(7:31–37) _____

_____

His leadership, we must…

(8:1–10) _____

_____

(8:11–21) _____

_____

_____

(8:22–26) _____

_____

_____

(8:27–30) _____

(8:31–33) _____

(8:34–38) _____

_____

His power, we must…

(9:1) _____

(9:2–13) _____

(9:14–29 _____

_____

(9:30–32) _____

_____

(9:33–37) _____

_____

(9:38–41) _____

(9:42–48) _____

_____

_____

(9:49–50) _____

BE GRATEFUL - WE SHOULD NOT BE PRESUMPTUOUS ABOUT...

His authority...

(11:1–10) _____

(11:11–26) _____

(11:27–33) _____

His provision for His people...

(12:1–12) _____

(12:13–17) _____

(12:18–27) _____

(12:28–37) _____

(12:38–44) _____

the future and...

(13:1–2) _____

(13:3–8) _____

_____

_____

(13:9–13) _____

(13:14–23) _____

_____

(13:24–27) _____

(13:28–32) _____

_____

(13:33–37) _____

MODELING SERVANT-LIKE HUMILITY

Who is not modeling "being humble in position and serving"? (14)

Chief priests/scribes/elders/council/officers – are seeking how to seize Jesus by stealth and kill Him (1-2); are glad that Judas wants to betray Jesus and offer Judas money to do so (10-11); send a crowd to seize Jesus (43-46, 53); and try to obtain false testimony against Jesus, accuse Him of blasphemy, condemned Him to be deserving of death, and spit on Him and beat Him (55-65)

Judas – goes to the chief priests to betray Jesus in exchange for money (10-11), is identified by Jesus as His betrayer (17-21, and betrays Jesus with a kiss (41-46)

Disciples – are indignant with and scold the woman who anoints Jesus (3-5), do not stay awake and keep watch (32-42), and leave Jesus and flee (50-52)

Peter – boasts that he will not fall away (29-31), cuts off the ear of the high priest's slave (47), follows Jesus at a distance and warms himself by the fire (54), and denies Jesus three times and weeps (66-72)

Who is modeling "being humble in position and serving"? (14)

Jesus – allows the woman to anoint His body (3-9), provides a place for He and His disciples to eat the Passover (12-16), provides a symbolic remembrance of His sacrifice for His disciples (22-25), prays to the Father (35-36, 39, 41), submits to the fulfillment of prophecy (48-49), does not respond to the false accusations against Him (60-61a), and does respond affirmatively to the question about His being the Christ (61b-62)

Who is not modeling "being thankful for provision and serving"? (15)

Chief priests/elders/scribes/council – deliver Jesus to Pilate because of envy (1, 10), accuse Jesus falsely (3), stir up the crowd to release Barabbas instead of Jesus (11), and mock Jesus on the cross (31-32a)

Pilate – chooses to please the crowd by having Jesus scourged and by handing Him over to be crucified (4-15)

The crowd – asks Pilate to release Barabbas and to crucify Jesus (8-14) and hurls abuse at Jesus on the cross (29-30)

The soldiers – mock Jesus (16-20), force a passerby to bear Jesus' cross (21), crucify Jesus and cast lots for His garments (22-26), and crucify two robbers with Him (27)

Robbers crucified with Jesus – insult Jesus (32b)

Who is modeling "being thankful for provision and serving"? (15)

Jesus – responds to Pilate as to who He is (2) and allows Himself to be scourged and crucified (15-39, Psalm 22)

The "women" – look on from a distance (40-41) and look on to see where Jesus is buried (47)

Joseph of Arimathea – asks Pilate for Jesus' body, wraps Him in a linen cloth, lays Him in a tomb, and rolls a stone against the entrance (42-46)

Who is not modeling "being grateful for status and serving"? (16)

Mary, Mary, and Salome do not tell the disciples what they saw at the tomb (7-8)

The disciples – do not listen to Mary Magdalene or the "two walking" about their seeing Jesus (9-14)

Who is modeling "being grateful for status and serving"? (16)

Mary, Mary, and Salome – go to the sepulcher (1-6)

Mary Magdalene – tells the disciples that Jesus is alive (9-11)

The "two walking" – tell the disciples that they have seen Jesus (12-13)

The disciples – respond to Jesus' directions (15-20)

Appendix VIII—B
The Gospel of John
Jesus-focused Spirituality

JESUS-FOCUSED SPIRITUALLY –THE GOSPEL OF JOHN

MAJOR THEMES

Think supernaturally past our...

    selves. (3:1–2a)

    reason. (3:2b-7)

    will. (3:8–12)

"See" and believe in Jesus, and we will...

    have eternal life. (3:13–16)

    be saved. (3:17)

    not be judged. (3:18–20)

    practice truth and come to the Light. (3:21)

Focus on Jesus by...

    hearing His voice so that our joy will be made full. (3:22–29)

    increasing Jesus and decreasing self. (3:30)

    listening to His words which are truth. (3:31–34)

    trusting in Him to eternal life (3:35–36)

OUT OF THE BOX - "THINK SUPERNATURALLY"

about...

the "Word" as being God and as creative activity. (1:1–3)

the life in the Word being the "Light of men." (1:4)

the Light which enlightens every man and which provides opportunity for people who believe in the Light to become the children of God by God's will. (1:5–13)

the Word becoming flesh and living among us in the form of Jesus Christ, the Son of God, through whom grace and truth are realized. (1:14–18)

the testimony of John the Baptist that Jesus is the Lamb of God who takes away the sins of the world, the One upon whom the Holy Spirit remains, the One who baptizes with the Holy Spirit, and the One who is the Son of God. (1:19–34, Isaiah 40:3)

following, and bringing others to follow, Jesus/the Lamb of God/Messiah/ Son of God/King of Israel/Son of Man as Andrew, Philip, Peter, and especially as Nathaniel did. (1:35–51)

and believe...

in Jesus because of His miracles, as the disciples did. (2:1–11)

in the scripture, the word Jesus had spoken, and that Jesus was raised from the dead, as a sign of His authority. (2:12–22)

in His name as the Christ and the Son of God from observing the signs that He is doing. (2:23–25)

LET THERE BE LIGHT - "SEE" JESUS AND BELIEVE THAT HE IS THE...

sum of all of the following which includes the...

Lord. (4:1–2)

source of the Holy Spirit springing up to eternal life. (4:3–15)

Christ who teaches that we must worship the Father supernaturally and genuinely. (4:16–30)

the One sent by God, the Father, who does the will of the Father and accomplishes the Father's work. (4:31–38)

Savior of the world revealed through His Word. (4:39–42)

prophet who draws people to himself through His miracles. (4:43–45)

the miraculous healer who heals people even at the point of death. (4:46–54)

One sent from God the Father and...

is equal with God the Father. (5:1–18)

has been given the power of life and all power of "judgment" by the Father.(5:19–23)

has life in himself and has been given authority by the Father to execute judgment. (5:24–29)

His judgment is just because He seeks the will of the Father. (5:30) the testimony concerning His being sent by God the Father comes from John the Baptist, from the works of Jesus, from God the Father Himself, and through the writing of Moses. (5:31–47)

"Bread of Life" and that…

He miraculously and abundantly provides food for the hungry people. (6:1–15; Ex. 23:15, Lev. 23:5–8, Num. 28:16–25, Deut. 16:1–8)

He miraculously walks on the water and delivers the disciples from a a storm at sea. (6:16–21)

He miraculously travels from one place to another. (6:22–25)

He gives the food that endures to eternal life. (6:26–40)

He is the living bread that comes down from heaven, and anyone who eats of this bread will live forever; this bread is His flesh which He will give for the life of the world. (6:41–51)

whoever eats His flesh and drinks His blood has eternal life. (6:52–59) those who believe that Jesus is the Bread of Life have the Holy Spirit, believe that His words are spirit and life, and have been chosen by God the Father. (6:60–65)

some disciples reject Jesus, some follow, one declares that Jesus is the Holy One of God, and one betrays Him. (6:66–70)

source of the "Living Water" and that…

He is selective in showing His power. (7:1–13; Lev.23:39–44; Feast of the Booths)

His powerful teaching is not His own but from God the Father and for the Father's glory. (7:14–24)

His powerful miracles are from the Father. (7:25–31)

those who reject Jesus will not go to heaven (7:32–36)

those who believe in Jesus will receive the Holy Spirit. (7:37–39; Lev. 23:39–44, Deut. 16:13–15, Zech. 14:16–19, Acts 2)

He is accepted by some and rejected by others. (7:40–53)

"Light of the World" (truth about sin) and that …

He chides those who condemn a sinner and instructs a sinner (destructive) to sin no more (restorative). (8:1–11)

those who follow Him will not walk in darkness but will have the Light of Life. (8:12–20; Psa. 62:11–12, Rom. 2:1–9)

unless we believe that He is from the Father, we will die in our sins and will not receive the truth. (8:21–30)

if we continue in His Word, we will know the truth and the truth will set us free (from our sins). (8:31–33)

we are in slavery to our sin; and if He frees us from our sin, we are free indeed, forever! (8:34–38)

those that reject Him cannot hear His Word (the truth) and are of their father the Devil (the father of lies). (8:39–47)

He is God (I AM); those who keep His Word will never see death! (8:48–59)

"Light of the World" (truth about healing) and that…

> He miraculously heals the man blind "from birth" on the Sabbath. (9:1–12, Deut. 28:45–46))

> the Pharisees say that Jesus is not from God because He healed on the Sabbath; others still wonder about His signs. (9:13–17)

> the Pharisees do not believe the blind man's testimony because they say that he was born in sin. (9:18–34)

> the blind man that is healed believes in Jesus; the Pharisees do not believe and will remain in their sin because of their spiritual blindness. (9:35–41)

"Door of the Sheep/the Good Shepherd" and that…

> anyone who enters the sheep fold through Him is saved. (10:1–10)

> He lays down His life for the sheep. (10:11–13)

> He knows His sheep and they know Him. (10:14–21)

> He gives His sheep eternal life, and no one can take them away from Him or the Father because Jesus and the Father are one. (10:22–30; Feast of Dedication)

> the Jews reject Jesus because they say that He is blaspheming by saying "the Father and I are one." (10:31–39; Psa. 82:6)

> many believe in Him because everything that John the Baptist said about Him is true. (10:40–42)

"Resurrection and the Life" and that...

> anyone who believes that Jesus is the Christ, the Son of God, will live forever! (11:1–27)

> He raises Lazarus from the dead, in the midst of unbelief. (11:28–44)

> some of the Jews believe in Jesus because they saw Him raise Lazarus from the dead and some we do not know about. (11:45–46)

> the chief priests and Pharisees reject Jesus, plan to kill Him, and threaten His followers because they want to keep their place and their nation. (11:47–59)

King and that...

> He is anointed in recognition that He is the king (12:1–8)

> the chief priests plan to kill Lazarus because many are seeing him as a living testimony and believing in Jesus as the king. (12:9–11; Ps. 118:26)

> His entry into Jerusalem as a king fulfills prophecy, and the testimony of those who saw Lazarus resurrected causes many to follow Him.
> (12:12–19; Zech. 9:9)

> anyone who serves Jesus (the king) must "follow" Him. (12:20–26)

> the Father glorifies His name through Jesus, the Jews reject Jesus, and some who believe are intimidated by the spiritual leaders (12:27–43) (Isa. 53:1, Isa. 6:10)

whoever sees Jesus, sees God the Father; whatever Jesus speaks is what the Father is telling Him; and whoever believes in Jesus will not remain in darkness. (12:44–50)

PUT ON THE BLINDERS - FOCUS ON JESUS AS THE...

"Master washing His disciples' feet" and...

> understand that one who is cleansed by Jesus needs only to have His *feet* washed by Jesus. (13:1–11; I John 1:9)

> wash each other's feet (of sin). (13:12–17)

> wash each others' feet even though we might be rejected or betrayed. (13:18–30)

> receive a new commandment that we love one another, as Jesus loved His disciples. (13:31–35)

> examine ourselves as to whether we are really ready to follow Jesus. (13:36–38)

"Way, the Truth, and the Life"; and...

> the only way to the Father. (14:1–7)

> understand that the words He says and the works He does are done by the the Father who abides in Him; ask Jesus anything in His name, and He will do it! (14:8–14)

> love Him and keep His commandments—He will send us the Holy Spirit. (14:15–17)

> love Him and keep His commandments—He will disclose Himself to us. (14:18–24)

> know that the Holy Spirit will teach us *all* things, and Jesus will give us *His* peace. (14:25–31)

"True Vine" and...

stay connected—abide in Him and He in us, ask Him and it will be done for us, bear much fruit, glorify the Father, prove to be Jesus' disciples, glorify the Father, abide in His love, keep His commandments, and our joy will be made full! (15:1–11)

know that we are Jesus' friends if we keep His commandments, that Jesus chose us and appointed us to bear fruit, and that He commands us to love one another! (15:12–17)

know that the world will hate us for His name's sake. (15:18–25)

know that when the Holy Spirit is sent to us, He will testify about Jesus; and we will testify about Jesus, also. (15:26–27)

Sender of the Holy Spirit...

who convicts the world of sin because of their unbelief in Jesus, of righteousness because Jesus is with the Father, and of judgment because Satan has been judged. (16:1–11)

who guides us all into all truth spoken from Jesus. (and the Father). (16:12–15)

who will give us whatever we ask the Father in Jesus name which will make our joy full. (16:16–28)

who will remind us that we can have peace in the world because Jesus has overcome the world! (16:29–33)

Great Unifier, praying to the Father that the Father would…

> glorify Him together with the Father. (17:1–5)

> sanctify believers in truth (God's Word) because Jesus has sent them into the world. (17:6–19; Psa. 41:9)

> perfect believers in unity so that the world will know that the Father sent Jesus and loves them, just as the Father loves Jesus. (17:20–24)

> cause believers to respond to the work of Jesus so that the Father's love for Jesus may be in believers and that Jesus, Himself, may be in believers. (17:25–26)

MODELING JESUS-FOCUSED SPIRITUALITY

Who is not modeling "thinking supernaturally? (18)

Judas—cannot think supernaturally past *himself* to "see" Jesus and betrays Jesus at night coming with a detachment of soldiers (vv. 1–3,5)

Peter—cannot think supernaturally past his *reason* to "see Jesus as he attempts to stop the capture of Jesus (v. 10), and cannot think past *himself* and his *will* to "see" Jesus as he denies Jesus three times (vv. 15–18, 25–27).

Annas, Caiaphas, Pilate, the Roman cohort, officers from the chief priests, the Pharisees, and the Jews—cannot think supernaturally past *themselves* and their *wills* as they deal with Jesus in a politically expedient manner (vv. 3–14, 19–24, 28–40)

Who is modeling "thinking supernaturally? (18)

Jesus—knows all the things that are coming upon Him (v. 4), fulfills scripture (vv. 8–9), tells Peter to put up his sword so that He can drink the cup that the Father has given Him (v. 11), and explains to Pilate that He is a king of a supernatural kingdom (vv. 33–37)

Who is not modeling "seeing" Jesus? (19)

Chief priests and officers—want Jesus to be crucified because they say that He made Himself out to be the Son of God (vv. 6–7), threaten Pilate with disloyalty to Caesar if he does not crucify Jesus (v. 12b), state that they have no other king but Caesar (v. 15), and argue about the title of king that Pilate puts on the cross (v. 21)

Pilate—finds no guilt in Jesus (vv. 4–6), makes an effort to release Him (vv. 8–12a), calls Him a king (vv. 13–15), and writes an inscription, "Jesus of Nazareth the King of the Jews," on Jesus' cross (vv. 19–22); *but* orders Jesus to be scourged (v. 1) and hands Him over, for politically expedient reasons, to be crucified (vv. 14–18)

Soldiers—abuse and mock Jesus (vv. 2–3) and cast lots for His garments (vv. 23–24)

Who is modeling "seeing Jesus?" (19)

"The disciple whom He loved"—takes Jesus' mother into his own household in response to Jesus' instructions from the cross (vv. 25–27)

Jesus—knowing that all things had been accomplished to fulfill scripture (and thereby making it easier for people to "see" Him), died (vv. 28–37)

Joseph of Arimathea—risks everything to ask Pilate for Jesus' body (v. 38) and, along with Nicodemus, places Jesus' body in a tomb (vv. 41–42)

Nicodemus—risks everything to bring myrrh and aloes for Jesus' body (v. 39) and, along with Joseph of Arimathea, places Jesus' body in a tomb (vv. 41–42)

Who is not modeling "believing" in Jesus? (20)

Mary—does not believe that Jesus has risen from the dead and tells Peter and John that "they" have taken Jesus' body out of the tomb and taken Him somewhere (vv. 1–2) and tells the two angels (vv. 11–13) and Jesus (vv. 14–15) the same thing

Peter—saw the grave clothes but there is no indication from John's writing that he believes (vv. 3–7)

the Disciples—do not believe yet because they did not understand the Scripture (vv. 9–10)

Thomas—does not believe and states that he will not believe until he see the imprint of nails in Jesus' hands, places his hand in the nail holes, and places his hand in the wound in His side (vv. 24–25)

Who is modeling "believing in Jesus? (20)

John—believes after seeing the grave clothes in the empty tomb (v. 8)

Mary—believes when Jesus speaks to her (vv. 16–18)

Disciples—believe when Jesus appears in their midst and shows them His wounds.
(vv. 19–23)

Thomas—believes when invited by Jesus to touch His wounds (vv. 26–29)

Us—John wrote these things that we might believe that Jesus is the Christ, the Son of God, and that by believing we may have life in His name (vv. 30–31)

Who is not modeling "focused on Jesus?" (21)

the Disciples—after seeing Jesus twice after His resurrection, focus back on fishing (vv. 1–3); because their focus is so much on fishing, do not recognize Jesus when He speaks to them (4–5); and recognize Jesus only after He does a miracle and feeds them some breakfast (vv. 6–14)

Peter—questioned by Jesus about the focus of his love (vv. 15–18), and is instructed by Jesus not to be focused on anyone else's ministry but to be focused only on *his* following Jesus (vv. 19–23)

Who is modeling "focused on Jesus?" (21)

John (the author)—testifies about the truth of his focus (v. 24) and the sufficiency of the detail on which *we* can focus (v. 25)

•

JESUS-FOCUSED SPIRITUALITY—THE GOSPEL OF JOHN
MAJOR THEMES

Think supernaturally past our…

(3:1–2a) _____

(3:2b-7) _____

(3:8–12) _____

"See" and believe in Jesus, and we will…

(3:12–16) _____

(3:17) _____

(3:18–20) _____

(3:21) _____

Focus on Jesus by…

(3:22–29) _____

(3:30) _____

(3:31–34) _____

(3:35–36) _____

OUT OF THE BOX—"THINK SUPERNATURALLY"

about…

(1:1–3) _____

(1:4) _____

(1:5–13) _____

_____

_____

(1:14–18) _____

_____

_____

(1:19–34) _____

_____

_____

_____

(1:35–51) _____

_____

_____

_____

_____

and believe…

    (2:1–11)   _____

    (2:12–22)   _____

                _____

    (2:23–25)   _____

LET THERE BE LIGHT - "SEE" JESUS AND BELIEVE THAT HE IS THE...

sum of all of the following which includes the...

(4:1–2) _____

(4:3–15) _____

(4:16–30) _____

_____

(4:31–38) _____

_____

_____

(4:39–42) _____

(4:43–45) _____

_____

(4:46–54) _____

_____

One sent by God the Father and...

(5:1–18) _____

(5:19–23) _____

_____

(5:24–29) _____

_____

_____

(5:30) _____

_____

(5:31–47) _____

_____

"Bread of Life" and that...

(6:1–15) _____

_____

(6:16–21) _____

_____

(6:21–25) _____

(6:26–40) _____

(6:41–51) _____

_____

_____

_____

(6:52–59) _____

_____

(6:60–65) _____

_____

_____

_____

(6:66–70) _____

_____

_____

_____

source of the "Living Water" and that...

(7:1–13) _____

(7:14–24) _____

_____

_____

(7:25–31) _____

(7:32–36) _____

(7:37–39) _____

_____

_____

(7:40–53)   _____

"Light of the World" (truth about sin) and that…

(8:1–11)   _____

_____

_____

(8:12–20)   _____

_____

(8:21–30)   _____

_____

_____

(8:31–33)   _____

_____

(8:34–38)   _____

_____

_____

(8:39–47)   _____

_____

_____

(8:48–59) _____

_____

"Light of the World" (truth about healing) and that…

(9:1–12) _____

_____

(9:13–17) _____

_____

_____

(9:18–34) _____

_____

_____

(9:35–41) _____

_____

_____

_____

"Door of the Sheep/the Good Shepherd" and that…

(10:1–10) _____

_____

(10:11–13) _____

(10:14–21) _____

(10:22–30) _____

_____

_____

_____

(10:31–39) _____

_____

_____

(10:40–42) _____

_____

"Resurrection and the Life" and that…

(11:1–27) _____

_____

(11:28–44) _____

(11:45–46) _____

_____

_____

_____

(11:47–59) _____

_____

_____

_____

King and that…

(12:1–8) _____

(12:9–11) _____

_____

_____

_____

(12:12–19) _____

_____

_____

_____

(12:20–26) _____

_____

(12:27–43) _____

_____

_____

_____

(12:44–50) _____

_____

_____

_____

PUT ON THE BLINDERS - FOCUS ON JESUS AS THE...

"Master washing His disciples' feet" and...

(13:1–11) _____

_____

_____

(13:12–17) _____

(13:18–30) _____

_____

(13:31–35) _____

_____

_____

(13:36–38) _____

_____

"Way, the Truth, and the Life"; and...

(14:1–7) _____

(14:8–14) _____

_____

_____

_____

(14:15–17) _____

_____

(14:18–24) _____

_____

(14:25–31) _____

_____

"True Vine" and…

(15:1–11) _____

_____

_____

_____

_____

_____

(15:12–17) _____

_____

_____

_____

(15:18–25) _____

_____

(15:26–27) _____

_____

_____

Sender of the Holy Spirit…

(16:1–11) _____

_____

_____

_____

_____

(16:12–15) _____

(16:16–28) _____

_____

(16:29–33) _____

_____

_____

Great Unifier, praying to the Father that the Father would…

(17:1–5) _____

(17:6–19) _____

_____

_____

(17:20–24) _____

_____

_____

_____

(17:25–26) _____

_____

_____

_____

MODELING JESUS-FOCUSED SPIRITUALITY

Who is not modeling "thinking supernaturally? (18)

Judas—cannot think supernaturally past *himself* to "see" Jesus and betrays Jesus at night coming with a detachment of soldiers (vv. 1–3,5)

Peter—cannot think supernaturally past his *reason* to "see" Jesus as he attempts to stop the capture of Jesus (v. 10), and cannot think past *himself* and his *will* to "see" Jesus as he denies Jesus three times (vv. 15–18, 25–27).

Annas, Caiaphas, Pilate, the Roman cohort, officers from the chief priests, the Pharisees, and the Jews—cannot think supernaturally past *themselves* and their *wills* as they deal with Jesus in a politically expedient manner (vv. 3–14, 19–24, 28–40)

Who is modeling "thinking supernaturally? (18)

Jesus—knows all the things that are coming upon Him (v. 4), fulfills scripture (vv. 8–9), tells Peter to put up his sword so that He can drink the cup that the Father has given Him (v. 11), and explains to Pilate that He is a king of a supernatural kingdom (vv. 33–37)

Who is not modeling "seeing" Jesus? (19)

Chief priests and officers—want Jesus to be crucified because they say that He made Himself out to be the Son of God (vv. 6–7), threaten Pilate with disloyalty to Caesar if he does not crucify Jesus (v. 12b), state that they have no other king but Caesar (v. 15), and argue about the title of king that Pilate puts on the cross (v. 21)

Pilate—finds no guilt in Jesus (vv. 4–6), makes an effort to release Him (vv. 8–12a), calls Him a king (vv. 13–15), and writes an inscription, "Jesus of Nazareth the King of the Jews," on Jesus' cross (vv. 19–22); *but* orders Jesus to be scourged (v. 1) and hands Him over, for politically expedient reasons, to be crucified (vv. 14–18)

Soldiers—abuse and mock Jesus (vv. 2–3) and cast lots for His garments (vv. 23–24)

Who is modeling "seeing Jesus?" (19)

"The disciple whom He loved"—takes Jesus' mother into his own household in response to Jesus' instructions from the cross (vv. 25–27)

Jesus—knowing that all things had been accomplished to fulfill scripture (and thereby making it easier for people to "see" Him), died (vv. 28–37)

Joseph of Arimathea—risks everything to ask Pilate for Jesus' body (v. 38) and, along with Nicodemus, places Jesus' body in a tomb (vv. 41–42)

Nicodemus—risks everything to bring myrrh and aloes for Jesus' body (v. 39) and, along with Joseph of Arimathea, places Jesus' body in a tomb (vv. 41–42)

Who is not modeling "believing" in Jesus? (20)

Mary—does not believe that Jesus has risen from the dead and tells Peter and John that "they" have taken Jesus' body out of the tomb and taken Him somewhere (vv. 1–2) and tells the two angels (vv. 11–13) and Jesus (vv. 14–15) the same thing

Peter—saw the grave clothes but there is no indication from John's writing that he believes (vv. 3–7)

the Disciples—do not believe yet because they did not understand the Scripture (vv. 9–10)

Thomas—does not believe and states that he will not believe until he see the imprint of nails in Jesus' hands, places his hand in the nail holes, and places his hand in the wound in His side (vv. 24–25)

Who is modeling "believing in Jesus? (20)

John—believes after seeing the grave clothes in the empty tomb (v. 8)

Mary—believes when Jesus speaks to her (vv. 16–18)

Disciples—believe when Jesus appears in their midst and shows them His wounds.
(vv. 19–23)

Thomas—believes when invited by Jesus to touch His wounds (vv. 26–29)

Us—John wrote these things that we might believe that Jesus is the Christ, the Son of God, and that by believing we may have life in His name (vv. 30–31)

Who is not modeling "focused on Jesus?" (21)

the Disciples—after seeing Jesus twice after His resurrection, focus back on fishing (vv. 1–3); because their focus is so much on fishing, do not recognize Jesus when He speaks to them (4–5); and recognize Jesus only after He does a miracle and feeds them some breakfast (vv. 6–14)

Peter—questioned by Jesus about the focus of his love (vv. 15–18), and is instructed by Jesus not to be focused on anyone else's ministry but to be focused only on *his* following Jesus (vv. 19–23)

Who is modeling "focused on Jesus?" (21)

John (the author)—testifies about the truth of his focus (v. 24) and the sufficiency of the detail on which *we* can focus (v. 25)

APPENDIX VIII – C
THE GOSPEL OF LUKE
STEADFAST FAITHFULNESS

STEADFAST FAITHFULNESS – THE GOSPEL OF LUKE

MAJOR THEMES

The "right kind of faith" relies on the Word of God, perseveres when circumstances hinder, and has a purpose to minister to the needy and preach the Gospel…

as exhibited by the disciples and as not exhibited by Herod who is only curious about Jesus. (9:1-10)

as not exhibited by the disciples who miss the opportunity to rely on the power of Jesus to minister to the needy. (9:11-17)

as not exhibited by the disciples who attempt to rely on their own power to drive out a demon. (9:37-43a)

as not exhibited by the disciples who attempt to abuse the power of Jesus. (9:51-56)

A forbearance to endure the suffering that accompanies the sacrifice is…

prophesied by Jesus about himself and required of all those who wish to follow Jesus. (9:18-27)

prophesied by Jesus as the "low" to follow the "high". (9:43b-45)

difficult because of physical discomfort, loss of respect, and social unacceptability to those that follow Jesus (9:57-61).

Staying the course by...

listening to Jesus alone. (9:28-36)

being humble. (9:46-50)

keeping "eyes front". (9:62)

THE "RIGHT KIND OF FAITH"

Who is not exhibiting the "right kind of faith"? (1)

Zacharias – does not rely on the Word of God in his lack of response to the angel of God (1:8-20)

Who is exhibiting the "right kind of faith"? (1)

Elizabeth – relies on the Word of God by being righteous and by walking blamelessly in the commands of the Lord (1:1-7), perseveres by keeping to herself in her pregnancy (1:24-25), perseveres and is blessed by Mary's presence (1:39-45), perseveres and gives birth to a son (1:57-58), and relies on the Word of God by praising God and quoting Scripture (1:46-56)

Mary – relies on the Word of God by responding to the angel, Gabriel, that she is "the bond slave of the Lord" and that "may it be done according to your word" (1:26-38), perseveres by traveling to Elizabeth's house while pregnant (1:39-45), relies on the Word of God by praising God and quoting Scripture (1:46-56)

Zacharias – relies on the Word of God by being righteous and by walking blamelessly in all the commands of the Lord (1:1-7), relies on the Word of God by naming his son "John" and praising the Lord quoting Scripture (1:62-79)

John the Baptist – perseveres by growing, becoming strong in spirit, and living in the desert (1:80)

Who is not exhibiting the "right kind of faith"? (2)

No one

Who is exhibiting the "right kind of faith"? (2)

Joseph – perseveres by traveling with his pregnant wife from Nazareth to Bethlehem where there was little shelter (2:1-7; relies on the Word of God by following the law of Moses concerning purification, presenting Jesus to the Lord in Jerusalem, and making a sacrifice to the Lord (2:22-24, 39), perseveres by returning to Nazareth (2:39)

Mary – perseveres by traveling with her husband, while pregnant, from Nazareth to Bethlehem (2:1-7), relies on God's Word by treasuring in her heart all the things told to her by the shepherds (2:19), relies on the Word of God by naming her son "Jesus" (2:21), relies on the Word of God by following the law of Moses concerning purification, presenting Jesus to the Lord in Jerusalem, and making a sacrifice to the Lord (2:22-24, 39), and relies on God's Word by treasuring in her heart "all these things" (2:51b)

shepherds – rely on the Word of God by quickly responding to the words of the angel of God and by going into Bethlehem to find Jesus (8:22)

Simeon – relies on the Word of God by being righteous and devout, looking for the Messiah, having the Holy Spirit upon him (2:25-26) and proclaiming that Jesus' ministry is a light of revelation to the Gentiles and the glory of God's people, Israel (2:27-32)

Anna – relies on the Word of God, as a widow, serving in the temple day and night with fasting and prayers (2:36-37) and ministers to those around her by telling them that Jesus is the Messiah (2:38)

Jesus – relies on the Word of God by growing in wisdom with the grace of God upon Him (2:40), by listening and questioning the teachers in the temple (2:41-47), by understanding His mission and being in subjection to His parents (2:48-51), and by increasing in wisdom and stature and being in favor with God and men (2:52)

AN EXAMINE-YOURSELF CHECKLIST – THE "RIGHT KIND" OF FAITH…

starts with…

a repentant attitude. (3:1-6)   ____

repentant behavior. (3:7-14)   ____

receiving the Christ (Son of God), Jesus. (3:15-38)   ____

is characterized by…

reliance on the Word of God in response
to temptation. (4:1-14)   ____

perseverance in doing and sharing the Word
even when circumstances hinder. (4:15-30)   ____

a purpose to minister to the needy with authority
and to teach the Word with authority. (4:31-44)   ____

by God's grace…

is increased by miracles of power and compassion. (5:1-15)____

is refreshed in private prayer. (4:42; 5:16; 6:12)   ____

results in the forgiveness of sin. (5:17-26, Lev. 14:2-32)   ____

understands that Jesus has the repentance of the sick
and sinners as the focus of His ministry. (5:27-32)   ____

knows that Jesus is the personification of the
Day of Atonement. (5:33-35)   ____

is single in its focus on Jesus (the new faith) and not the accomplishment of the Law (the old faith). (5:36-39)   ____

differs from the "old faith" in its…

permission to override the misinterpreted rigidity of the Law in order to minister to those in need. (6:1-11)   ____

recognition that the "call to be sent"
is from Jesus. (6:12-16)   ____

realization that the miracles of Jesus are available for both Jews and Gentiles. (6:17-19)   ____

requirement to have a faithful heart attitude as described by Jesus. (6:20-45)   ____

being built on an obedient foundation of acting upon the "faithful attitude". (6:46-49)   ____

focuses on Jesus…

and His authority (power). (7:1-10)   ____

and His compassion (love). (7:11-17)   ____

as the Messiah. (7:18-23, Isa. 61:1))   ____

and is received by those who are prepared. (7:24-29) (but is rejected by those who prefer to "play games" with the truth) (7:30-35)   ____

and has a passion for Him because of the forgiveness of our sins. (7:36-50)   ____ is responsive by…

      supporting others in ministry. (8:1-3)   ____

      hearing the Word of God in an honest and good heart, holding it fast, and bearing fruit with perseverance. (8:4-15)   ____

      sharing with others what we hear from the Word of God (8:16-18)   ____

      being faithful to hear the Word of God and do it. (8:19-21)   ____

      relying on the power and love of Jesus in the midst of the "storms". (8:22-25)   ____

      coming to Jesus, being healed by Him and telling others what great things Jesus does for us. (8:26-39)   ____

      reaching out to touch Jesus in times when personal healing is needed   ____

      and telling others what great things Jesus does for us. (8:43-48)   ____

      asking Jesus for help, not being afraid, and believing that faith in Jesus results in resurrection. (8:40-42; 49-56)   ____

REJECTION ADVICE – ENDURING THE "SUFFERING" THAT ACCOMPANIES THE SACRIFICE REQUIRES AN UNDERSTANDING THAT...

our suffering may come from...

> evil and that we speak and walk away if not received, that Jesus has defeated Satan, that we have been given power over wickedness, that we will not be injured (by the spirits), that our names are recorded in heaven, and that the Father reveals Himself to us through Jesus. (10:1-24)

> the world and that we must risk possible loss in order to minister to the sick and needy. (10:25-37)

> friends, family, fellow believers, etc., and that we need to keep focused on what Jesus has called us to do. (10:38-42)

opposition to our ministry may come from...

> ourselves and necessitates persistent prayer for God's provision through the Holy Spirit. (11:1-13)

> skeptics (followers of Satan and prideful people) who respond in an unbelieving way to our good works done in the power of the Holy Spirit. (11:14-36)

> false teachers who are hostile to our obedience and truthfulness about God. (11:37-54)

we must not be distracted by the "world" but we must...

> fear God, not man. (12:1-12)

> be concerned with spiritual, not temporal, matters. (12:13-34)

be doing, faithfully, the work to which the Lord has called us and watching for His return. (12:35-59)

the Kingdom of God will...

not look like the Israel of Jesus' time – unrepentant, unproductive, and hypocritical. (13:1-17)

start small but grow large; grow quietly but end fully. (13:18-21)

consist of those who are faithful and will be withheld from Jerusalem until Jesus comes to judge it. (13:22-35)

concerning service to others we must...

be compelled to do so no matter what suffering the circumstances may cause. (14:1-6)

be humble. (14:7-11)

not be seeking service in return but unconditionally serving the needy. (14:12-14)

know that our service may be rejected by those who feel they are not in need; then we must go and serve the needy. (14:15-24)

love Jesus the most and know that following Jesus will be costly – consider the cost, be prepared to give up everything, and do not lose your purpose and resolve. (14:25-35)

concerning the lost that we must...

seek them and celebrate those that are found, as part of the whole (15:1-10) be patient in looking for them and celebrate the repentance of a sinner even if we think it is unfair (15:11-32)

our stewardship must be wise in the use of…

money in order to prepare for our use of the spiritual riches. (16:1-13)

the riches of the Old Testament law and the prophets by connecting it to the preaching of the "Kingdom of God". (16:13-31)

FINISH WELL – STAY THE COURSE BY...

humbly...

having faith to do the difficult things such as rebuking our brother when he sins and forgiving him when he repents. (17:1-6)

not expecting special attention for doing things that God has commanded us to do. (17:7-10)

being grateful and giving glory to God for His work in our life. (17:11-19)

realizing that the Kingdom of God is in our midst, even in us. (17:20-21)

not chasing after signs but <u>losing</u> our <u>lives</u> in <u>Jesus</u>! (17:22-37)

persisting in...

prayer resulting in justice. (18:1-8)

humility resulting in our...

justification and exultation. (18:9-14)

entrance into the Kingdom of God. (18:15-17)

treasure in heaven. (18:18-27)

rewards in this life and eternal life. (18:28-30)

understanding the meaning of Jesus' death and resurrection. (18:31-34)

faith and healing. (18:35-43)

ministry to others, no matter who they are. (19:1-10)

the investment of our God-given gifts (the gospel message and spiritual gifts).
(19:11-27)

obedience and the proclamation that Jesus is the King! (19:28-40)

pursuing the things of peace in our relationship with God, receiving Jesus, and thereby avoiding the fate of Jerusalem. (19:41-48)

bewaring of false teachers who question the authority of Jesus over...

the things that He has done. (20:1-8)

Israel. ((20:9-19)

discerning what is right. (20:20-26)

the afterlife. ((20:27-40)

the Kingdom of God – Jesus is the Christ. (20:41-44)

the right to all the glory! (20:45-47)

being aware of...

the need to give humbly out of our need knowing that everything belongs to the Lord. (21:1-4)

not being misled by false messiahs nor being terrified by wars, etc. (21:5-11) the opportunity persecution provides for testimony and the gain that will accompany our endurance. (21:12-19)

the prophecy. (21:20-33)

the need to be on guard, alert and praying so that we have strength to "escape all these things" and stand before the Son of Man. (21:34-36)

the need to listen to Jesus! (21:37-38)

MODELING STEADFAST FAITHFULNESS

Who is not modeling the "right kind of faith"? (22)

Chief priests, teachers of the law, council of elders – seek how to put Jesus to death (2), bribe Judas (5), arrest Jesus like a robber (52-53), take Jesus to the Council chamber and question Him (66-71)

Guards – mock Jesus and beat Jesus (63-64), say many blasphemous things against Him (65)

Judas – possessed by Satan (3), consents to betray Jesus for money (4-6), betrays Jesus with a kiss (47-48)

Disciples – discuss about who is to betray Jesus (21-23), have a dispute among themselves about who is the greatest (24), sleep from sorrow instead of praying and watching (39-40, 45-46), cut off the ear of the slave of the high priest (49-50)

Peter – denies Jesus three times and weeps bitterly (54-62)

Who is modeling the "right kind of faith"? (22)

Jesus – makes provision for the Passover for His disciples (7-13), instructs His disciples about remembering Him and His sacrifice through the eating of the bread and drinking from the cup (14-20), teaches His disciples about the priority of serving (25-27), promises the disciples that they will sit at His table in His kingdom and sit on thrones judging the twelve tribes of Israel (28-30), tells Peter that He will pray for him and that he will deny Him three times (31-34), warns His disciples to be prepared to protect themselves in His absence (35-38) prays to the father about the events about to happen and submits to the Father's will (41-44), heals the slave's ear (51), perseveres through the abuse of the men holding Him (63-65), states to the Council of Elders that from now on He will be seated at the right hand of the power of God and that He is the Son of God, knowing that it would result in His death (67-70)

Who is not modeling "enduring the suffering"? (23)

Pilate – acts in a manner that is politically expedient in order not to "suffer" by first sending Jesus to Herod and then giving the crowds a choice between Jesus and Barabbas (1-7, 13-25)

Herod – acts in a manner that is politically expedient in order not to "suffer" by sending Jesus back to Pilate, mocks Jesus, and treats Jesus with contempt (8-12)

the chief priests, the rulers, and the people – bring Jesus before Pilate (1-2), accuse Jesus before Herod (10), choose Barabbas over Jesus (18-19), call out for Jesus to be crucified (21, 23), stand by looking on Jesus being crucified (35), and beat their breasts (48, 18-13)

the soldiers – mock Jesus, treat Jesus with contempt (11, 36-37)

Who is modeling "enduring the suffering"? (23)

Simon of Cyrene – without choice, carries Jesus' cross (26)

Jesus – suffers at the hands of the chief priests and scribes (2, 18, 21, 23), Herod (11), Pilate (24-25, the "rulers" (35), the soldiers (36-37), the "sign" (38), one of the criminals (39), and the cross (33, 44-46)

Jesus during his suffering – warns the "women" (27-31), forgives the people persecuting Him (34), and promises the repentant criminal that he will be with Him in paradise (40-43)

Jesus in His death – causes the temple curtain to be torn allowing the direct access of the people to God the Father (44) and is a testimony of God the Father to the centurion (47)

Joseph of Arimathea – as a member of the Council; risks losing everything, perhaps even his life, by not consenting to the Council's plan and action, by asking Pilate for Jesus' body, and by providing a tomb for Jesus' body (50-53)

the **"women"** – risk their lives to be at the cross, to follow Jesus' body to the tomb, and to prepare for the caring of Jesus' body (54-56)

Who is not modeling "staying the course"? (24)

disciples – do not believe the women (11), two leave town (13-35), are startled and frightened at Jesus' appearance to them (36-37), and still can not believe even though Jesus shows them His hands and feet (38-43)

Who is modeling "staying the course"? (24)

the **"women"** – go to the tomb when there was a stone across the entrance (1-2), do not run away was they see the two men (3-7), remember Jesus' Words (8), and report to the disciples what they had seen at the tomb (9-10)

Peter – goes to the tomb and marvels at what has happened (12, 34)

disciples (after Jesus' reassurance) – have their minds opened by Jesus so that they can understand the scriptures (45-47), are instructed by Him (48-49), worship Jesus after witnessing His ascension, are joyful, and are continually in the temple praising God (50-53)

Jesus – fulfills prophecy about his resurrection (13-51)

STEADFAST FAITHFULNESS – THE GOSPEL OF LUKE

MAJOR THEMES

The "right kind of faith" relies on the Word of God, perseveres when circumstances hinder, and has a purpose to minister to the needy and preach the Gospel…

(9:1-9)   _____

_____

_____

(9:10-17)   _____

_____

_____

(9:37-43a)   _____

_____

_____

(9:51-56)   _____

_____

A forbearance to endure the suffering that accompanies the sacrifice is...

(9:18-27) _____

_____

_____

(9:43b-45) _____

(9:57-61) _____

_____

_____

Staying the course by...

(9:28-36) _____

(9:46-50) _____

(9:62) _____

THE "RIGHT KIND OF FAITH"

Who is not exhibiting the "right kind of faith"? (1)

Zacharias – does not rely on the Word of God in his lack of response to the angel of God (1:8-20)

Who is exhibiting the "right kind of faith"? (1)

Elizabeth – relies on the Word of God by being righteous and by walking blamelessly in the commands of the Lord (1:1-7), perseveres by keeping to herself in her pregnancy (1:24-25), perseveres and is blessed by Mary's presence (1:39-45), perseveres and gives birth to a son (1:57-58), and relies on the Word of God by praising God and quoting Scripture (1:46-56)

Mary – relies on the Word of God by responding to the angel, Gabriel, that she is "the bond slave of the Lord" and that "may it be done according to your word" (1:26-38), perseveres by traveling to Elizabeth's house while pregnant (1:39-45), relies on the Word of God by praising God and quoting Scripture (1:46-56)

Zacharias – relies on the Word of God by being righteous and by walking blamelessly in all the commences of the Lord (1:1-7), relies on the Word of God by naming his son "John" and praising the Lord quoting Scripture (1:62-79)

John the Baptist – perseveres by growing, becoming strong in spirit, and living in the desert (1:80)

Who is not exhibiting the "right kind of faith"? (2)

No one

Who is exhibiting the "right kind of faith" (2)

Joseph – perseveres by traveling with his pregnant wife from Nazareth to Bethlehem where there was little shelter (2:1-7): relies on the Word of God by following the law of Moses concerning purification, presenting Jesus to the Lord in Jerusalem, and making a sacrifice to the Lord (2:22-24, 39), perseveres by returning to Nazareth (2:39)

Mary – perseveres by traveling with her husband, while pregnant, from Nazareth to Bethlehem (2:1-7), relies on God's Word by treasuring in her heart all the things told to her by the shepherds (2:19), relies on the Word of God by naming her son "Jesus" (2:21), relies on the Word of God by following the law of Moses concerning purification, presenting Jesus to the Lord in Jerusalem, and making a sacrifice to the Lord (2:22-24, 39), and relies on God's Word by reassuring in her heart "all these things" (2:51b)

shepherds – rely on the Word of God by quickly responding to the words of the angel of God and by going into Bethlehem to find Jesus (8:22)

Simeon – relies on the Word of God by being righteous and devout, looking for the Messiah, having the Holy Spirit upon him (2:25-26) and proclaiming that Jesus' ministry is a light of revelation to the Gentiles and the glory of God's people, Israel (2:27-32)

Anna – relies on the Word of God, as a widow, serving in the temple day and night with fasting and prayers (2:36-37) and ministers to those around her by telling them that Jesus is the Messiah (2:38)

Jesus – relies on the Word of God by growing in wisdom with the grace of God upon Him (2:4o), by listening and questioning the teachers in the temple (2:41-47), by understanding His mission and being in subjection to His parents (2:48-51, and by increasing in wisdom and stature and being in favor with God and men (2:52)

AN EXAMINE-YOURSELF CHECKLIST – THE "RIGHT KIND" OF FAITH...

starts with...

a repentant attitude. (3:1-6) ____

repentant behavior. (3:7-14) ____

receiving the Christ (Son of God), Jesus. (3:15-38) ____

is characterized by...

reliance on the Word of God in response
to temptation. (4:1-14) ____

perseverance in doing and sharing the Word
even when circumstances hinder. (4:15-30) ____

a purpose to minister to the needy with authority
and to teach the Word with authority. (4:31-44) ____

by God's grace...

is increased by miracles of power
and compassion. (5:1-15) ____

is refreshed in private prayer. (4:42; 5:16; 6:12) ____

results in the forgiveness of sin. (5:17-26, Lev. 14:2-32) ____

understands that Jesus has the repentance of the sick
and sinners as the focus of His ministry. (5:27-32) ____

knows that Jesus is the personification
of the Day of Atonement. (5:33-35) ____

is single in its focus on Jesus (the new faith) and not the accomplishment of the Law (the old faith). (5:36-39) ____

differs from the "old faith" in its...

permission to override the misinterpreted rigidity of the Law in order to minister to those in need. (6:1-11) ____

recognition that the "call to be sent" is from Jesus. (6:12-16) ____

realization that the miracles of Jesus are available for both Jews and Gentiles. (6:17-19) ____

requirement to have a faithful heart attitude as described by Jesus. (6:20-45) ____

being built on an obedient foundation of acting upon the "faithful attitude". (6:46-49) ____

focuses on Jesus...

and His authority (power). (7:1-10) ____

and His compassion (love). (7:11-17) ____

as the Messiah. (7:18-23, Isa. 61:1)) ____

and is received by those who are prepared. (7:24-29) (but is rejected by those who prefer to "play games" with the truth) 7:30-35) ____

and has a passion for Him because of the forgiveness of our sins. (7:36-50) ____ is responsive by…

    supporting others in ministry. (8:1-3)   ___

    hearing the Word of God in an honest and
good heart, holding it fast, and bearing
fruit with perseverance. (8:4-15)   ___

    sharing with others what we hear
from the Word of God (8:16-18)   ___

    being faithful to hear the Word of
God and do it. (8:19-21)   ___

    relying on the power and love of Jesus
in the midst of the "storms". (8:22-25)   ___

    coming to Jesus, being healed by Him and telling
others what great things Jesus does for us. (8:26-39)   ___

    reaching out to touch Jesus in times when personal
healing is needed and telling others what great
things Jesus does for us. (8:43-48)   ___

    asking Jesus for help, not being afraid, and believing that
faith in Jesus results in resurrection. (8:40-42; 49-56)   ___

REJECTION ADVICE – ENDURING THE "SUFFERING" THAT ACCOMPANIES SACRIFICE REQUIRES AN UNDERSTANDING THAT...

our suffering may come from...

(10:1-24)   _____

_____

_____

_____

_____

_____

_____

(10:23-37)   _____

_____

_____

(10:38-42)   _____

_____

_____

opposition to our ministry...

(11:1-13)   _____

_____

(11:14-36) _____

_____

_____

_____

(11:37-54) _____

_____

we must not be distracted by the world but we must...

(12:1-12) _____

(12:13-34) _____

(12:35-59) _____

the Kingdom of God will...

(13:1-17) _____

(13:18-21) _____

(13:22-35) _____

_____

_____

concerning service to others we must…

(14:1-6) _____

_____

(14:7-11) _____

(14:12-14) _____

_____

(14:15-24) _____

_____

_____

_____

(14:25-35) _____

_____

_____

_____

concerning the lost we must…

(15:1-10) _____

_____

(15:11-32) _____

_____

_____

our stewardship must be wise in the use of...

(16:1-15) _____

_____

(16:16-31) _____

_____

_____

FINISH WELL – STAY THE COURSE BY...

humbly...

    (17:1-6)   _____

    _____

    _____

    (17:7-10)   _____

    _____

    (17:11-19)   _____

    _____

    (17:20-21)   _____

    (17:22-37)   _____

persisting in...

    prayer resulting in justice

    (18:1-8)   _____

    humility resulting in our...

    (18:9-14)   _____

    (18:15-17)   _____

    (18:18-27)   _____

(18:28-30) _____

(18:31-34) _____

(18:35-43) _____

ministry to others no matter who they are

(19:1-10) _____

the investment of our God-given gifts (the gospel message and spiritual gifts

(19:11-27) _____

_____

obedience and the proclamation that Jesus is the King!

(19:28-40) _____

pursuing the things of peace in our relationship with God, receiving Jesus, and thereby avoiding the fate of Jerusalem.

(19:41-48) _____

_____

bewaring of false teachers who question the authority of Jesus over...

(20:1-8) _____

(20:9-19) _____

(20:20-26) _____

_____

(20:27-40) _____

(20:41-44) _____

(20:45-47) _____

being aware of…

(21:1-4) _____

_____

(21:5-11) _____

_____

(21:12-19) _____

_____

_____

(21:20-33) _____

_____

(21:34-36) _____

_____

_____

_____

(21:37-38) _____

MODELING STEADFAST FAITHFULNESS

Who is not modeling the "right kind of faith"? (22)

Chief priests, teachers of the law, council of elders – seek how to put Jesus to death (2), bribe Judas (5), arrest Jesus like a robber (52-53), take Jesus to the Council chamber and question Him (66-71)

Guards – mock Jesus and beat Jesus (63-64), say many blasphemous things against Him (65)

Judas – possessed by Satan (3), consents to betray Jesus for money (4-6), betrays Jesus with a kiss (47-48)

Disciples – discuss about who is to betray Jesus (21-23), have a dispute among themselves about who is the greatest (24), sleep from sorrow instead of praying and watching (39-40, 45-46), cut off the ear of the slave of the high priest (49-50)

Peter – denies Jesus three times and weeps bitterly (54-62)

Who is modeling the "right kind of faith"? (22)

Jesus – makes provision for the Passover for His disciples (7-13), instructs His disciples about remembering Him and His sacrifice through the eating of the bread and drinking from the cup (14-20), teaches His disciples about the priority of serving (25-27), promises the disciples that they will sit at His table in His kingdom and sit on thrones judging the twelve tribes of Israel (28-30), tells Peter that He will pray for him and that he will deny Him three times (31-34), warns His disciples to be prepared to protect themselves in His absence (35-38) prays to the father about the events about to happen and submits to the Father's will (41-44), heals the slave's ear (51), perseveres through the abuse of the men holding Him (63-65), states to the Council of Elders that from now on He will be seated at the right hand of the power of God and that He is the Son of God, knowing that it would result in His death (67-70)

Who is not modeling "enduring the suffering"? (23)

Pilate – acts in a manner that is politically expedient in order not to "suffer" by first sending Jesus to Herod and then giving the crowds a choice between Jesus and Barabbas (1-7, 13-25)

Herod – acts in a manner that is politically expedient in order not to "suffer" by sending Jesus back to Pilate, mocks Jesus, and treats Jesus with contempt (8-12)

the chief priests, the rulers, and the people – bring Jesus before Pilate (1-2), accuse Jesus before Herod (10), choose Barabbas over Jesus (18-19), call out for Jesus to be crucified (21, 23), stand by looking on Jesus being crucified (35), and beat their breasts (48, 18-13)

the soldiers – mock Jesus, treat Jesus with contempt (11, 36-37)

Who is modeling "enduring the suffering"? (23)

Simon of Cyrene – without choice, carries Jesus' cross (26)

Jesus – suffers at the hands of the chief priests and scribes (2, 18, 21, 23), Herod (11), Pilate (24-25, the "rulers" (35), the soldiers (36-37), the "sign" (38), one of the criminals (39), and the cross (33, 44-46)

Jesus during his suffering – warns the "women" (27-31), forgives the people persecuting Him (34), and promises the repentant criminal that he will be with Him in paradise (40-43)

Jesus in His death – causes the temple curtain to be torn allowing the direct access of the people to God the Father (44) and is a testimony of God the Father to the centurion (47)

Joseph of Arimathea – as a member of the Council; risks losing everything, perhaps even his life, by not consenting to the Council's plan and action, by asking Pilate for Jesus' body, and by providing a tomb for Jesus' body (50-53)

the "women" – risk their lives to be at the cross, to follow Jesus' body to the tomb, and to prepare for the caring of Jesus' body (54-56)

Who is not modeling "staying the course"? (24)

disciples – do not believe the women (11), two leave town (13-35), are startled and frightened at Jesus' appearance to them (36-37), and still can not believe even though Jesus shows them His hands and feet (38-43)

Who is modeling "staying the course"? (24)

the "women" – go to the tomb when there was a stone across the entrance (1-2), do not run away was they see the two men (3-7), remember Jesus' Words (8), and report to the disciples what they had seen at the tomb (9-10)

Peter – goes to the tomb and marvels at what has happened (12, 34)

disciples (after Jesus' reassurance) – have their minds opened by Jesus so that they can understand the scriptures (45-47),

are instructed by Him (48-49), worship Jesus after witnessing His ascension, are joyful, and are continually
    in the temple praising God (50-53)

Jesus – fulfills prophecy about his resurrection (13-51)

APPENDIX VIII – D
THE GOSPEL OF MATTHEW
DEVOTED OBEDIENCE

DEVOTED OBEDIENCE – THE GOSPEL OF MATTHEW

MAJOR THEMES

Commune with God in secret by...

giving (sign of commitment to God). (6:1-4)

praying (speaking to God). (6:5-15)

fasting (listening to God). (6:16-18)

Have singleness toward God of...

heart (desire). (6:19-21)

eye (thought). (6:22-23)

hand (service). (6:24)

Seek God first by...

not worrying about seeking provisions for our life. (6:25-32)

seeking His kingdom and His righteousness and <u>He</u> will provide for us. (6:33)

taking life one day at a time. (6:34)

HE REIGNS - JESUS, THE KING...

has the right royal lines according to ...

His genealogy related to the Davidic covenant. (1:1-17, Isaiah 7:10-14, Jeremiah 23:5-6)

His genealogy related to the Holy Spirit. (1:18-25, Isaiah 7:14)

had an unusual birth ...

accompanied by the appearance of a star over His birthplace, which resulted in worship by some and fear by others. (2:1-12)

the details of which were fulfillment of prophecy. (2:13-23, Numbers 24:17, Micah 5:2, Hosea 11:1, Jeremiah 31:5)

is coroneted by ...

having His way prepared by a herald, John the Baptist. (3:1-12)

being anointed by the Holy Spirit and announced by God the Father. (3:13-17)

begins His reign by ...

being tested by His enemy. (4:1-11)

bringing hope to His kingdom. (4:12-17)

appointing ministers. (4:18-22)

ministering throughout His kingdom. (4:23-25)

proclaims the requirements of His law related to "attitude":

> be happy – poor in spirit (humble), mourn (grieve, possibly for our sin), gentle (mild, not caustic), hunger and thirst after righteousness (compelled to do right), merciful (actively compassionate), pure in heart (clean in thought and feelings, having no personal agenda), peacemakers (opposite to fire-builders), those insulted and persecuted because of Jesus (will not sin against their conscience, won't bend when tribulation comes) (5:1-12)

> be actively salty, influencing others. (5:13)

> be a shining light, as a living testimony to others. (5:14-16)

> keep and teach the commandments. (5:17-19)

> be truly righteous. (5:20)

> do not be angry but be reconciled with others. (5:21-26)

> remove the things that cause our stumbling. (5:27-30)

> avoid divorce. (5:31-32)

> keep our word. (5:33-37)

> respond to evil with good.(5:38-42, Deut. 19:21)

> love enemies and pray for those that persecute us. (5:43-47)

> be spiritually mature. (5:48)

proclaims the requirements of His law related to "process":

> commune with God in secret – give, pray, and fast. (6:1-18)

have singleness of heart, mind's eye, and hand. (6:19-24)

seek first His kingdom and His righteousness. (6:25-34)

proclaims the requirements of His law related to "outcomes":

do not judge others but do self-examination and reformation before giving advice to others (7:1-5)

be discerning in spiritual giving. (7:6)

ask God and He will provide. (7:7-11)

treat others in the same way we want them to treat us. (7:12)

follow the narrow way of obedience to God. (7:13-14)

discern false prophets by their fruits and beware of them. (7:15-20)

do the will of God the Father, not your own. (7:21-23)

build you life on the Rock; <u>hear</u> and <u>act</u> on the words of Jesus. (7:24-27)

be amazed at the words and authority of Jesus, the King. (7:28-29)

teaches, by example, the "natural" side of His new law (physical ministry) in that He...

is <u>willing</u> to heal even the most unclean. (8:1-4)

has the authority to heal. (8:5-13)

fulfills prophecy by healing infirmities and diseases. (8:14-17, Isa. 53:4-6)

requires sacrifice and discipline on the part of His followers. (8:18-22)

requires trust/faith on the part of His followers. (8:23-27)

is rejected by some people for the carrying out His law. (8:28-34)

teaches, by example, the "supernatural" side of His new law (spiritual ministry) by...

forgiving sins. (9:1-8)

calling sinners to follow Him. (9:9)

desiring compassion for sinners. (9:10-13)

not requiring His disciples to fast because He is the personification of the Day of Atonement. (9:14-15)

requiring His followers to give up their sinful old life completely. (9:16-17)

responding to a synagogue official's faith through the healing of his daughter. (9:18-19; 23-26)

interrupting an important mission by stopping to heal a woman who had faith in Him. (9:20-22)

healing two blind men who had faith in Him as the Messiah. (9:27-31, Isa. 35:5)

being misrepresented by the spiritual leaders because of His spiritual ministry. (9:32-34) persevering in teaching and proclaiming the gospel and healing sickness and disease. (9:35)

having compassion for the distressed and dispirited people and calling His followers to ask God to send out workers to help save the people. (9:36-38)

STAY TUNED - COMMUNE WITH GOD IN SECRET...

by...

being called by Jesus to be one of His disciples and given authority to be His apostles. (10:1-4)

giving freely in ministry. (10:5-8)

fasting to hear and to rely on God in our ministry. (10:9-15)

praying for wisdom and direction in ministry. (10:16-20)

following as a disciple of Jesus and...

enduring to the end in the face of hatred. (10:21-23)

being maligned as one of His followers. (10:24-25)

proclaiming <u>boldly</u> and <u>fearlessly</u> what Jesus tells us. (10:26-31)

confessing Jesus before men. (10:32-33)

causing division for the Lord's sake, if need be, within our family. (10:34-36, Mic. 7:5-8)

loving Jesus the "most", "taking up our crosses" and following Jesus, and "losing our life" for Jesus' sake. (10:37-39)

receiving Jesus' prophets and righteous men. (10:40-41)

ministering to " spiritually young" disciples. (10:42)

TOTALLY COMMITTED - HAVE SINGLENESS OF OUR...

heart...

being controlled by Jesus...

as John the Baptist seeks to do. (11:1-6, Isaiah 61:1)

by allowing John the Baptist to prepare our hearts for Jesus. (11:7-15, Mal. 3:1)

by not rejecting Jesus because we can not have Him on our terms. (11:16-19)

by repenting. (11: 20-24, Ezek. 26-28, Isaiah 23)

by being humble and receiving God's revelations through Jesus. (11:25-27)

by allowing Jesus to direct our lives. (11:28-30)

in its condition toward Jesus by...

desiring compassion (not sacrifice). (12:1-8, Hosea 6:6)

helping others even when we are accused of doing wrong. (12:9-24, Isaiah 42:1-2)

being "with" Jesus and "gathering" with Him. (12:25-30)

not blaspheming against the Holy Spirit. (12:31-32)

being good (fruitful) and speaking what is good. (12:33-37)

not looking for signs but being humble and repentant before Jesus. (12:38-42) not being empty and open to evil spirits. (12:43-45)

doing the will of God the Father. (12:46-50)

in its consecration through Jesus by...

having and understanding the Word of God and bearing fruit. (13:1-9; 18-23)

seeing, hearing and understanding the parables. (13:10-17, Isa. 6:8-10)

knowing that at the end of the age, the righteous will shine forth as the sun and that the unrighteous will be destroyed. (13:24-30, 36-43; Dan. 12:3)

having faith that the Kingdom of Heaven will be victorious. (13:31-32)

having faith that the Kingdom of Heaven will spread in victory throughout the world. (13:33)

understanding that Jesus spoke parables to fulfill prophecy. (13:34-35, Psa. 78:1-4)

sacrificing everything joyfully for the Kingdom of Heaven. (13:44-46)

being righteous and therefore saved from the fiery furnace. (13:47-50)

teaching things of value out of the Old and New Testaments. (13:51-52)

being able to withstand criticism from those who knew us before our conversion and are offended by our testimony. (13:53-58)

eye...

in the clearing of it by...

> not holding to man's words before men but to God's Word. (14:1-12, Lev.20:21)

> not trusting in on our own power, but God's (14:13-21)

> not being afraid of the "storms" of life. (14:22-27)

> keeping our focus off of circumstances and on Jesus, the Son of God. (14:28-33)

> trusting in the miraculous power and love of Jesus. (14:34-36)

which is turned away from man's traditions...

> that invalidate the Word of God. (15:1-9, Lev. 20:9, Deut. 5:16, Isa. 29:13)

> that wrongly identify the source of sin. (15:10-20, Lev. 22:1-16)

> and has compassion on <u>everyone</u> of faith. (15:21-28)

> and has our works result in the glorification of God. (15:29-31)

> and on the work of God. (15:32-38)

> and always pushing on. (15:39)

that does not look for signs but instead...

> bewares of false teachers who <u>look</u> for signs, except the sign of Jonah. (16:1-12)

acknowledges that Jesus is the Christ, the Son of the living God. (16:13-17)

continues in faith, building the church. (16:18-20, Isa. 22:22)

sets itself on God's interests. (16:21-23)

denies self, takes up its cross and follows Jesus. (16:24-26, Psa. 62:12, Pro. 24:12)

looks for Jesus coming in His Kingdom. (16:27-28)

focused on…

listening to Jesus alone. (17:1-13)

drawing on the power of Jesus alone and not on our own. (17:14-21)

the inevitability of sacrifice in service. (17:22-23)

God's interests and not distracted by the things of the world. (17:24-27)

hand…

in serving our less mature "brothers and sisters" by…

being humble, receiving them, and not causing them to stumble. (18:1-7)

cutting out of our life those things that cause us, and others, to stumble. (18:8-9, Romans 14:13)

not despising them. (18:10-11)

helping to restore those that have gone astray. (18:12-14)

attempting to be reconciled with them following the process of restoration. (18:15-20)

forgiving them an infinite number of times. (18:21-22)

forgiving them from the <u>heart</u>. (18:23-35)

in <u>humbly</u> giving all that we have to Jesus by serving…

our spouse, if we have one. (19:1-12, Deut. 24:1)

the children. (19:13-15)

the poor. (19:16-26)

Jesus. (19:27-30)

in gratefully working for Jesus' kingdom by…

not expecting greater rewards than our fellow workers. (20:1-16)

not expecting an easy way to deliverance. (20:17-19)

humbly not expecting (presumptuously) that others serve us but, rather, that we serve others sacrificially as Jesus did. (20:20-28)

humbly asking Jesus to open our eyes and gratefully following Him. (20:29-34)

NUMERO UNO - SEEK FIRST THE KINGDOM OF GOD AND HIS RIGHTEOUSNESS...

acknowledging who Jesus is by...

praising Him as the King. (21:1-11, v. 5 - Zech. 9:9, v. 9 - Psa. 118:26)

keeping the King's house as a house of prayer. (21:12-13, Isa. 56:7)

praising Him as children in the face of adversity. (21:14-17, Psa. 8:2)

being fruitful for Jesus. (21:18-19)

believing we will receive what we ask of Him in prayer. (21:20-22)

believing in His authority and that His authority is from heaven. (21:23-27, Phil. 2:8-11)

being obedient to His direction. (21:28-32)

understanding the consequence of not respecting God the Father – a wretched end and losing the promise. (21:33-41)

understanding the consequence of rejecting Him – broken in pieces, scattered like dust, and losing the promise. (21:42-44, v. 42 - Psa. 118:22)

understanding the unrepentant attitude of those who reject Him – worrying about the consequences from man rather than from God. (21:45-46) by responding…

to God's invitation to us to come into His kingdom. (22:1-10)

by having the "right" clothes to wear in His kingdom. (22:11-14; Rev. 3:4-5, 19:8)

in recognizing the supernatural nature of His kingdom. (22:15-22)

in recognizing the eternity of His kingdom. (22:23-33, Ex. 3:6)

in recognizing the heart of God's law. (22:34-40, Deut. 6:5, Lev. 19:18)

in recognizing that Jesus is the Christ, God's Son. (22:41-46, Psa. 110:1)

bewaring of false teachers and leaders and not following those that…

are proud. (23:1-12)

are not in the Kingdom of Heaven itself and prevent others from entering. (23:13)

take advantage of those who are vulnerable and make long prayers as a pretense. (23:14)

lead converts astray. (23:15)

do not know what is important. (23:16-22)

neglect doing the important things such as justice, mercy, and faithfulness and replace them by doing less important things. (23:23-24) clean the outside of things but not the inside of themselves. (23:25-26)

appear to be righteous but inwardly are full of hypocrisy and lawlessness. (23:27-28)

honor dead prophets but not living ones. (23:29-33)

treat prophets and the Messiah poorly. (23:34-39)

readying ourselves for Jesus' second coming by...

not relying on the things of man. (24:1-2)

knowing the prophetic signs (24:3)

listening to Jesus concerning "When will these things happen?" (24:4-28, Daniel 9:27; 11:31, 12:11)

listening to Jesus concerning "What will be the sign of Your coming?" (24:29-31, Revelations 1:7)

listening to Jesus concerning "What will be the sign of the end of the age?" (24:32-41, I Thessalonians 4:16-17)

being on the alert for Jesus' second coming. (24:42-44)

doing the Lord's work diligently until He comes again. (24:45-51) serving the Lord by...

staying prepared for Jesus' coming. (25:1-13)

being fruitful in the work that the Lord has given to us to do. (25:14-30)

feeding the hungry, giving drink to the thirsty, inviting strangers in, clothing the naked, visiting the sick, and going to those in prison. (25:31-46)

MODELING DEVOTED OBEDIENCE

Communing with God in Secret (26)

Who is not modeling "giving in secret"? (26:1-35)

Who is taking?
Chief priests, scribes, and elders – planning to take and kill Jesus (3-6)
Disciples – indignant about the "woman" (7-9), insecure about their relationship Jesus (20-22)
Judas – money for betrayal (14-16, 23-25)

Who is modeling "giving in secret? (26:1-35)

Who is giving? (26:1-25)
The "woman" at Simon the Leper's house - poured oil on Jesus head (6-7, 12-13)
Jesus – (26-35) – telling of how he will provide for the forgiveness of many

Who is not modeling "praying to God in secret"? (26:36-46)

Disciples – Jesus tells them to watch and pray (41, 44), Jesus finds them sleeping (40, 43, 45)

Who is modeling "praying to God in secret? (26:36-46)

Jesus – praying to God in secret (36-39, 42, 44)

Who is not modeling "fasting (listening) before God in secret"? (26:47-75)

Judas – betrays Jesus (47-50)
Disciple - who cuts off ear (51)
Crowds – want to arrest Jesus (55)

Disciples – run away (56)

Caiaphas, chief priests, and the whole Council – trying to obtain false witnesses against Jesus, saying that He blasphemed, saying He deserved death, beating Him, and mocking Him (57-67)

Peter – denies Jesus (69-75)

Who is modeling "fasting (listening) before God in secret"? (26:47-75)

Jesus – chooses not to use the 12 legions of angels available to Him (52-53), allows capture (47-56), chooses not to defend Himself in an unfair trial (57-63), makes a statement that results in His death sentence (65-68)

Singleness of Heart, Eye, and Hand for God (27)

Who does not have "singleness of heart" for God? (27:1-11)

Chief priests/elders – desire to put Jesus to death (1), refuse responsibility for Jesus' betrayal (4, 6-10)
Judas – has a divided heart (3-5)

Who has a "singleness of heart" for God? (27:1-12)

Jesus – admits to Pilate that He is the King of the Jews knowing that it would seal His death (11)

Who does not have "singleness of eye" for God? (27:12-13)

Chief priests/elders – accuse Jesus (12-14)

Who does have "singleness of eye" for God? (27:12-14)

Jesus – clear and single on the Father, knows what righteousness is (He is it), no need to respond to accusations because His actions have been righteous (12-14)

Who does not have "singleness of hand" for God? (27:15-66)

Pilate – orders Jesus to be scourged and crucified as a matter of political expediency and then washes his hands (15-26) and orders the tomb to be guarded (62-66)
Soldiers – use Jesus as a means of entertainment and provision (27-31, 33-37)
Simon of Cyrene – service is coerced (32)
Robbers/crowds – justifying their own behavior, mob mentality, sense of security in numbers (38-44)
Chief priests and Pharisees – convince Pilate to guard the tomb and do so (62-66)

Who does have "singleness of hand for God? (27:15-66)

Jesus – places His life in the Father's hands (45-46, Psalm 22), the veil of the Temple is torn (51), bodies of the saints are resurrected (52-53), testimony to non-believers – centurion (54)

"Women" – continue to follow Jesus (55-56, 61)

Joseph of Arimathea – gets Jesus' body and provides tomb (58-60)

Seeking First His Kingdom and His Righteousness (28)

Who is not "seeking first His kingdom and His righteousness?

Guards/soldiers – choose money over truth (11-15)

Chief priests/elders – choose to bribe the soldiers over truth (11-15)

Some disciples – doubtful about Jesus (17b)

Who is "seeking first His kingdom and His righteousness?

"Two Mary's" – Angel tells them to tell the disciples (1-7), they go (8), they worship Jesus (9), they go (11a)

Some disciples – worship Jesus (17a)

Jesus – instructs the disciples to go and make disciples of all nations; baptizing them in the name of the Father, Son, and Holy Spirit; and teaching them to observe all things that He had commanded them; and reminds His disciples that he is with them always (18-20)

DEVOTED OBEDIENCE – THE GOSPEL OF MATTHEW

MAJOR THEMES

Commune with God in secret by...

(6:1-4) _____

(6:5-15) _____

(6:16-18) _____

Have singleness toward God of...

(6:19-21) _____

(6:22-23) _____

(6:24) _____

Seek God first by...

(6:25-32) _____

(6:33) _____

_____

(6:34) _____

HE REIGNS - JESUS, THE KING...

has the right credentials according to ...

    (1:1-17)   _____

    (1:18-25)   _____

had an unusual birth ...

    (2:1-12)   _____

    _____

    _____

    (2:13-23)   _____

    _____

is coroneted by ...

    (3:1-12)   _____

  _____

    (3:13-17)   _____

    _____

begins His reign by ...

    (4:1-11)   _____

    (4:12-17)   _____

    (4:18-22)   _____

    (4:23-25)   _____

proclaims the requirements of His law related to "attitude":

(5:1-12) _____

_____

_____

_____

_____

_____

_____

_____

_____

_____

(5:13) _____

(5:14-16) _____

(5:17-19) _____

(5:20) _____

(5:21-26) _____

(5:27-30) _____

(5:31-32) _____

(5:33-37) _____

(5:38-42) _____

(5:43-47) _____

(5:48) _____

proclaims the requirements of His law related to "process":

(6:1-18) _____

(6:19-24) _____

_____

(6:25-34) _____

proclaims the requirements of His law related to "outcomes":

(7:1-5) _____

_____

_____

(7:6) _____

(7:7-11) _____

(7:12) _____

_____

(7:13-14) _____

_____

(7:15-20) _____

(7:21-23) _____

(7:24-27) _____

_____

(7:28-29) _____

_____

teaches, by example, the "natural" side of His law in that He...

(8:1-4) _____

(8:5-13) _____

(8:14-17) _____

(8:18-22) _____

_____

(8:23-27) _____

(8:28-34) _____

_____

teaches by example, the supernatural side of His law by...

(9:1-8)   _____

(9:9)   _____

(9:10-13)   _____

(9:14-15)   _____

               _____

(9:16-17)   _____

               _____

(9:18-19; 23-26)   _____

               _____

(9:20-22)   _____

               _____

(9:23-31)   _____

(9:32-34)   _____

               _____

(9:35)   _____

               _____

AND HOW SHALL YOU KNOW ALL PARABLES

(9:36-38) _____

_____

_____

_____

STAY TUNED - COMMUNE WITH GOD IN SECRET...

by...

    (10:1-4) _____

    _____

    (10:5-8) _____

    (10:9-15) _____

    (10:16-20) _____

following as a disciple of Jesus and...

    (10:21-23) _____

    (10:24-25) _____

    (10:26-31) _____

    (10:32-33) _____

    (10:34-36) _____

    _____

    (10:37-39) _____

    _____

    _____

    (10:40-41) _____

    _____

    (10:42) _____

TOTALLY COMMITTED - HAVE SINGLENESS OF OUR...

heart...

being controlled by Jesus...

(11:1-6) _____

(11:7:15) _____

_____

(11:16-19) _____

_____

(11:20-24) _____

(11:25-27) _____

(11:28-30) _____

in its condition toward Jesus by...

(12:1-8) _____

(12:9-24) _____

_____

(12:25-30) _____

(12:31-32) _____

(12:33-37) _____

(12:38-42) _____

_____

(12:43-45) _____

(12:46-50) _____

in its consecration through Jesus by...

(13:1-9, 18-23) _____

_____

(13:10-17) _____

(13:24-30, 36-43) _____

(13:31-32) _____

_____

(13:33) _____

_____

(13:34-35) _____

_____

(13:44-46) _____

_____

(13:47-50) _____

_____

(13:51-52) _____

_____

(13:53-58) _____

_____

eye...

in the clearing of it by...

(14:1-12) _____

_____

(14:13-21) _____

(14:22-27) _____

(14:28-33) _____

_____

(14:34-36) _____

which is turned away from man's traditions...

(15:1-9) _____

(15:10-20) _____

(15:21-28) _____

(15:29-31) _____

_____

(15:32-38) _____

(15:39) _____

that does not look for signs but instead...

(16:1-12) _____

_____

(16:13-17) _____

_____

(16:18-20) _____

(16:21-23) _____

(16:24-26) _____

(16:27-28) _____

focused on...

(17:1-13) _____

(17:14-21) _____

_____

(17:22-23) _____

(17:24:27) _____

hand...

in serving our "brothers and sisters" by...

(18:1-7) _____

_____

(18:8-9) _____

_____

(18:10-11) _____

(18:12-14) _____

(18:15-20) _____

_____

(18:21-22) _____

(18:23-35) _____

in <u>humbly</u> giving all that we have to Jesus by...

(19:1-12) _____

(19:13-15) _____

(19:16-26) _____

(19:27-30) _____

in gratefully working for Jesus' kingdom by...

(20:1-16) _____

(20:17-19) _____

(20:20-28) _____

_____

_____

(20:29-34) _____

NUMERO UNO - SEEK FIRST THE KINGDOM OF GOD AND HIS RIGHTEOUSNESS...

acknowledging who Jesus is by...

(21:1-11) _____

(21:12-13) _____

(21:14-17) _____

(21:18-19) _____

(21:20-22) _____

_____

(21:23-27) _____

_____

(21:28-32) _____

(21:33-41) _____

_____

_____

(21:42-44) _____

_____

_____

(21:45-46) _____

by responding...

(22:1-10) _____

(22:11-14) _____

_____

(22:15-22) _____

(22:23-33) _____

(22:34-40) _____

(22:41-46) _____

bewaring of false teachers and leaders and not following those that...

(23:1-12) _____

(23:13) _____

_____

(23:14) _____

_____

(23:15) _____

(23:16-22) _____

(23:23-24) _____

_____

_____

(23:25-26) _____

_____

(23:27-28) _____

_____

(23:29-33) _____

(23:34-39) _____

readying ourselves for Jesus' second coming by…

(24:1-2) _____

(24:3) _____

(24:4-28) _____

_____

(24:29-31) _____

_____

(24:32-41) _____

_____

(24:42-44) _____

(24:45-51) _____

serving the Lord by…

(25:1-13) _____

(25:14-30) _____

_____

(25:31-46) _____

_____

_____

_____

MODELING DEVOTED OBEDIENCE

Communing with God in Secret (26)

Who is not modeling "giving in secret"? (26:1-35)

Who is taking?
Chief priests, scribes, and elders – planning to take and kill Jesus (v. 3-6)
Disciples – indignant about the "woman" (7-9), insecure about their relationship Jesus (20-22)
Judas – money for betrayal (14-16, 23-25)

Who is modeling "giving in secret? (26:1-35)

Who is giving? (26:1-25)
The "woman" at Simon the Leper's house - poured oil on Jesus head (6-7, 12-13)
Jesus – (26-35) – telling of how he will provide for the forgiveness of many

Who is not modeling "praying to God in secret"? (26:36-46)

Disciples – Jesus tells them to watch and pray (41, 44), Jesus finds them sleeping (40, 43, 45)

Who is modeling "praying to God in secret? (26:36-46)

Jesus – praying to God in secret (36-39, 42, 44)

Who is not modeling "fasting (listening) before God in secret"? (26:47-75)

Judas – betrays Jesus (47-50)
Disciple - who cuts off ear (51)
Crowds – want to arrest Jesus (55)

Disciples – run away (56)

Caiaphas, chief priests, and the whole Council – trying to obtain false witnesses against Jesus, saying that He blasphemed, saying He deserved death, beating Him, and mocking Him (57-67)

Peter – denies Jesus (69-75)

Who is modeling "fasting (listening) before God in secret"? (26:47-75)

Jesus – chooses not to use the 12 legions of angels available to Him (52-53), allows capture (47-56), chooses not to defend Himself in an unfair trial (57-63), makes a statement that results in His death sentence (65-68)

Singleness of Heart, Eye, and Hand for God (27)

Who does not have "singleness of heart" for God? (27:1-11)

Chief priests/elders – desire to put Jesus to death (1), refuse responsibility for Jesus' betrayal (4, 6-10)
Judas – has a divided heart (3-5)

Who has a "singleness of heart" for God? (27:1-12)

Jesus – admits to Pilate that He is the King of the Jews knowing that it would seal His death (11)

Who does not have "singleness of eye" for God? (27:12-13)

Chief priests/elders – accuse Jesus (12-14)

Who does have "singleness of eye" for God? (27:12-14)

Jesus – clear and single on the Father, knows what righteousness is (He is it), no need to respond to accusations because His actions have been righteous (12-14)

Who does not have "singleness of hand" for God? (27:15-66)

Pilate – orders Jesus to be scourged and crucified as a matter of political expediency and then washes his hands (15-26) and orders the tomb to be guarded (62-66)
Soldiers – use Jesus as a means of entertainment and provision (27-31, 33-37)
Simon of Cyrene – service is coerced (32)
Robbers/crowds – justifying their own behavior, mob mentality, sense of security in numbers (38-44)
Chief priests and Pharisees – convince Pilate to guard the tomb and do so (62-66)

Who does have "singleness of hand for God? (27:15-66)

Jesus – places His life in the Father's hands (45-46, Psalm 22), the veil of the Temple is torn (51), bodies of the saints are resurrected (52-53), testimony to non-believers – centurion (54)
"Women" – continue to follow Jesus (55-56, 61)
Joseph of Arimathea – gets Jesus' body and provides tomb (58-60)

Seeking First His Kingdom and His Righteousness (28)

Who is not "seeking first His kingdom and His righteousness?

Guards/soldiers – choose money over truth (11-15)
Chief priests/elders – choose to bribe the soldiers over truth (11-15)
Some disciples – doubtful about Jesus (17b)

Who is "seeking first His kingdom and His righteousness?

"Two Mary's" – Angel tells them to tell the disciples (1-7), they go (8), they worship Jesus (9), they go (11a)
Some disciples – worship Jesus (17a)
Jesus – instructs the disciples to go and make disciples of all nations; baptizing them in the name of the Father, Son, and Holy Spirit; and teaching them to observe all things that He had commanded them; and reminds His disciples that he is with them always (18-20)

APPENDIX VIII – E
THE BOOK OF ACTS
SPIRITUAL PRODUCTIVITY

SPIRITUAL PRODUCTIVITY – THE BOOK OF ACTS

MAJOR THEMES

Minister in unity to the needy in the power of the Holy Spirit...

by discerning the need. (3:1-6)

by meeting the need. (3:7-8)

to the wonder and amazement of those watching. (3:9-10)

Humbly explain about the source of the power to those who are "amazed" that the...

ministry is not accomplished in our own power or piety. (3:11-12)

effect of the ministry is accomplished through the power of the name of Jesus. (3:13-16)

Persevere in boldly sharing about Jesus with those that are "amazed" that...

the prophecy concerning the Christ is fulfilled in Jesus. (3:17-18)

they need to repent and turn back to God so that their sins may be wiped away in order that times of refreshing may come from the presence of the Lord and that He may send Jesus, the Christ, preached to them. (3:19-21)

they need to listen to Jesus. (3:22-26, Deut 18:15, Gen. 22:15)

SPIRITUAL PRODUCTIVITY OCCURS IN JERUSALEM THROUGH...

responding to Jesus in unity and...

obeying Jesus' commands and waiting upon the Holy Spirit. (1:1-5)

being Jesus' witnesses, in the power of the Holy Spirit, to the remotest parts of the the world. (1:6-11, Isa. 43:8-13)

being of one mind and continuing in prayer (1:12-14)

replacing witnesses of Jesus. (1:15-26, Psa. 69:25, 109:8)

explaining the source of the power to those amazed by the work of the Holy Spirit...

falling on each believer. (2:1-4, Gen. 11:1-4))

amazing some and causing mocking by others. (2:5-13)

in fulfillment of prophecy about the Holy Spirit. (2:14-21, Joel 2:28-32)

that Jesus ministered on earth doing miracles, wonders, and signs and was put to death on a cross. (2:22-23, kerygama - part 1)

that God, the Father, raised Jesus from the dead, to which the apostles were witnesses. (2:24-32, Psa. 16:8-11, kerygama - part 2)

that Jesus, exalted to the right hand of God, pours out the Holy Spirit on those who believe the Old Testament prophecies that Jesus is both Lord and Christ. (2:33-36, Psa. 110:1, kerygama - part 3) that they need to repent of their sins, be baptized in the name of Jesus Christ for the forgiveness of their sins, and receive the gift of the Holy Spirit. (2:37-41, kerygama - part 4)

resulting in believers who are "together", sharing property and possessions with other believers as one might have need, continuing daily with one mind, eating together with gladness and sincerity of heart, praising God, having favor with all the people, and adding to their numbers those who are being saved. (2:42-47)

perseverance of the saints in boldly sharing about Jesus…

in spite of being arrested and interrogated. (4:1-12)

in spite of being commanded by authorities not to speak about Jesus. (4:13-22)

being delivered from confinement, being filled with the Holy Spirit, praising God, and speaking the Word of God with boldness. (4:23-31)

being of one heart and soul, sharing possessions, and sharing about the resurrection of Jesus. (4:32-35)

through sacrifice of their possessions for the good of the Body as a whole. (4:36-37)

maintaining unity in the Body…

by confronting a lack of integrity as the Apostles did…

with Ananias and Sapphira. (5:1-11, Joshua 7:1-26)

even though some believers refused to associate with those leading in ministry. (5:12-16) by boldly sharing the "whole message of this Life" (resurrection) in spite of persecution. (5:17-26)

by boldly proclaiming obedience to God rather then men. (5:27-32)

and being delivered again. (5:33-40)

by boldly teaching and preaching that Jesus is the Christ, even after being subjected to suffering and shame for His name. (5:41-42)

by dealing with a lack of equity as the Apostles did...

by confirming "deacons" chosen by the congregation to serve. (6:1-7)

in spite of those chosen being persecuted for ministering in the power of the Holy Spirit. (6:8-15)

by defending the faith, as Stephen did, and telling others that they should not...

reject the "deliverers" (especially Jesus). (7:1-29, 52)

be disobedient to the spiritual leaders. (7:30-43, 53)

resist the Holy Spirit. (7:44-51)

by standing firm in the faith, as Stephen did, even if it means our death. (7:54-60)

(See Appendix XI and Appendix XII for a visual summary of Acts 1-7)

SPIRITUAL PRODUCTIVITY OCCURS IN JUDEA/SAMARIA THROUGH...

the perseverance of the saints in spite of persecution. (8:1-4)

Philip's responding to Jesus by ministering to the Samaritans in the power of the Holy Spirit and boldly proclaiming Jesus to be the Son of God.(8:5-8)

Philip's boldly explaining the source of the power to those amazed by the work of the Holy Spirit, a gift from God. (8:9-24

perseverance of Philip, following the leading of God in boldly sharing about Jesus.
(8:25-40)

SPIRITUAL PRODUCTIVITY OCCURS IN THE UTTERMOST PARTS OF THE WORLD THROUGH...

Saul's responding to Jesus by proclaiming Him to be the Son of God to the Jews in the power of the Holy Spirit through...

his dramatic conversion and bold preaching in Damascus. (9:1-22)

his daring escape from the Jews at Damascus. (9:23-25)

his "bold speaking" about Jesus in Jerusalem. (9:26-29)

his being sent to Tarsus for his safety and for peace and increase of the Church. (9:30-31)

Peter's responding to Jesus in unity by ministering to the needy in the power of the Holy Spirit in...

> Lydda by healing Aeneas, and those that saw turned to the Lord. (9:32-35)

> Joppa by bringing Tabitha back to life and many believed in the Lord. (9:36-43)

> Caesarea by...

>> Cornelius' vision to send for Peter. (10:1-8)

>> Peter's vision that what God has cleansed is not unholy. (10:9-16)

>> Peter's speaking about Jesus with Cornelius' relatives and friends. (10:17-43)

>> the pouring out of the Holy Spirit on Cornelius' relatives and friends who are <u>Gentiles</u>! (10:44-48)

Peter's explanation to the Jews in Jerusalem of the amazing outpouring of the Holy Spirit on...

> the Gentiles (11:1-18)

the Church's responding to Jesus in unity by ministering to the needy in the power of the Holy Spirit through...

> sending Barnabas (and Saul) from Jerusalem to Antioch to teach the new Gentile Christians there. (11:19-26)

> the Gentile believers in Antioch sending financial support to the Jewish believers in Judea. (11:27-30)

the perseverance of the saints through...

overcoming the obstacles of persecution – fervent prayer by the church. (12:1-5)

the miraculous deliverance of Peter by God. (12:6-17)

the vengeance of God against those who oppose the saints. (12:18-23)

the spreading of the Word of God and the fulfilling of the mission of Barnabas and Saul. (12:24-25)

SPIRITUAL PRODUCTIVITY OCCURS IN THE UTTERMOST PARTS OF THE WORLD (PAUL'S FIRST MISSIONARY JOURNEY) THROUGH...

the church in Antioch responding to the Holy Spirit in unity by...

the consecration of Barnabas and Saul for the work to which God had called them (13:1-3)

Paul's exhibiting the miraculous power of the Holy Spirit to...

an amazed Sergius Paulus in Paphos who believes. (13:4-12)

perseverance of the saints sharing about Jesus by...

Paul's effective teaching in the synagogue at Pisidian Antioch. (13:13-43)

Paul's and Barnabas' declaring that salvation was available to the Gentiles, even though persecution followed. (13:44-52)

Paul's and Barnabas' teaching in the synagogue at Iconium, even though persecution followed. (14:1-7)

Paul's and Barnabas' explaining the source of the healing power of the Holy Spirit to...

an amazed people of Lystra. (14:8-18)

perseverance of the saints boldly sharing about Jesus by...

Paul's surviving a stoning by Jews from Antioch and Iconium. (14:19-21a)

Paul's and Barnabas' encouragement and appointing of elders in Derbe, Lystra, Iconium, and Antioch. (14:21b-23)

Paul's and Barnabas' teaching in Perga. (14:24-25)

Paul's and Barnabas' report to the sending church at Antioch of all that God had done with them and how He had opened the door of faith to the Gentiles. (14:26-28)

the responding of the church to Jesus in unity, through compromise, in...

Paul's and Barnabas' return to Jerusalem to clarify the divisive issue concerning the circumcision of gentile believers. (15:1-5, 12)

Peter's presenting the case for resolution. (15:6-11)

James' presenting a compromise for resolution. (15:13-21)

the apostles and elders agreeing on a solution and making it public to the whole church. (15:22-29)

bringing joy and encouragement to the church in Antioch by the decision. (15:30-35)

Paul's and Barnabas' separate return to ministry through compromise. (15:36-41)

Paul's circumcision of Timothy, which is another compromise as he brought the news of the "decision" to the "cities", strengthening them and increasing their faith. (16:1-5)

SPIRITUAL PRODUCTIVITY CONTINUES TO THE UTTERMOST PARTS OF THE WORLD (PAUL'S SECOND MISSIONARY JOURNEY) THROUGH...

Paul's responding to the Holy Spirit, the Spirit of Jesus, and a vision to...

go to Macedonia instead of Asia. (16:6-10)

perseverance of Paul in sharing Jesus...

with Lydia, a woman, in Philipi. (16:11-15)

and casting out a spirit of divination from a slave girl who was hindering their work, resulting in persecution. (16:16-21)

with his jailer after being imprisoned and then delivered by God. (16:22-40)

in Thessalonica where the brethren were persecuted by jealous Jews because of Paul's teaching. (17:1-9)

in Berea where crowds were stirred up against Paul by the Jews from Thessalonica. (17:10-15)

in Athens using the Athenian's own beliefs as a starting point. (17:16-34)

with the Gentiles after lack of response from the Jews. (18:1-8)

in responding to a vision to remain in Corinth for a year and a half despite possibilities of persecution. (18:9-11)

in spite of being brought to the judgment seat of the Roman proconsul by the Jews. (18:12-17)

in Ephesus where he reasoned with the Jews. (18:18-21)

in finishing his journey by returning to the church in Antioch. (18:22)

SPIRITUAL PRODUCTIVITY CONTINUES TO THE UTTERMOST PARTS OF THE WORLD (PAUL'S THIRD MISSIONARY JOURNEY) THROUGH...

the perseverance of the saints in boldly sharing Jesus by...

Paul's strengthening all of the disciples in the Galatian region and Phrygia. (23)

Priscilla's and Aquilla's explaining to Apollos more accurately the way of God. (18:24-28)

Paul's responding to the Lord by...

going to Ephesus, baptizing 12 men in the name of Jesus, and watching the Holy Spirit come upon the men when he laid hands on them. (19:1-7, 18:21)

perseverance of Paul in boldly sharing about Jesus...

as conditions in Ephesus dictated. (19:8-10)

God doing extraordinary miracles...

by Paul's hands. (19:11-20)

Paul's responding to the Holy Spirit by...

planning to pass through Macedonia and Achaia on his way to Jerusalem and then on to Rome. (19:21-22)

perseverance of Paul in boldly sharing about Jesus in...

Ephesus when challenged by the artisans who made idols to Artemis. (19:23-41)

Paul's responding to the Holy Spirit in...

passing through Macedonia. (20:1-6, 19:21)

Paul's responding to Jesus by...

healing the boy in the power of the Holy Spirit. (20:7-12)

Paul's responding to the Holy Spirit in...

going to Jerusalem. (20:13-16, 19:21)

Paul's responding to Jesus in unity to minister to the needy in the power of the Holy Spirit, explaining the source of the power to those amazed by the power of the Holy Spirit, and persevering in sharing about Jesus in his speech to...

the elders of the church at Ephesus. (20:17-35)

the brethren responding to Jesus...

in the manner in which they parted with Paul. (20:36-38)

SPIRITUAL PRODUCTIVITY CONTINUES IN JERUSALEM THROUGH PAUL'S...

responding to the Holy Spirit to...

return to Jerusalem despite warnings. (21:1-16, 19:21)

responding to Jesus in unity by submitting to...

the process of purification in the Temple. (21:17-26)

perseverance in boldly sharing about Jesus in...

the temple, resulting in his persecution at the hands of the Jewish mob. (21:27-40)

the face of the Jewish mob, telling them that Jesus had sent him to the Gentiles. (22:1-21)

SPIRITUAL PRODUCTIVITY CONTINUES TO THE UTTERMOST PARTS OF THE WORLD (ROME) THROUGH PAUL'S...

responding to the Holy Spirit to go to Rome by...

telling the Roman commander that he was a Roman citizen. (22:22-30)

foiling the procedures of the Council by setting the Pharisees and Sadducees against each other and maintaining himself under Roman control. (23:1-10)

responding to Jesus to go to Rome by...

listening to Jesus' encouragement. (23:11)

perseverance...

under God's protection from the Jews. (23:12-24:9)

perseverance in boldly sharing about Jesus to...

the Roman governor. (24:10-27)

responding to Jesus by...

appealing to Caesar which would protect him from the Jews trying to kill him and would guarantee that he would be able to reach Rome. (25:1-27)

MODELING SPIRITUAL PRODUCTIVITY

Who is modeling "sharing about Jesus"? (26)

Paul – boldly sharing about Jesus with Agrippa and Festus: his position as a Pharisee and his belief in resurrection (4-8), his zeal in persecuting followers of Jesus (9-11), his personal encounter with Jesus in which he is instructed by Jesus to open the eyes of the Jew and Gentiles about Jesus, the Savior (12-18), his testimony about his obedience to Jesus in telling the Jews and Gentiles about Jesus that they might turn from darkness to light and from the dominion of Satan to God and that they might receive forgiveness of sins and an inheritance among those who have been sanctified by faith in Jesus (19-21), his teaching that the Christ was to suffer and, that by His resurrection from the dead, He would be the first to proclaim light to the Jewish people and to the Gentiles (23); is rejected as mad by Festus and is laughed off by Agrippa (24-32)

Who is modeling "explaining the source of the power to those amazed by the work of the Holy Spirit"? (27)

Paul – his ministry rejected at first by the proud centurion (1-12), his ministry to all aboard the ship with an encouraging prophecy from an angel of God (13-26), his ministry accepted by a humble centurion not to let some of the sailors abandon the ship (27-32), his ministry to the crew by encouraging them to eat - after publically giving thanks to God (33-38), and his salvation from execution by a convicted centurion (39-44)

Who is modeling "ministering to the needy in the power of the Holy Spirit"? (28)

Paul – ministering to the Gentiles in Malta (1-10), to the Jews in Rome (11-29, and with anyone who comes to him (30- 31)

SPIRITUAL PRODUCTIVITY – THE BOOK OF ACTS

MAJOR THEMES

Ministry to the needy in the power of the Holy Spirit...

    (3:1-6)   _____

    (3:7-8)   _____

    (3:9-10)   _____

Humbly explain about the source of the power to those who are amazed that the...

    (3:11-12)   _____

               _____

    (3:13-16)   _____

               _____

Persevere in boldly sharing about Jesus with those that are "amazed" that...

    (3:17-18)   _____

               _____

    (3:19-21)   _____

               _____

               _____

_____

_____

(3:22-26)   _____

SPIRITUAL PRODUCTIVITY OCCURS IN JERUSALEM THROUGH...

responding to Jesus in unity and...

    (1:1-5)   _____

                           _____

    (1:6-11) _____

_____

    (1:12-14) _____

    (1:15-26) _____

explaining the source of the power to those amazed by the work of the Holy Spirit...

    (2:1-4)   _____

    (2:5-13) _____

    (2:14-21) _____

    (2:22-23) _____

                           _____

                           _____

    (2:24-32) _____

                           _____

                           _____

(2:33-36) _____

_____

_____

_____

(2:37-41) _____

_____

_____

_____

(2:42-47) _____

_____

_____

_____

_____

_____

_____

perseverance of the saints in boldly sharing about Jesus...

(4:1-12) _____

(4:13-22) _____

_____

(4:23-31) _____

_____

_____

(4:32-35) _____

_____

_____

(4:36-37) _____

_____

maintaining unity in the Body...

by confronting a lack of integrity as the Apostles did...

(5:1-11) _____

(5:12-16) _____

_____

(5:17:26) _____

_____

(5:27-32) _____

(5:33-40) _____

(5:41-42) _____

_____

_____

by dealing with a lack of equity as the Apostles did...

(6:1-7) _____

(6:8-15) _____

_____

by defending the faith and telling others that they should not...

(7:1-29, 52) _____

(7:30-43, 53) _____

(7:44-51) _____

by standing firm in the faith, as Stephen did, even if it means our death. (7:54-60)

(see Appendix XI and XII for visual summary of Acts 1-7.)

SPIRITUAL PRODUCTIVITY OCCURS IN JUDEA/SAMARIA THROUGH...

(8:1-4)   _____

(8:5-8)   _____

               _____

               _____

(8:9-24)   _____

               _____

(8:25-40)   _____

               _____

SPIRITUAL PRODUCTIVITY OCCURS IN THE UTTERMOST PARTS OF THE WORLD THROUGH...

Saul's responding to Jesus by proclaiming Him to be the Son of God to the Jews in the power of the Holy Spirit through...

(9:1-22)   _____

(9:23-25)   _____

(9:26-29)   _____

(9:30-31)   _____

               _____

Peter's responding to Jesus in unity by ministering to the needy in the power of the Holy Spirit in...

Lydda (9:32-35) _____

_____

Joppa (9:36-43) _____

_____

Caesarea by...

(10:1-8) _____

(10:9-16) _____

(10:17-43) _____

(10:44-48) _____

_____

Peter's explanation to the Jews in Jerusalem of the amazing outpouring of the Holy Spirit on...

(11:1-18) _____

the Church's responding to Jesus in unity by ministering to the needy in the power of the Holy Spirit through...

(11:19-26) _____

_____

_____

(11:27-30) _____

_____

_____

the perseverance of the saints by...

(12:1-5) _____

_____

(12:6-17) _____

(12:18-23) _____

_____

(12:24-25) _____

_____

_____

SPIRITUAL PRODUCTIVITY OCCURS IN THE UTTERMOST PARTS OF THE WORLD (PAUL'S FIRST MISSIONARY JOURNEY) THROUGH...

the church in Antioch responding to the Holy Spirit in unity by...

(13:1-13) _____

_____

Paul's explaining the source of the miraculous power of the Holy Spirit to...

(13:4-12) _____

perseverance of the saints boldly sharing about Jesus by...

(13:13-43) _____

(13:44-52) _____

_____

_____

(14:1-7) _____

_____

_____

Paul's and Barnabas' explaining the source of the healing power of the Holy Spirit to...

(14:8-18) _____

perseverance of the saints boldly sharing about Jesus by…

(14:19-21a) _____

(14:21b-23) _____

_____

_____

(14:24-25) _____

(14:26-28) _____

_____

_____

_____

the responding of the church to Jesus in unity by…

(15:1-5, 12) _____

_____

_____

(15:6-11) _____

(15:13-21) _____

(15:22-29) _____

_____

(15:30-35) _____

_____

(15:36-41) _____

_____

(16:1-5) _____

_____

_____

SPIRITUAL PRODUCTIVITY CONTINUES TO THE UTTERMOST PARTS OF THE WORLD (PAUL' SECOND MISSIONARY JOURNEY) BY...

Paul's responding to the Holy Spirit, the Spirit of Jesus, and a vision to...

(16:6-10) _____

perseverance of Paul in boldly sharing about Jesus...

(16:11-15) _____

(16:16-21) _____

_____

_____

(16:22-40) _____

AND HOW SHALL YOU KNOW ALL PARABLES

(17:1-9) _____

_____

_____

(17:10-15) _____

_____

_____

(17:16-34) _____

_____

(18:1-8) _____

(18:9-11) _____

_____

(18:12-17) _____

_____

_____

(18:18-21) _____

(18:22) _____

_____

SPIRITUAL PRODUCTIVITY CONTINUES TO THE UTTERMOST PARTS OF THE WORLD (PAUL'S THIRD MISSIONARY JOURNEY) THROUGH...

perseverance of the saints in sharing about Jesus by...

(18:23) _____

_____

(18:24-28) _____

_____

Paul's responding to the Lord by...

(19:1-7, 18-21) _____

_____

_____

perseverance of Paul in boldly sharing about Jesus...

(19:8-10) _____

God doing extraordinary miracles...

(19:11-20) _____

Paul's responding to the Holy Spirit by...

(19:21-22) _____

_____

perseverance of Paul in boldly sharing about Jesus in...

(19:23-41) _____

_____

Paul's responding to the Holy Spirit in...

(20:1-6, 19:21) _____

Paul's responding to Jesus by...

(20:7-12) _____

Paul's responding to the Holy Spirit in...

(20:13-16, 19:21) _____

Paul's responding to Jesus in unity to minister to the needy in the power of the Holy Spirit, explaining the source of the power to those amazed by the power of the Holy Spirit, and persevering in sharing about Jesus in his speech to...

(20:17-35) _____

the brethren responding to Jesus...

(20:36-38) _____

SPIRITUAL PRODUCTIVITY CONTINUES IN JERUSALEM THROUGH PAUL'S...

responding to the Holy Spirit to...

(21:1-16, 19:21) _____

responding to Jesus in unity by submitting to...

(21:17-26) _____

_____

perseverance in boldly sharing about Jesus in...

(21:27-40) _____

_____

(22:1-21) _____

_____

SPIRITUAL PRODUCTIVITY CONTINUES TO THE UTTERMOST PARTS OF THE WORLD (ROME) THROUGH PAUL'S...

responding to the Holy Spirit to go to Rome by...

(22:22-30) _____

_____

(23:1-10) _____

_____

_____

_____

responding to Jesus to go Rome by...

(23:11) _____

perseverance...

(23:12-24:9) _____

perseverance in boldly sharing about Jesus to...

(24:10-27 _____

responding to Jesus by...

(25:1-27) _____

_____

_____

_____

MODELING SPIRITUAL PRODUCTIVITY

Who is modeling "perseverance in boldly sharing about Jesus"? (26)

Paul – boldly sharing about Jesus with Agrippa and Festus: his position as a Pharisee and his belief in resurrection (4-8), His zeal in persecuting followers of Jesus (9-11), his personal encounter with Jesus in which he is instructed by Jesus to open the eyes of the Jew and Gentiles about Jesus, the Savior (12-18), his testimony about his obedience to Jesus to tell the Jews and Gentiles about Jesus that ehy might turn from darkness to light and from the dominion of Satan to God and that they might receive forgiveness of sins and an inheritance among those who have been sanctified by faith in Jesus (19-21), his teaching that the Christ was to suffer and, that by His resurrection from the dead, He would be the first to proclaim light to the Jewish people and to the Gentiles (23), is rejected as mad by Festus and is laughed off by Agrippa (24-32)

Who is modeling "ministering to the needy in the power of the Holy Spirit? (27)

Paul – his ministry rejected at first by the proud centurion (1-12), his ministry to all aboard the ship with an encouraging prophecy from an angel of God (13-26), his ministry accepted by a humble centurion not to let some of the sailors abandon the ship (27-32), his ministry to the crew by encouraging them to eat- after publically giving thanks to God (33-38), and his salvation from execution by a convicted centurion (39-44)

Who is modeling "ministering to the needy in the power of the Holy Spirit" and perseverance in boldly sharing about Jesus"? (28)

Paul – ministering to the Gentiles in Malta (1-10), to the Jews in Rome (11-29), and with anyone who comes to him (30-31)

Appendix IX
Coming To Jesus

Servant-like humility is being ...

humble in position (Mark 10:1-16)
thankful for provision (Mark 10:17-34)
grateful for status (Mark 10:35-45)

Bartimaeus is an example of servant-like humility (Mark 10:46-52). When he "comes" to Jesus, Bartimaeus is capable of "seeing" Jesus because of his humility. Nicodemus is prideful (John 3:1-12). When he "comes" to Jesus, Nicodemus can not see beyond himself, his reason, or his will. As a result of his pride, he is not able to "see" Jesus. We need to humble ourselves, and then we will be in a position to be able to "see" Jesus".

Jesus-focused spirituality is ...

"Seeing" Jesus and believing (John 3:13-21) that He is the ...

Lord/Source of the Holy Spirit/Christ/Messiah/Savior/Prophet/Healer - all in one (John 4)

One sent by God the Father – given all authority by the Father (John 5).

"Bread of Life" – the person of substance (John 6) who provides for our spiritual and eternal *security.*

source of the **"Living Water"** – the person of life (John 7) who enlivens and *empowers* us with the Holy Spirit.

"Light of the World" – the person of truth (John 8) who *frees* us from all the lies about remaining in condemnation for our sin.

"Light of the World" – the person of truth (John 9) who *frees* us from all the lies about Him not being able to heal us (including from our sin).

"Door of the Sheep/Great Shepherd" – the person of care (John 10) who gives us a sense of *worth* through His love and acceptance.

"Resurrection and the Life" – the person of hope (John 11) who gives us *joy* in that if we believe, we will never die and will see the glory of God.

King – the spiritual King and Savior (John 12) who gives us *meaning* by providing us the opportunity to serve in His kingdom and to glorify God.

"Seeing and believing in Jesus" requires no other response on our part other than simply choosing to believe in Jesus!

Focusing on Jesus (John 3:22-36) as the ...

"Master washing His disciples' feet" (John 13) and responding by **humbly** washing each other's feet.

"Way, the Truth, the Life, and the only way to the Father (John 14) and responding by being **focused on Jesus** and communing with the Father through the Holy Spirit.

"True Vine (John 15) and responding by having **faith** in Jesus alone (not in yourself nor any other person or thing).

"Sender of the Holy Spirit" (John 16) and responding by being **obedient** to the Word of God (Jesus) and the Holy Spirit.

"Great Unifier praying to the Father for unity" (John 17) and responding by allowing ourselves to be sanctified in truth and perfected in unity in that we may be **spiritually productive** (that the world may know that the Father sent Jesus and loves them).

Focusing on Jesus compels a response!

If we begin to lose our focus on Jesus, we need to refocus. Jesus helps us to refocus on Him by ...

getting our attention (John 21:6-7).

inviting us to have a little breakfast with Him (John 21:9-13).

asking us a tough question, followed by a reminder of our main vocation (John 21:15-17).

giving us a unequivocal command about where our focus should be (John 21:18-22).

Refocusing on Jesus compels a response!

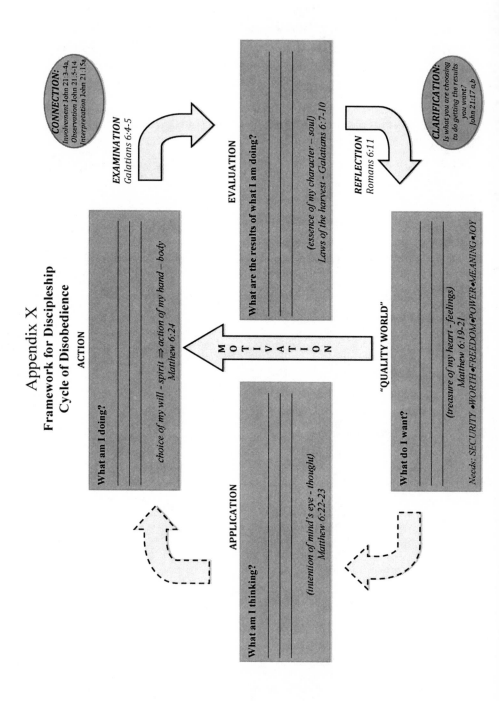

Appendix X
Framework for Discipleship
Cycle of Disobedience

CONNECTION:
Involvement John 21:3-4a
Observation John 21:5-14
Interpretation John 21:15a

EXAMINATION
Galatians 6:4-5

EVALUATION

What are the results of what I am doing?

(essence of my character – soul)
Laws of the harvest - Galatians 6:7-10

CLARIFICATION:
Is what you are choosing to do getting the results you want?
John 21:17 a,b

REFLECTION
Romans 6:11

ACTION

What am I doing?

choice of my will - spirit ⇒ action of my hand – body
Matthew 6:24

APPLICATION

What am I thinking?

(intention of mind's eye - thought)
Matthew 6:22-23

M O T I V A T I O N

"QUALITY WORLD"

What do I want?

(treasure of my heart - feelings)
Matthew 6:19-21
Needs: SECURITY ●WORTH●FREEDOM●POWER●MEANING●JOY

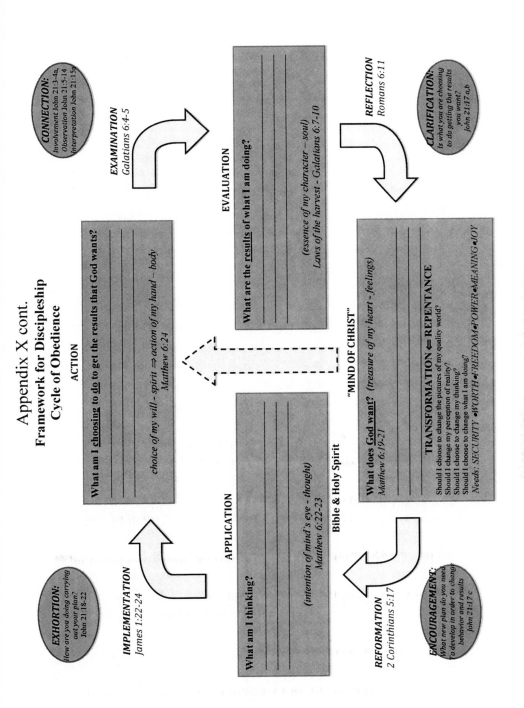

Appendix X cont.
Framework for Discipleship
Cycle of Obedience

CONNECTION:
Involvement John 21:3-4a,
Observation John 21:5-14
Interpretation John 21:15a

REFLECTION
Romans 6:11

CLARIFICATION:
*is what you are choosing
to do getting the results
you want?*
John 21:17 a,b

EXAMINATION
Galatians 6:4-5

EVALUATION

What are the results of what I am doing?

(essence of my character – soul)
Laws of the harvest - Galatians 6:7-10

ACTION

What am I choosing to do to get the results that God wants?

choice of my will – spirit ⇒ action of my hand – body
Matthew 6:24

"MIND OF CHRIST" *(treasure of my heart - feelings)*

What does God want?
Matthew 6:19-21

TRANSFORMATION ⇐ REPENTANCE

Should I choose to change the picture of my quality world?
Should I change my perception of reality?
Should I choose to change my thinking?
Should I choose to change what I am doing?
Needs: SECURITY •WORTH •FREEDOM•POWER•MEANING•JOY

APPLICATION

What am I thinking?

(intention of mind's eye - thought)
Matthew 6:22-23

Bible & Holy Spirit

IMPLEMENTATION
James 1:22-24

EXHORTION:
*How are you doing carrying
out your plan?*
John 21:18-22

REFORMATION
2 Corinthians 5:17

ENCOURAGEMENT:
*What new plan do you need
to develop in order to change
behavior and results*
John 21:17 c

APPENDIX X-A

FRAMEWORK FOR DISCIPLESHIP DYNAMIC

The "Framework for Discipleship" is based on the "process of obedience" that I see in Matthew 6:19-24 and Galatians 6:7-10 (see Chapter 11).

The "Cycle of Disobedience" is a pattern that needs to be stopped. In the "Cycle of Disobedience" the *motivation* to *act* starts with an *emotional desire* to meet one or more *needs* listed at the bottom of the *"Quality World"* box. Most of the time, the desire to get what one *wants* goes directly to *action* as represented by the *solid* arrow going from what one *wants*, *"Quality World"*, to what one *does*, *action*. It usually does <u>not</u> (but is possible) involve a lot of *thinking* as represented by the *dotted* arrows on the left side of the page. The progression of this pattern, when *examined*, usually *results* in an *evaluation* that is negative and/or unproductive. Even though the *results* may be negative and/or unproductive, the one involved may find the *results* to be what is *wanted*. As a result, one will continue this pattern as represented by the *solid* arrows between the boxes. Only when one's *reflection* leads to a determination that the *action* is not getting the *results* that are *wanted*, will the pattern be broken and the possibility that the "Cycle of Obedience" can be realized. This change may happen in any or all of the four possibilities listed under the *"transformation < repentance"* piece in the *"Mind of Christ"* box of the "Cycle of Obedience".

The "Cycle of Obedience" is a pattern that needs to be going and ongoing. In the "Cycle of Obedience" the individual has gone through a stage of *repentance* and *transformation* as illustrated in the box, *"Mind of Christ"*. Finding the meeting of one's personal *needs* in God changes one's desire to want what God wants. Following <u>this</u> pattern necessitates avoiding going <u>directly</u> from *"wants"* to *"doing"* and is represented by the *dotted* arrow going from what one *wants* to what one *does*. In order to determine what it is that God *wants*, one needs to *think* about what it is that God *wants*. This *reformation* is accomplished with the help of the *Bible* and the *Holy Spirit*. One's *thinking* about what God wants is *applied* to existing circumstances and results in a plan. With this plan in mind, one can now *implement* the plan into *action*. During and after the *action*, one can *examine* the *results* of the *action* and *evaluate* its effectiveness and productivity. Next one can *reflect* on the *results* in order to adjust one's understanding of what it is that God *wants* and go on around the pattern again. All of this is represented by the *solid* arrows between the boxes.

The questions in the boxes need to be asked and answered by the one being discipled. The discipler may need to help by suggesting the questions that the disciples needs to be asking of self. The ovals represent the activity (*connection, clarification, encouragement, exhortation*) of the discipler in the various stages of the disciple's progression and contain questions that would help the discipler to execute the specific activity. Appendix X – B provides a scriptural example (John 21) of how the activity of the discipler in the blue ovals plays out with the disciple. In this example, Jesus is the discipler; Peter is the disciple

Appendix X – C shows the practical application of the "Framework for Discipleship" applied to a discipline situation that might involve parents with a child or a teacher with a student. The child/student would be required to write their own answers to the questions.

Note: The "Framework for Discipleship" overlays the "Framework for Spiritual Maturity". (Appendix III)

Repentance	Servant-like Humility
Transformation	Jesus-focused Spirituality
Application	Steadfast Faithfulness
Action	Devoted Obedience
Evaluation	Spiritual Productivity

APPENDIX X - B
FRAMEWORK FOR DISCIPLESHIP - EXAMPLE

JESUS – *THE DISCIPLER*   PETER – *THE DISCIPLE*

CONNECTION

Observation – "Simon Peter said to them (the other disciples), 'I am going fishing'. They said to him, 'We will also come with you'. They went out and got into the boat; and that night they caught nothing. But when the day was now breaking, Jesus stood on the beach; yet the disciples did not know that it was Jesus. (John 21:3-4a)

Involvement – "So Jesus said to them, 'Children, you do not have any fish, do you?' They answered Him, 'No'. And He said to them, 'Cast the net on the right hand side of the boat and you will find a catch.' So they cast, and then they were not able to haul it in because of the great number of fish. Therefore that disciple whom Jesus loved said to Peter, 'It is the Lord'. So when Simon Peter heard that it was the Lord, he put his outer garment on (for he was stripped for work), and threw himself into the sea. But the other disciples came in the little boat, for they were not far from the land, but about one hundred yards away, dragging the net full of fish. So when they got out on the land, they saw a charcoal fire already laid and fish place on it, and bread. Jesus said to them, 'Bring some of the fish which you have now caught.' Simon Peter went up and drew the net to land, full of large fish, a hundred and fifty-three; and although there were so many, the net was not torn. Jesus said to them, 'Come and have breakfast.' None of the disciple ventured to question Him, 'Who are You?' knowing that it was the Lord. Jesus came and took the bread and gave it to them, and the fish likewise." (John 21:5-14)

Interpretation – "So when they had finished breakfast, Jesus said to Simon Peter, 'Simon, son of John, do you love Me more than these?" (John 21:15a)

CLARIFICATION – "So when they had finished breakfast, Jesus said to Simon, Peter, 'Simon, son of John, do you love Me more than these? He said to Him, 'Yes Lord, You know that I love You.'" (John 21:15a,b) "He said to Him a second time, 'Simon, son of John, do you love Me?' He said to Him, 'Yes, Lord, You know that I love You.'" (John 21:16a,b) "He said to him the third time, 'Simon, son of John, do you love Me?'" Peter was grieved because He said to him the third time. 'Do you love Me?' And He said to Him, 'Lord, You know all things, You know that I love You.'" (John 21:17a,b)

ENCOURAGEMENT – "He said to him, 'Feed My lambs.'" (John 21:15c) "He said to him, 'Shepherd My sheep.'" (John 21:16c) "Jesus said to him, 'Tend my sheep.'" (John 21:17c)

EXHORTATION – "'Truly, truly, I say to you, when you were younger, you used to gird yourself and walk wherever you wished; but when you grow old, you will stretch out your hands and someone else will gird you, and bring you where you do not wish to go.' Now this He said signifying by what kind of death he would glorify God. And when He had spoken this, He said to him, 'Follow Me!' Peter, turning around, saw the disciple whom Jesus love following them, the one who also had leaned back on His bosom at the supper and said, 'Lord, who is the one who betrays you?' So Peter seeing him said to Jesus, 'Lord, and what about this man?' Jesus said to him, 'If I want him to remain until I come, what is that to you? You follow Me!'" (John 21:18-22)

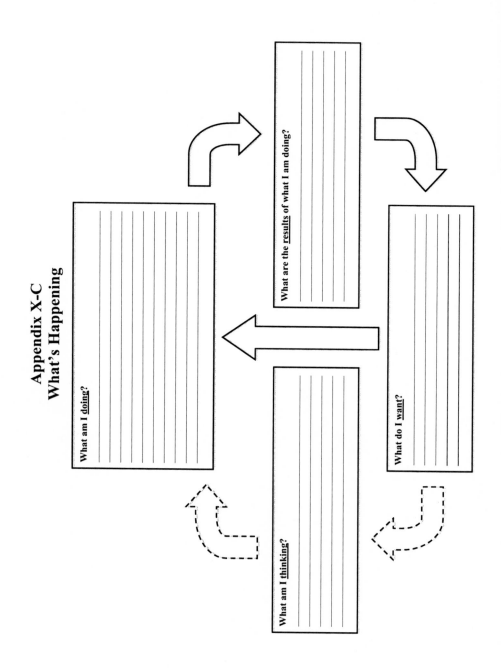

Appendix X-C
What's Happening

What am I doing?

What are the results of what I am doing?

What do I want?

What am I thinking?

Appendix X-C cont.
Transformation Plan

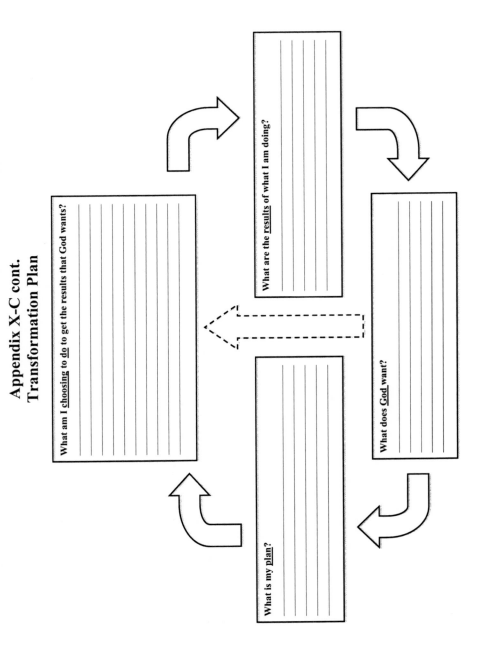

What are the results of what I am doing?

What does God want?

What is my plan?

What am I choosing to do to get the results that God wants?

Appendix XI

Spiritual Productivity
The Book of Acts

The World

Bold
Acts 4-28

Minister to the needy in the power of the Holy Spirit...

- by discerning the need.
- by meeting the need (anyone's).
- to the wonder and amazement of those watching.
  Acts 3:1-10

Explain to those that are amazed that the...

- ministry is not accomplished through our own power or piety.
- effect of the ministry is accomplished through the power of the name of Jesus (the Holy Spirit which is a gift from God).
  Acts 3:11-16

Perseverant
Acts 4-28

Share with those that are amazed that...

- Jesus ministered on the earth doing miracles, wonders and signs, and was put to death on a cross.
- God, the Father, raised Jesus from the dead, to which the apostles were witnesses.
- Jesus, exalted to the right hand of God, pours out the Holy Spirit on those who believe in Jesus
- they need to repent of their sins, be baptized in the name of Jesus Christ for forgiveness of their sins, and receive the gift of the Holy Spirit.
  Acts 3:17-26

Acts 1:8

Acts 2:47b; 5:14-16; 6:7

Body of Believers

In the context of **UNITY** believers:

- Devote themselves to the apostles' teaching
- Fellowship
- "Break bread"
- Pray
- Share possessions
- Eat together with glad and sincere hearts
- Praise God and singing
- Enjoy favor with all people
  Acts 2:42-47a; 4:32-35

In the context of **UNITY** leadership:

- Confronts lack of integrity
  Acts 5:1-16
- Addresses lack of equity
  Acts 6:1-6
- Contends for the faith
  Acts 7:1-53
- Stands firm in the faith
  Acts 7:54-60

Appendix XII

Framework for Spiritual Community

LOVE ONE ANOTHER

with the attitude of the Beatitudes reminding each other to keep the faith in Christ. *(John 15:12-17; Matt 5:1-12)*

Poor in spirit • Mourn • Meek • Hunger & thirst after righteousness • Merciful • Pure in heart • Peacemakers • Those persecuted for righteousness sake

EDIFY ONE ANOTHER

to unity through the gifts of the Spirit. *(John 17:20-23; Romans 12:4-15, 1 Corinthians 14:12. 1 Corinthians 14:12, Ephesians 4:1-16)*

Prophecy • Exhortation • Mercy • Faith • Service • Giving • Wisdom • Healing • Distinguishing spirits • Teaching • Leading • Knowledge • Miracles • Tongues • Interpretation of tongues

A spiritual community moving together toward Christ

ENCOURAGE ONE ANOTHER

by walking in the Spirit, exhibiting the fruits of the Spirit. *(John 16:7-15; Galatians 5:13-26)*

Love • Joy • Peace • Patience • Kindness • Goodness • Faithfulness • Gentleness • Self-control

APPENDIX XII (CONT.)

NOTES ON THE "FRAMEWORK FOR SPIRITUAL COMMUNITY"

LOVE ONE ANOTHER with the attitude of the Beatitudes reminding each other to keep faith in Christ (John 15:12-17, Matthew 5:1-12).

First group – having to do with self
- *poor in spirit* – poor in human spirit, "poor" in the sense of being totally dependent on God, as a beggar.
- *mourn* – to grieve (possibly for our sin), capable of being sensitive
- *meek* – mild (not caustic)
- *hunger and thirst after righteousness* – doing what is ethically right and immediately seeking vindication from God when we do sin (confess our sins and ask forgiveness)

Second group – having to do with others
- *merciful* – actively compassionate
- *pure in heart* – clean in thoughts and feelings, having no personal agenda
- *peacemakers* – opposite to fire-builders
- *those who are persecuted for righteousness sake* – will not sin against their conscience; won't bend when the tribulation comes

Our living out the attitudes of the Beatitudes is directly related to our faith in Christ.

ENCOURAGE ONE ANOTHER by walking in the spirit, exhibiting the fruits of the Spirit (John 16:7-15, Galatians 5:13-26).

Background
- Fruit of the sinful nature vs. fruit of the Spirit (Gal. 5:16-18)
- "fruit" – the word in the Greek means fruit that has been plucked, harvested, ready to be consumed
- The fig is a fruit in Mark 11:12-20. There is an analogy between the temple and the withered fig tree. If one is being disobedient to God, he will not be able to bear "fruit" that is ripe, mature, harvested and ready to be consumed by others.
- When we walk in the Spirit, exhibiting the fruit of the Spirit, others can eat of that "fruit" that is plucked, harvested and ready to be consumed. Others will benefit from our actions that are the result of the fruits of the Spirit and are encouraged to persevere in their walk in the Spirit.

Fruits of the Spirit
- *Love* – agape (love in a social or moral sense; sees something infinitely precious as its object). The Greek translation of the Old Testament uses the word 95% of the time to describe love from God to man, man to God, man to neighbor. We can start with the attitude of the Beatitudes.
- *Joy* – cheerfulness, calm, delight (John 3:29, 15:9-11)
- *Peace* – from a primitive verb, "to join"; one, peace quietness, rest, and "set at one again" (suggesting that "not peace" is division)
- *Patience* – from the words "long" and "passion" (as if breathing hard, fiercely); forbearance, long-suffering (by implication to sacrifice)
- *Kindness* – usefulness, i.e., moral excellence in character and demeanor
- *Goodness*- good, virtue or beneficence

- *Faithfulness* – trustworthy, proven
- *Gentleness* – same word root as in "blessed are the meek"; here it implies humility
- *Self-control* – vigorous/strong in a thing, self-controlled in appetite, etc., temperate

The fruit of the Spirit in our lives is directly related to our obedience to Christ.

EDIFY ONE ANOTHER to unity through the gifts of the Spirit (John 17:20-23, Romans 12:4-15, I Corinthians 12:4-31, I Corinthians 14:12, Ephesians 4:1-16).

<u>*Romans 12:6-8, Gifts of the Spirit*</u> – divine gratuity

<u>Context (v. 1-6)</u> – We are not to think more highly of ourselves (no room for the Holy Spirit and leads to division), but to think so as to have sound judgment (safe, reined in, self-controlled, room for the Holy Spirit and no division/unity)

<u>Gifts of the Spirit.</u>
- Prophecy – foretell, inspired speaking
- Service – run errands, "gopher"
- Teaching – instruction
- Exhortation – implore, entreat
- Giving – give
- Diligence in leading – lead with earnestness, speed
- Mercy – actively compassionate

<u>*I Corinthians 12:8-11, Gifts of the Spirit*</u> – divine gratuity

<u>Context (v. 1-7,12-13)</u> – You can only say "Jesus is Lord" by means of the Holy Spirit. Each one is given the manifestation of the Spirit for the <u>common good</u>. All members of the Body, though many, are <u>one</u>. All are baptized into <u>one</u> body...and all are made to drink of

<u>one</u> Spirit. The body is not one member, but many. So that there may be <u>no</u> <u>division</u> in the Body, but that the members may have the same care for one another. We are to earnestly desire the greater (stronger/more powerful) gifts.

<u>Gifts of the Spirit</u>.

- *Word of wisdom* – something said, clear/wise, worldly or spiritual
- *Word of knowledge* - something said; to make known, understood
- *Faith* – convicted of a religious truth, especially upon Christ for salvation
- *Healing* – a cure, the effect of healing
- *Miracles* – force, power, a miracle itself
- *Prophecy* – prediction
- *Distinguishing spirits* – discerning, to separate thoroughly
- *Various kinds of tongues* – "some" "kinds (kindred)" "tongues"; by implication, language, specifically one naturally acquired
- *Interpretation of tongues* – "translate" "tongues", by implication, language

The gifts of the Spirit in our lives is directly related to our willingness to minister in the power of the Holy Spirit.

GEESE ANALOGY.

- When a goose is sick or wounded and falls to the ground, two other geese follow it down and stay with it until it dies or is ready to resume flying (Love one another with the attitudes of the Beatitudes).
- The geese in the rear of the formation honk in order to encourage the ones in the front to keep going, breaking

the wind resistance (Encourage one another by walking in the Spirit, exhibiting the fruits of the Spirit).

- When the geese fly in their "V" formation, the lift of the goose in front helps to lift the goose following. Geese flying in formation can fly 71 times farther than one goose flying alone (Edify one another through the gifts of the Spirit).

CONCLUSION

When we are loved with the attitude of the Beatitudes, our hearts feel a sense of worth that reminds us of whence our worth comes – Jesus, and our faith in Jesus becomes more steadfast.

Our hearts are encouraged by seeing someone walking in the Spirit exhibiting the fruits of the Spirit. This reminds us that the <u>power</u> of the Spirit is entrusted to us, as well, so that our obedience to Jesus can go to an even higher level of devotion.

Our hearts are edified by witnessing the gifts of the Spirit in God's people as they work together in meaningful unity. We are stimulated to exercise the gifts given to us in order to be more spiritually productive.

Why do our hearts need to feel love, encouragement, and edification? The reason is that our hearts are in a great battle with our flesh, the world, and Satan. We need to help one another to guard our hearts. We need to fight to protect the hearts of one another!

A SPIRITUAL COMMUNITY MOVING TOGETHER TOWARD CHRIST IS ONE THAT LOVES ONE ANOTHER, ENCOURAGES ONE ANOTHER, AND EDIFIES ONE ANOTHER.

Appendix XIII
FRAMEWORK FOR SPIRITUAL
MATURITY – AN OVERVIEW
(Themes from the Parable of the Sower)

<u>Wayside</u> <u>soil</u> represents **"hard"** people. The need is *worth*; the way in which the need is satisfied is through *love and acceptance*.

The problem with the **"hard"** people is their selfish **pride**. They want to raise themselves up so that others will *love and accept* them and give them a sense of *worth*.

They have pride of position (Mark 10: 1-16).

They have pride of provision (Mark 10: 17-34).

They have pride of presumption that others should serve them (Mark 10: 35-45).

The way <u>not</u> to be a "hard" person is to have **servant-like humility** in position, in provision, and in status. In our **humility** we begin to see that God will raise us up and give us a sense of *worth* through <u>His</u> *love and acceptance* (Mark 10:46-52).

<u>Germination</u> <u>of the seed</u> represents **spiritual birth**. The need is *freedom*; the way in which the need is satisfied is through having *choice*.

The problem with people who have been born naturally is that they need to be **born again spiritually**. Their choices are limited to the natural realm only.

They do not think supernaturally past their self, their reason, and their will (John 3: 1-12).

They do not "see" and believe in Jesus (John 3:13-21).

They do not focus on Jesus (John 3: 22-36).

The way to be **born again spiritually** is to think supernaturally beyond your self, your reason, and your will; to "see" and believe in Jesus; and to focus on Jesus. Through this transformation we find *freedom* by being able to make *choices* in the supernatural realm.

Rocky soil represents **"shallow"** people. The need is *power*; the way in which the need is satisfied is through *trust*. The shallow people vary their *trust* in a myriad of things according to which seems to provide them with the most *power*.

The problem with the **"shallow"** people is their **lack of faith**.

> They have the wrong kind of faith – one in which they expect God to do other than empower them and provide for them in order to serve Him (Luke 9: 1-17, 37-43a, 51-56).
>
> They avoid suffering (Luke 9: 18-27, 43b-45, 57-61).
>
> They do not stay the course in their faith (Luke 9: 28-36, 46-50, 62)

The way <u>not</u> to be a **"shallow"** person is to have the right kind of faith (one that expects no more from God than His empowerment and provision in order to serve Him), to choose to endure the suffering that results from serving Him, and to stay the course in our faith. In this way we *trust* in God and experience the ultimate *power* (the Holy Spirit) that God has entrusted to us, and we have a **steadfast faith**.

Thorny soil represents **"unproductive"** people. The need is *security*; the way in which the need is satisfied is through *physiological provision*.

The problem with the **"unproductive"** people is their **disobedience**. They seek *physiological provision* from a myriad of sources in order to gain a sense of *security*.

> They do not commune with God in secret (Matthew 6: 1-18).
>
> They do not have a devoted singleness of heart, mind's eye, and service to God (Matthew 6: 19-24).
>
> They do not seek God first in their life (Matthew 6: 25-34).

The way <u>not</u> to be an **"unproductive"** person is to commune with God in secret; to have a devoted singleness of heart, mind's eye, and service to God (devoted obedience to God); and to seek God first in our life. In our **obedience** we find *security* through God's *physiological provision*.

Good **soil** represents **"productive"** people. The need is *meaning*; the way in which the need is satisfied is through having a *purpose*.

The characteristic of the **"productive"** people is their **ongoing fruitfulness**. They find *meaning* through their *purpose* of being **productive** for God.

> They respond to Jesus in unity and minister to the needy in the power of the Holy Spirit, to the amazement of those watching. (Acts 3:1-10)
>
> They explain to those amazed that what ministry they do is accomplished through the power of the Holy Spirit, which comes from faith in the name of Jesus. (Acts 3:11-16)
>
> They share the Gospel message with others in order that they would have the opportunity to receive Jesus and the power of the Holy Spirit. (Acts 3:17-26).

The way to be a **"productive"** person is to minister to others in the power of the Holy Spirit, to help others understand that the ministry is done through the power of the Holy Spirit, and to share the Gospel message in order that they would have the opportunity to receive Jesus and the power of the Holy Spirit. In our ongoing ministry we find *meaning* by fulfilling our *purpose* of being **productive** for God.

Appendix XIV
Framework for an Effective Disciple

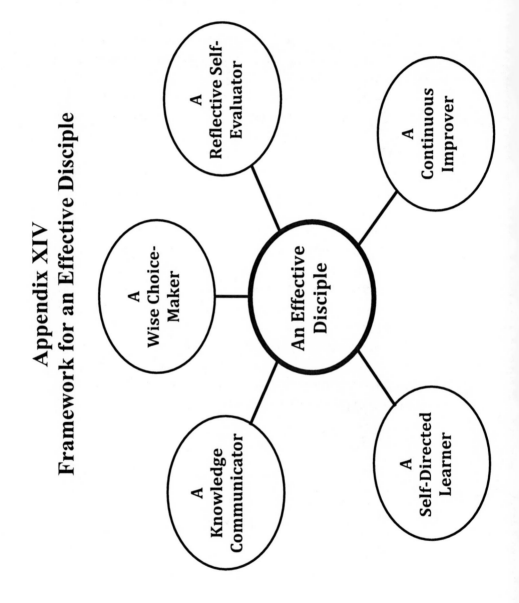

APPENDIX XII (continued)
AN EFFFECTIVE DISCIPLE

A wise choice-maker

Has a heart for Jesus – "Do not store up for yourselves treasures on earth, where moth and rust destroy, and where thieves break in or steal. But store up for yourselves treasures in heaven where neither moth nor rust destroys, and where thieves do not break in or steal; for where your treasure is, there your heart will be also." (Matthew 6:19-21)

Has a clear eye for Jesus – "The eye is the lamp of the body; so then if your eye is clear, your whole body will be full of light. But if your eye is bad, your whole body will be full of darkness. If then the light that is in you is darkness, how great is the darkness." (Matthew 6:22-23)

Has a serving hand for Jesus – "No one can serve two masters, for either he will hate the one and love the other, or he will be devoted to one and despise the other. You cannot serve God and wealth." (Matthew 6:24)

A self-directed learner

Hears the Word – "And the one on whom the seed was sown on the good soil, this the man who <u>hears the word</u>...(Matthew 13:23)

Understands the Word – "And the one on whom the seed was sown on the good soil, this is the man who hears the word and <u>understands it</u>...(Matthew 13:23)

Does the Word – "And the one on whom the seed was sown on the good soil, this is the man who hears the word and understands it; who indeed <u>bears fruit and brings forth, some a hundredfold, some sixty, and some thirty.</u>" (Matthew 13:23)

A knowledgeable-communicator

Witnessing about Jesus – "But you will receive power when the Holy Spirit has come upon you; and you shall be My witnesses both in Jerusalem and in all Judea and Samaria, and even to the remotest part of the earth." (Acts 1:8)

Preaching the gospel – "And He said to them, 'Go into all the world and preach the gospel to all creation.'" (Mark 16:15)

Teaching the commandments of Jesus – "Go therefore and make disciples of all nations, baptizing them in the name of the Father and the Son and the Holy Spirit, teaching them to observe all that I have commanded you; and lo, I am with you always, even to the end of the age". (Matthew 28:18-20)

A reflective self-evaluator

About knowledgeable communication, self-directed learning, and wise choice- making – "But each must examine his own work, and then he will have reason for boasting in regard to himself alone, and not in regard to another. For each one will bear his own load." – (Galatians 6:4-5)

A continuous improver

In knowledgeable communication, self-directed learning, and wise choice- making – "Therefore, leaving the elementary teaching about Christ, let us press on to maturity...For God is not unjust so as to forget your work and the love which you have shown toward His name, in having ministered and in still ministering to the saints, and we desire that each one of you show the same diligence so as to realize the full assurance of hope until the end". (Heb. 6:1-11)

ABOUT THE AUTHOR

John Wedlock has a BA in history from Yale University and MEd from American University. He served as an officer in the U.S. Navy and was a secondary-school history teacher, department chairman, high-school basketball coach, and a public school superintendent. He has served as a Sunday-school teacher, Sunday school superintendent, Christian school headmaster, and elder board chairman; and for 45 years has discipled men to be more consecrated and committed followers of Jesus. He lives with his wife of 56 years, Louise, in St. Petersburg, Florida, and is blessed with 3 children, 7 grandchildren, and 2 great grandchildren.

CPSIA information can be obtained
at www.ICGtesting.com
Printed in the USA
FFOW03n0445280817
39333FF